BHAGAVAN SRI
(An Int

BOOKS BY THE AUTHOR

*(1) *The Song of Life* (Poems) (*Hind Kitabs*)

 (2) *In Life's Temple* (Poems) (*Blackie's*)

*(3) *The Poetic Approach to Language* (*O.U.P.*)

 (4) *English in India* (*Asia*)

 (5) *India and World Culture* (*Vikas*)

 (6) *Studies in Indo-Anglian Poetry* (*Sai Ratan*)

 (7) *D.R. Bendre : Poet and Seer* (*Somaiya*)

 (8) *Narahari Prophet of New India* (a novel) (*Somaiya*)

 (9) *Sri Aurobindo : Seer and Poet* (*Abhinav Publications*)

(10) *Coleridge's Aesthetics* (*Abhinav Publications*)

(11) *An Integral View of Poetry* (*Abhinav Publications*)

(12) *Bhagavan Sri Sathya Sai Baba—An Interpretation* (*Abhinav Publications*)

EDITED

*(1) *The Literatures in the Indian Languages* (*Union Ministry of Information, New Delhi*)

 (2) *The Golden Treasury of Indo-Anglian Poetry* (*Sahitya Akademi*)

 (3) *The Golden Book of Sathya Sai Lyrics* (*Sathya Sai Publication Foundation*)

 (4) *Twentyone Indo-Anglian Poems* (*Sahitya Akademi*)

*Out of print.

Bhagavan Sri Sathya Sai Baba
(AN INTERPRETATION)

Vinayak Krishna Gokak

BHAGAVAN SRI SATHYA SAI BABA
(An Interpretation)

Abhinav Publications New Delhi-110016

© V K GOKAK

2nd edition 1983
3rd edition 1989

Published by :
Shakti Malik
Abhinav Publications
E—37 Hauz Khas
New Delhi-110016

ISBN 81-7017-258-6

Printed at Delux Printers, Old Rohtak Road, Delhi

AUM

This book is dedicated in all love and reverence to **Bhagavan Sri Sathya Sai Baba** at whose feet I learnt the lesson of pure love, of an uncompromising devotion to truth regarding oneself and the world and of confidence and peace in the midst of tumult both within and without. May his blessings lead me from the Unreal to the Real.

PREFACE

I AM glad to offer my homage to Bhagavan Sri Sathya Sai Baba on the occasion of his fiftieth birthday, 23rd November 1975. This book indicates the light that I have received from him, along with millions of other seekers, and I am happy to put it in the hands of readers at the time of these golden jubilee celebrations held in many parts of the world.

Baba's personality is too multi-faceted and elusive to be captured by any camera or contained in any biography. The best that one can do is to focus a few lights on some of the remote cliffs and peaks and the foothills of this himalayan personality. This is what I have attempted in this book. For this book I have drawn on my own experiences of eye and ear, my mind and intellect, my heart and psyche. No other account can be more authentic than the one which draws upon one's own experiences. Here is an image of Baba as reflected in the pool of my vision and understanding.

I am aware of the fact that, for a multi-faceted personality like his, there can be numerous interpretations, emphasizing one aspect or the other. All that I can say is that there is undoubtedly a nectar-drop of truth authenticating this interpretation.

I have divided the volume into five parts: Personality; Philosophy; Work; Sayings and Writings; Impact. This is only for the sake of convenience. The entire book is an attempt to touch the intangible and view the invisible.

vii

Baba is to be understood more in silence than in talk, more in the impersonal range than in the personal perspective.

I have added an appendix to the book, giving biographical particulars about Baba in a systematic form. This has been compiled by Shri D.S. Habbu, Lecturer in History, Sri Sathya Sai Arts and Science College, Whitefield, at my request. I am grateful to him for it.

I am also grateful to Abhinav Publications for having published this book so promptly.

Brindavan,   **VINAYAK KRISHNA GOKAK**
Whitefield,
Bangalore.

CONTENTS

BHAGAVAN SRI SATHYA SAI BABA
(An Interpretation)

I. Personality

1. AN INTRODUCTION

THERE is the man of the world, the man of genius, the man of God and the universal man or *visva-manava* of Tagore's conception. We have perhaps to add to these categories another that consists of god-men, however small the number. One may even say that these are the salt of the earth.

Sri Sathya Sai Baba is a god-man belonging to this category.

He is a phenomenon and one has to understand him and the mission which is his.

The unique feature that makes his appearance distinctive, apart from the subtle and even occasionally unfathomable expression in his eyes and on his face, is the shock or aura of hair on his head.

He takes no milk, fruits or sweet dishes because he says his devotees who are not so well-to-do also try to serve him with costly dishes when he goes to their homes.

He has hardly a few hours of sleep. He is ready to give *darshan* at 7 A.M. in the morning. He is busy granting interviews to the afflicted and the aspiring from 9 A.M. to 12.30 in the noon.

He himself reads the hundreds of letters that he receives every day between 1 P.M. and 4 P.M. These letters may be in different languages; but no one else is allowed to open them. He even replies to a few letters himself. He is ready to grant *darshan* again in the afternoon;

3

has committee meetings for discussing the affairs of the colleges and hospitals founded by him; and he chats with a few disciples, giving them guidance in their quest for Truth. He writes every month for *Sanathana Sarathi* and he does his writing in the evenings. As for *bhajans* and songs, which are so enchantingly lyrical and musical, there is no time fixed for them. They flow from him in conversation or while addressing large meetings. One can see that this is a packed programme for a day.

His passion for the service of humanity knows no bounds. His love flows forth to all alike and this is life to him. He has said that his one mission in life is to uphold Dharma and the Law, restore India to her former glory of Spirit and bring the world back to the message of Spirit.

He is a great giver and a great benefactor of mankind.

II

Born of a Raju family with a tradition of piety and culture, on 23rd November, 1926, at Puttaparthi, Anantapur District, Andhra Pradesh, Sri Sathya Sai Baba is now nearing fifty. Puttaparthi was the back of the beyond before Baba was born there. Today it is a centre of pilgrimage for lakhs of people from all over India and abroad.

The miraculous pranks that Baba played at home and as a school-going boy are now well-known.

He was subjected to great suffering by the family because they called in exorcisers to treat him, believing that he was possessed by the devil. He used to go into trance for hours, chanting Sanskrit verses like a scholar, and was altogether an unpredictable child. One day when he was in his 13th year, he declared: "I am SAI BABA. I shall not remain here any longer. My devotees are calling me." He left the house and went to a nearby garden

and chanted there, to an audience of devotees that had
gathered around him, the first of his enchanting *bhajans*:

Manasa Bhajare Gurucharanam
Dustara Bhavasagarataranam

and the audience repeated these lines in an ecstasy of
joy. Millions of people have, since then, repeated the
numerous *bhajans* that have flowed from his lips. The
sweet music and the noble sentiments that animate the
bhajans must only be experienced in order to be assessed.

It took some time for Baba to be known for what he
is. There were a few disciples around him and he lived
in comparative obscurity; but he used to tell them:
"You have easy access to me now. A few years hence,
you will have to get a glimpse of me standing miles away
from me; there will be such huge crowds." His fame
grew steadily and spread far and wide.

III

One thinks of the Christ, the Buddha, Sankara and
Vivekananda when one thinks of Baba. There is the
same compassion for fellow-men and the same urge for
relieving human suffering. One can find there also the
healing touch of the Christ and the heart-easing speech
of the Buddha.

He stands on a level where all knowledge lies at his
feet. He has only to pick up what portion of it he requires as the occasion demands it. He lectures in two
languages, Telugu and Kannada, and converses freely in
two others, Tamil and Malayalam. He can even play with
Hindi and English. From one who has hardly had a
smattering of the English language, it is thrilling to listen
to sentences like "One should not only do the work that
one likes, but also like the work that one has to do";

5

"Begin the day with love, spend the day with love and end the day with love: that is the way to God".

What overawes one is the catholicity of Baba. It does not matter to him what master a disciple comes from. All are one. He becomes to each disciple the master he has accepted.

The uniqueness of Baba lies in the fact that he did not have to practise any penance or achieve any *siddhi* or realization in this life. He was born with them.

The sun cannot help being resplendent and the miraculous man miraculous. What is a miracle or an oracle to us is, to the god-man, the most natural thing in the world to happen, the simplest thing to say.

Even more miraculous, if there can be grades in miraculousness, is his subtle entry into the innermost thoughts of people anywhere and everywhere!

Most miraculous of all are the countless cures he effects directly, even thousands of miles away. They are breath-taking cures, inexplicable to medical science.

What can one make of all this? It means that here is a manifestation, not only of Truth or Love, but Power.

Further, this power manifests itself through one who is human like the rest of us.

There is another aspect of Baba's miracles that needs to be touched upon. He says that their function is to draw people back to the life of Spirit. He gives them what they want so that they may begin to want what he would like them to want.

With all this miraculousness, Baba has the heart of a child. He can sport and prattle away like an innocent child and, at the same time, be a more shrewd judge of men and events than any statesman or diplomat. He can rise to the heights of humour as well as sublimity.

IV

Baba's philosophy is meant for the common man, even the villager who is illiterate but is an heir to great traditions. The charming *bhajans* and the simple but moving parables which flow unendingly from his lips— sometimes reminiscent of the Buddha, the Indian saints and the Christ, but very often his own—go home to common men's businesses and bosoms. At the same time, the insights that they bring are challengingly profound to the scholar and the philosopher.

The four key words of his teaching are *Satya* (Truth), *Dharma* (Loyalty to the Law), *Shanthi* (Peace) and *Prema* (Love). The seeker has to speak, love and live the Truth at all costs and in any circumstances. *Dharma* consists of right action.

Peace is the foundation of the spiritual life. Not only is Peace a negation of the chaos or disorder within one-self; it is also a positive experience building up towards spiritual delight. When the bedrock of Peace has been achieved, intuition, the psyche within, opens up. The river of Love begins to flow endlessly on the bedrock of Peace. It is this flowering of the human personality that Baba aims at. The symbol of Prashanthi Nilayam is the symbol of the unfolding lotus and the uprising flame.

V

Baba's programme of action is designed for the indivi- dual as well as the collectivity. It is a programme meant for individual and national regeneration. It is a clarion call for the regeneration of humanity. His impassioned eloquence keeps lakhs of people moved and spell-bound. His whirlwind tours, his discourses to the elite, the students and the masses, kindle in us the fire of hope and renewal at a time when the national scene almost makes us feel that all is lost. The confidence he inspires and the assurance he gives infuse into us a new enthusiasm. They proceed from a centre of power which convinces us of its certainty and invincibility.

The injunction that he lays on the wealthy that come to him is to feed the poor. Whenever there is a plan to feed the poor, he himself moves about the kitchen and the eating *maidan*, serving them with his own hands. In a poor country like India, this is the first offering and consecration. He asks the thousands of *Sai Samitis* that function in the country and abroad to meet every week to chant *bhajans* and meditate. The chanting of God's name is the easiest way to God in this ungodly age. He calls on them to have '*nagar sankirtan*', itinerary singing in the locality in which they live, at least once a month. This is how they can bring God into the lives of men. He asks the *Samitis* and *Sai Seva Dals* organised in cities, towns and villages, to help fellow-men in distress, comfort the sick in hospitals with their visits and *bhajans* and take charge of public functions and assemblies in a spirit of disinterested service. He permits *Sai Mahila Mandals* to organise themselves for similar purposes and bring about a spiritual transformation among Indian womanhood. Women are going to be mothers of the nation and it is they who will bring up the heroes of tomorrow. He prevails upon all to form *Sai Balamandirs* where children can be introduced to the beauty of the spiritual life through *bhajans*, songs, parables drawn from the great and his own teachings and simple lessons in good living. He encourages the formation of *Sai Study Circles* where spiritual classics can be read by groups of aspirants. In the *vidwan mahasabhas* or learned assemblies which he loves to have organised, he gets the more

8

gifted to share their knowledge and experience with their brethren. He helps to publish the writings of scholars and men of letters. He starts and finances *veda patha-shalas*, hospitals and schools and colleges. His idea is to start a Sathya Sai College in every State in India, for the young must be taught to cultivate their personality in the right manner if India is to regain her lost soul. Dharma Kshetra in Bombay is a spiritual centre aiming at the all-round shaping of the human personality. The millionaires in Bombay spent lakhs of rupees on buil-ding it.

In the midst of ceaseless talk all around about the amelioration of the masses and the regeneration of our people, Baba works night and day, modestly and silently, to achieve these aims. No one can work in a more self-effacing manner. An American writer had been to Baba some time back. It was his desire to write Baba's bio-graphy so that the world might know him. Baba listen-ed to him with humility and said gently to him: "Wait for ten years before you write it. Please find out first whether I am really acceptable to you. What is the good of writing a biography which, after five years, you your-self may feel like rejecting? Please verify for yourself what you wish to write about. If, after ten years, you still feel like writing my biography, you may do so."

2. BABA AND THE CONCEPT OF AVATARHOOD

(I)

AN affirmation of the sovereignty of consciousness over matter is not an unfamiliar idea in the West. Idealistic European philosophers have spoken about it. Berkeley was one of them. Consciousness comes first. Matter is only a gross form that consciousness assumes.

But matter is not to be shunned or rejected. Spirit and Matter, the infinite and the finite and eternity and the moment have to meet and mingle in the domain of life. These are the great lines that William Blake wrote:

"To see a world in a grain of sand
And heaven in a wild flower
Hold infinity in the palm of your hand
And eternity in an hour."

As things stand today, *maya* comes from the West and not the East. We are surfeited with the Atomic Age, the Push-Button Era and all the gadgets that they have brought into the world. They all indicate the prosperity of the body but not of the soul. We must turn from this depressing emptiness and think of bringing about a marriage of heaven and earth as Blake did:

"I shall not cease from mental fight
Nor shall this sword rest in my hand
Till I have built Jerusalem
in England's green and pleasant land."

This is what India has stood for in the golden moments of her history. There is a surprising absence of dogma in her philosophy and religion. She is prepared to contemplate the Divine in any form or formlessness and through any symbol. It is not surprising that Shri Ramakrishna Paramahamsa and Bhagavan Baba viewed and view the Crescent and the Star, the Cross, the Wheel of Law, the Sacrificial Fire and Aum as symbols expressing the same divine truth.

Each prophet has his own speciality and modern India has had a galaxy of prophets. Each of them stands for promoting, in his own way, the evolution of man towards the discovery of his inmost self.

The West has been reconciled to prophets. But it is shocked by the concept of *avatarhood* except, of course, in the case of Jesus Christ. An *avatar* is God Himself descending into human flesh. But how can a two-legged thing be God? How can such an ephemeral creature govern the universe? *Avatarhood* is therefore dubbed a piece of Indian fantasy or *maya*.

But the West is not, after all, so alien to this concept. Let us think of the concept of Being and Becoming in Plato and Plotinus and of the idealism of Berkeley. Let us think of Schelling, the German philosopher and of the British Coleridge. Coleridge said that all knowledge rests on the coalescence of subject and object. He remarked that it is possible for the subject to understand the object because the same Reality that transcends both of them also permeates them.

Indian seers have held that Reality is both personal and impersonal. It can be adored either as Shri Krishna or as the Virat or Infinite Person described in the eleventh canto of the *Gita*.

Nature and its laws—What poets have called Necessity

—are the product of a cosmic ignorance—a power-cons-
ciousness that has been separated from its original source.
They have a role to play in the scheme of creation. The
Law or Order sustains the worlds. It is a multiplicity that
has forgotten the underlying unity.

But these Laws of Nature can be transcended whenever a ray, direct from the Supreme, penetrates the
universe. This ray is Power,—will, thought and feeling
combined in a solar flash. The Word, which is at the
very root of Creation, is a complex seed-symphony of
Truth, Beauty, Goodness, Love, Delight and Power.

When does the Ray descend? As the Gita says, whenever righteousness is at a low ebb and the unrighteous
ride on the crest of the wave, the Ray takes human
form to establish the reign of Truth again, to protect the
good and to punish the wicked.

The question may be asked: how does the Avatar
fulfil his mission? What the Avatar does in his own
personal, human capacity can only have limited application. It will, in fact, be symbolic of what the divine part
of him will achieve by changing the spirit of an age, the
ideals that nations set before themselves and the trends
in the thinking of humanity.

The greater the need, the more frequently do avatars
descend on the human scene. The Avatar moves like a
colossus among men. The past, the present and the
future lie open to his gaze. What is more, he has the
power of Grace. An avatar has sixteen *kalas* or phases.
Five of these he shares with human beings and other
animals,—the five doors of perception,—sight, hearing,
smell, taste and touch. Another four he shares with human beings,—mind, heart, intelligence and the *turyavastha*
or transcendence of intuitive experience. The seven phases
that follow are characteristic of a *purnavatar*, an integral

or all-inclusive *avatar*: Grace or reward for effort that fails to be rewarded though it has come from the deserving; *anugraha* or special Grace whether the recipient merits it or not; the power to create a new order of life in society, new states of consciousness in individuals or new objects; the power to support and sustain what is inherently good, which may happen to be defenceless; the power to destroy what is evil; the assumption of a *form* which, whenever it is recalled mentally or in the presence of a photograph, results in the immediate spiritual presence (sometimes even physical) of the Avatar himself, affording a solution to the problem that the beholder has in mind; and the assumption of a *name* which has a similar potency.

An avatar is always at work and always at rest. His vision is worldwide and it embraces all the dimensions of Time. He has an effortless command over metempsychosis, *paranthahkarana pravesh* or entry into the innermost hearts of others, the power to open up new channels of thinking, the power to exercise the will for the benefaction of individuals or the race and the power to restore life to the dead. An Avatar is an integral manifestation of the Divine.

An *avatar* is generally called a *bhagavan*. According to ancient Sanskrit lexicographers, the word *bhaga* connotes six unique attributes: *sriyah* or material prosperity; *yashah* or fame, prosperity due to the intellect, creative ability, generosity, etc.; *aishvarya*, which is a third form of wealth, authority derived from inherent power; *virya* or heroism; *jnanam* or wisdom; and *vairagya* or detachment. A *bhagavan* is one who possesses these six attributes. There is also the Sanskrit verse:

Utpattincha vinashancha
Bhutanam agatim gatim

13

Vetti vidyam avidyam cha
Sa vachya bhagavan iti.

An avatar has also the four attributes of the Divine: omnipresence, omniscience, omnipotence and omnifelicity.

An avatar comes to usher in a new age for humanity, to enable humanity to take another step in its evolution towards its ultimate goal.

(II)

The popular notion of *avatars* is that there are ten of them: the Matsya or Fish Incarnation; the Koorma or Tortoise; the Varaha or Boar; Nrisimha or Man-Lion; Vamana; Parasurama; Rama; either Balarama or the Buddha; Sri Krishna; Kalki.

Those who wish to include the Buddha in this list usually drop Balarama.

But the Bhagavata mentions twentytwo *avatars*. The first one is the *Purushavatar*, the form that God assumed when he set out to create the universe. This form was in the likeness of a man, possessing the five organs of perception (ear, eye, tongue, skin and nose), the five organs of action (voice or larynx; hand; foot; organ of excretion and the organ of generation), the five elements, and *manas* or mind. This *avatar* is basic to all the others which merge in it after they have fulfilled their mission. It is from the lotus in the solar plexus of this *Purushavatar* that the four-faced Brahma is born. It is from the five elements which were part of this Purusha that the universe took shape. It is this Infinite Purusha that became himself the many incarnations that followed.

The first incarnation of the Purusha is said to be that of the four immortal celibates—Sanaka, Sanandana, Sanatsujata and Sanatkumara. This is known as the

Kaumaravatar. This was followed by the Boar. Then came Narada who composed the *Pancharatragama*. He was followed by the Nara-Narayana incarnation. The fifth was Kapila, author of Sankhya Shastra. The sixth was Dattatreya, who taught Prahlad, Alarka and others the spiritual way of life. Then followed Yajna; Rishabha; Pruthu; the Fish; the Tortoise; Dhanvantari who came with the goblet of the nectar of immortality when the ocean was churned by the gods and demons; Mohini who secured the nectar for the gods, depriving the demons of it; Nrisimha or Man-Lion; Vamana; Parasurama; Vyasa who compiled the Vedas; Rama; Balarama; Krishna; the Buddha; Kalki, who is predicted to be born of a brahmin called Vishnuyasha.

It will be seen from this account of the various incarnations that the list given is quite a miscellaneous one. Nor is it easy to see why the *avatars* should be only twentytwo even according to the Hindu conception. Several prophets and saints have been claimed as *avatars* in the centuries that followed: Sankaracharya; Gauranga; Sri Ramakrishna; Sri Aurobindo; Ramana Maharshi and several others. There are, of course, quite a few outside the Hindu fold, Jesus Christ being one of them.

There is a way out of this confusion. Not each one is an integral *avatar* (*Purnavatar*), for a complete manifestation, all the sixteen criteria discussed above have to be in evidence. Where only a few of these criteria are manifest, we have an *amshavatar* or a fractional avatar. Even Sri Rama is not acknowledged as an integral avatar. Some great men are also regarded as *vibhutis* or embodiments of certain qualities of the Divine or emanations from the gods or goddesses who represent these qualities. Only Sri Krishna, among the past incarnations, is known as an integral avatar.

15

Another point of interest regarding *avatars* is whether they are instances of *descent*, of the Divine descending into human flesh or of *ascent*,—of man climbing into godhood by his own heroic effort and renunciation. The Bhagavata view is one of descent. The view that the Jains take regarding their *tirthankaras* is one of ascent. But the *tirthankara* is also regarded as capable of all that an avatar can do.

The *avatar* appears whenever, as the Gita says, the world is passing through a spiritual and moral crisis. The *avatar* comes in order to uphold *dharma* and to reveal the next evolutionary step in creation. It is easy to see how the modern world, through its tremendous scientific progress and moral regress, is ripe for avatars. But the avatar, according to Sri Aurobindo's interpretation of the Gita (IV-9), is here mainly to raise man from his manhood to supermanhood by his own example and influence: "Divine is My birth as well as My work. One who knows this in true principle, comes not to rebirth after leaving his body; he, O Arjuna, comes to Me." Sri Aurobindo remarks: "The growth of the god in man is man's proper business; the steadfast turning of this lower into the divine nature is the carefully hidden meaning of human life." (*Essays on the Gita*, pp. 312-13)

Sri Aurobindo says that the Divine appears as Avatar to aid the great transitional stages and as *vibhuti* during the lesser transitions. A *vibhuti* embodies some power of the Divine. But his consciousness is not that of an inborn Divinity. There is a double element in the Avatar—human in front, Divine behind: "If you look upon the human alone, looking with the external eye only and not willing or ready to see anything else, you will see a human being only." The terms *Avatar* and *vibhuti* are not "concerned with morality or immorality, perfection

16

or imperfection according to small human standards... they are not at all the essence of the matter." Sri Aurobindo defines an *Avatar* as one who is conscious of the presence and power of the Divine born in him or descended into him and governing from within his will and life and action; he feels identified inwardly with this divine power and presence.

The Personal and the Impersonal are two aspects of the Divine. It is easier to seek the Divine in the Personal manifestation than in the Impersonal. Says the Gita in the 5th verse of the XIIth canto: "Kleshodhika-tarastheshamavyaktasaktachetasam."

(III)

The Avatar, therefore, is not the crude thing that he is made out to be by the common people. There are avatars as there are men of genius and varying degrees of avatarhood make their appearance through the ages. Just as there are only a few colossi in science or in the fine arts, there are only a few integral avatars.

Baba speaks of his three incarnations, Shirdi Sai, Sathya Sai and Prem Sai. Prem Sai is the third and last in this sequence and it is assumed that he will be an incarnation of Sakti. Shirdi was an incarnation of Siva. There is a chapter on the childhood of Shirdi Baba in this book. The Sathya Sai incarnation stands for the combined glory of Siva and Sakti,— both consciousness and executive force. This makes for greater complexity.

The Divine himself is the supreme paradox. He is the One in the Many, Spirit and Matter at the same time. Himself transcendental, the Divine has become the universe itself. He is infinity which can also crowd itself into a little room. Immortality itself, He is also Death. He is both Time and Eternity. He is Love, but this Love

17

also is red in tooth and claw. Formless, the Divine is yet the father of all forms.

An avatar is a paradox cut in the image of the Divine. He is divine though human. Most people know how Baba, when the right half of his body was completely paralysed, sprinkled a little water over it with his left hand and was 'whole' again. He is human though divine, as when Shirdi Baba shed tears over the death of the cook whom he had loved so well. Sathya Sai Baba is the loving Sai mother pouring her love over her little children. But he is also a real task-master, sometimes relentless when a devotee is at fault and has to be taught a lesson.

Krishna is the deity in our bosom, the indwelling Divine. But he also manipulates well his strings as the producer of this puppet-show,—he subjects each son of man to the wiles of *maya* or illusion. He is supreme in wisdom like Maheshwari and also perfect in executive skill like Maha Saraswati. He stands for harmony, love and beauty like Maha Laxmi, but is irresistible in the destruction of evil like Maha Kali.

A poet and an enchanting singer, Baba is also a philosopher and a social worker. He talks away sometimes like a simple and innocent child. But he can be a master diplomat when the occasion requires it. Approach him as a friend and you will find that he is too remote from you. Speak to him with awe as to Universal Man and you will see that he is speaking to you as a friend by your bedside.

The Avatar is there to separate the subtle from the gross, grain from chaff and soul from the desire-self. He sets free invisible forces which change the destinies of nations.

Whose Avatar is Baba? Is he an Avatar of Sri Krishna?

The lovely statue in the meditation hall at Prashanti
Nilayam is sure to tempt us to accept this suggestion.
Krishna, the flute-player of Brindavan, is about to play
on his flute, manipulate the stops and flood the world
with divine music. But he suddenly hears the agonising
cry of humanity and is startled from the ecstasy of music.
His fingers hover in midair and there is an expression of
deep concern on his face. The statue accounts for the
very genesis of this avatar in Puttaparti.

Is he Siva? A staunch Saivite had been to Puttaparti.
Seeing the Krishna statue in the Meditation Hall, he felt
antipathetic and did not feel like meditating in that hall.
He went to the riverside, had a dip in the Chitravati and
sat on the bank of the river to worship the Lingam. But
as he held the Lingam in his left hand and concentrated on it, he caught a glimpse of Baba on the surface
of the soft stone of the Lingam. He turned back to see
whether Baba was standing there behind him, his image
being reflected in the stone. This was not so. But it
happened every time he concentrated on the Lingam.
Puzzled, he proceeded again towards the meditation hall.
And he met Bhagavan there just when he was about to
enter it. Bhagavan, who had never spoken to him before,
asked him smilingly: "Why have you come away? You
wanted to worship Siva by the riverside."

Many other devotees have found in Baba their own
Masters or the particular deities they worship. Baba has
been Murughan, Sakti and all the Masters by turns. The
fact is that each avatar is there as a manifestation of the
Divine. And the Divine is all-encompassing, for He is
the substance in the symbols.

(IV)

We should never forget the fact that, as Sri Aurobindo

19

says, when the Divine descends, he takes upon himself
the burden of humanity in order to exceed it—he
becomes human in order to show humanity how
to become divine. Those who have turned their back
on the Divine in Baba have admitted that Baba's
lasting appeal lies in the human touch, "his ability to
enter into the hearts of men and plant a seed of
faith." But the double element is there and we will
not be able to understand Baba unless we realise that he
is an amalgam of the human and Divine. I wrote about
Narahari in my novel, *Narahari, Prophet of New India*
(p. 145): "Inspiration flowed to his instrumental personality from the Divine in him. His instrumental self addressed stirring songs of love and devotion to this divine element within himself. His mortal self was only a projection of the other one, the Immortal in him. But this
dichotomy, which was only a temporary phenomenon,
created endless opportunities for turning life into a co-
operative adventure between the human and divine."

I regard the cook episode in the life of Shirdi Baba as
one that throws a great deal of light on this nexus of
the human and divine in an Avatar. A male cook had
served Shirdi Baba loyally and with love for many years.
When the cook died, big tears trickled down the cheeks
of Shirdi Baba. He had loved him deeply with such a
warm and human love. But the very next moment Shirdi
Baba recollected himself and said calmly: "where have
you gone, after all? You have become a part of Me."

I have referred earlier to the idea that Baba is the
combined manifestation of Siva and Sakti (the psychological masculine and feminine, and not the biological).
There must be an integration of these two aspects in
man's psyche. There is a world crisis today because the
masculine aspect of man's consciousness has outstripped

its feminine counterpart. One associates Grace with the feminine aspect of the Godhead. Grace comes through the feminine aspect and promotes the psychological transformation of the individual as well as the collectivity. When Grace acts,

"Then miracle is made the common rule,
One mighty deed can change the course of things,
A lonely thought becomes omnipotent."

When Baba writes about Sri Krishna in *Bhagavata Vahini* we get to know what an Avataric personality has to say about an Avatar. Baba makes Arjun say, after the self-slaughter of the Yadavas, when he had to return alone tragically from Dwaraka: "We have failed to understand his play. With that deluding human form he moved with us, mixed with us, behaved with us as if he was our kinsman and well-wisher, our friend and guide and saved us from many a calamity. We were carried away by pride that we had His Grace. We sought from him mere external victory and temporal benefits. We ignored the vast treasures with which we could have filled our hearts. We never contemplated his real reality."

This is what his most intimate disciple has to say about Sri Kishna as an Avatar. Sage Suka gives a picture of Sri Krishna, such as would be painted by a good observer: "He treated the world as a puppet-show. He was always radiant with his smile. He never knew anxiety, disappointment or distress. He behaved sometimes as a common man, sometimes as an innocent child, at other times as a near kinsman, or as an intimate friend, or as a masterful monarch. He had the capacity and cleverness to play all roles with a unique distinction."

The impression that one finally has of an Avatar is

21

this unique blend of the human and the divine,—the attributes that go to make up *aishvarya* or divinity and all those human qualities that make him so sweet and lovable, qualities that may be summed up as *madhurya* or sweetness.

3. BABA'S MISSION AND MESSAGE

BHAGAVAN Sathya Sai Baba has been a name to conjure with in recent years. Lakhs of people who have been to Puttaparti have returned with hope in their eyes and peace in their hearts. Millions of people who have listened to the magic chanting of his *bhajans* and his thrilling eloquence carry in their minds an unforgettable memory of what they have seen and heard. Thousands of people in North and East India have become his devoted disciples because of the miraculous cures he wrought for them from a distance or the wondrous signs of his presence that he vouchsafed them. Hundreds of Europeans and Americans have been drawn to him by the books written about him, the film strips on festival days in the *Nilayam* and on Baba and the gramophone records they have listened to.

Sai Samitis have been formed all over India and abroad. Sai literature consisting of collections of Baba's speeches and his writings is available in the original in Telugu, in English and in the leading Indian languages. There is a centre like Dharmakshetra in Bombay, a distinctive architectural landmark. Similar centres have come up in Madras and at several other places also. A few Sathya Sai arts and science colleges have already been functioning and Baba desires to start at least one college in each state in India. Prashanthi Nilayam itself has developed into a modern ashram with the construction of hundreds of apartments. At

the Sathya Sai World Conference held in Bombay in
1968, he declared that it was his mission to restore India
to her former spiritual glory. He said that he would not
rest from his labours till this had been achieved.

Even a few sayings of Baba give us an idea of his
personality. One of the key words of his philosophy is
Love. "Start the day with love", he says, "fill the day
with love, spend the day with love, end the day with
love: This is the way to God." *Truth* is another word.
"There are three I's", he says, "the one you think you
are; the one that others think you are; and the one you
really are." He prescribes *Dharma* or right action is
another word. "Start early", says Baba, "drive slowly
and reach safely." Those who enter the Nilayam at
Puttaparti read this legend of peace: "You are in the
light. The light is in you. You are the light."

Even if we approach him on the moral and ideological plane, the purity of his living and the width of his
thinking are breath-taking. He has said that love is his
own image or *swarupa*; peace is his own abiding attitude
or *swabhava*; *Dharma* or right action his unfailing way
of doing things and *sathya* or truth the element he lives
and breathes in. He is Purity itself.

As for his largeness of vision, one has to remember
his affirmation that all religions are pathways to the
Divine. The Hall of Meditation in Prashanti Nilayam
has, on its walls, portraits of the Buddha and Jesus
Christ, Zoroaster and Guru Nanak, Sankaracharya
and Madhwacharya. The Prashanti symbol of the unfolding lotus is itself encompassed by Aum, the Wheel
of *Dharma*. the Sacred Fire, the Crescent and the Star
and the Cross. He has also warned us again and again
that we should not be limited by the form and name of
Sai. All other names and forms are equally divine and

we should have the same respect and affection for them. What matters is the one effulgent Spirit behind many names and forms.

Baba's is a presence that is felt everywhere. He knows every thing for he has access to what W.B. Yeats calls the Earth Memory. His psycho-kinetic and other powers transcend cosmic laws.

The omnifelicity that he diffuses through his universal love has been widely felt and experienced.

As for the individual, Baba leads him all the way from desire to illumination. He showers on the devotee the affection of a mother, *Sai Janani*. He has the power to fulfil the legitimate desires of the devotee and succour him in distress. He is also the relentless hammerer and shaper of souls passing human beings through the furnace of sorrow or the streams of joy as the occasion requires it. His field of sports is eternity, not Time. He has neither pity nor hate but love,—the love that cuts an agate and the love that saves.

God can transform the collectivity in a miraculous way. Baba is not a pawn but a player who has the strength derived from the Unfailing Champion in the game of chess played on the cosmic chequerboard. The transformation has to be achieved humanly and through human means.

For this purpose, Baba has sketched out a comprehensive programme. A citizen has to be trained in right action through *seva dal* discipline—attending to patients in hospitals and erring children in remand homes and helping those in distress. It is the sacred duty of the rich to feed the poor and look after them. The coming generation has to be trained for right action through well-devised courses in *bal vihars, mahila vibhags* and colleges for men and for women especially started for the purpose.

Through Sathya Sai study circles and *Vidvan Mahasa-bhas* or contacts with the learned through their dis-courses, one has to develop one's vision of Truth. This has also to happen through *veda pathashalas* by studying ancient Indian culture, performing sacrifices in the vedic manner and observing great festival days and the birthdays of *avatars* and saints.

The Sathya Sai samitis work for peace and concord. They draw their members from all castes and creeds, all communities and language groups. They learn to work together as a fraternity. They chant the heart-easing songs or *bhajans* of Baba and move for *nagar sankirtan* or itinerant devotional singing in the early hours of the morning, waking up fellow-citizens with the utterance of the name of God. They worship Him in all names and forms.

To the sceptic who thinks it is absurd to take any human being as God, Baba says: "Yes, I am God. What capacity do you have, as you stand, to test this statement? Plunge into your own soul and see from there. You will then realise the truth of the statement. I may add that you are also God." The concept of *Avatarhood* has to be understood in its proper context. An *avatar* is the saviour who takes the human evolution a step higher. He is a ray direct from the Supreme and it is because of his presence in a world hemmed in by cosmic laws that there is the possibility of transcendent grace.

4. A MULTI-FACETED PERSONALITY

I

BABA'S has been a name to conjure with for millions of people in India and for thousands in different parts of the world. Every day has been a day of miracles in his life. No one has a closer grip over his own life than Baba has. We tend to be slaves, but he is always the master of his movements. He had his sports of boyhood during the first sixteen years of his life. When these *balalilas* or pranks were over, the next sixteen years were devoted to *Mahimas*, to breath-taking miracles. The period from his thirty-second to his forty-eighth year, was devoted to *Upadesh* or delivering discourses on spiritual topics for the benefit of the people. Everything has been planned and it all proceeds according to plan. The period of sixteen years from his fortyeighth year onwards, it seems, will lead to intensive instruction in *sadhana* or spiritual discipline to select groups. Prashanthi Nilayam is preparing itself for this change, as it were, by rebuilding itself, from the small hamlet that it was for a thousand people, into a real international township with modern amenities for more than five thousand. At the Navaratra festival in September 1973, a devotee presented a crown with a gold base, so studded over with diamonds, that the gold could hardly be seen. This was meant for the statue of Shirdi Baba sitting in his characteristic pose, the right leg resting across the left. This was priced at two lakhs of rupees. Bhagavan remarked smiling that everything happens at the right time. Prashanthi Nilayam was the residence of a private individual. Three domes have now risen upon it, turning it into a *mandir* or temple. (This coincides strangely with the prophecy of a mystic American couple that the himalayan temple with three domes, built by the two Masters, Arun and Rama, where the ancient religion, which is the fountainhead of all the great religions of the world, was propounded, and which had gone down owing to a shift in the earth's movement, would come up again in 1968, announcing the advent of a new world order.) There is a will ruling this dedicated life and shaping everything around it according to a divine plan.

A few members of Parliament called on Bhagavan some months ago and they requested Bana to tell them something about himself. Bhagavan said: "When among men, I am a man. When among women, I am a woman. Among children, I am a child. Alone, I am God." One has to ruminate on these words to know the many layers of meaning contained in the statement.

Baba's plans for another life are also complete. He says that he will live in this body till he is ninetysix years of age, in order to complete his mission. Thereafter, he will be born as Prem Sai in a village in Mandya District in Karnataka, to fix the spire, as it were, on the temple he has built or the work that he has accomplished.

The thought indeed strikes one that the Sathya Sai movement will spread far and wide with each succeeding year. I was present at the Silver Jubilee function of the temple consecrated to Shirdi Baba at the instance of Bhagavan Sathya Sai Baba at Guindy, Madras. Bhagavan insisted that the Shirdi form, and not the Sathya Sai form, should be installed at the temple. The organisers had erected a *Dhwaja Sthamba* or Flag-pillar to celebrate the occasion, featuring the unfolding lotus-bud and divine flame. They had inscribed on its beautiful panels the legend of some of Baba's teachings about love and so on. This was an unusual inscription for a pillar and it looked like an Ashoka pillar to me, reborn in another form after more than two thousand years. One may expect these new Ashokan pillars to rise all over different parts of the country in the coming years.

II

Bhagavan Baba's personality is like a sunbeam. Several rainbow colours have been fused into it. It would be interesting to identify them, if only to understand the complex structure of a personality which is essentially so simple and innocent.

Baba is, first and foremost, the enchanting *bhajan* singer of Brindavan. To listen to him singing to the many, many thousands who sit thrilled before him and recite after him in the midst of a momentous silence, is to experience the process of a social revolution in progress before our eyes and in our very ears. The very first *bhajan* he sang: *Manasa Bhajare Gurucharanam Dustara Bhavasagara Taranam* is a *mantra* or an integrated utterance in which melody, meaning and image are fused together in the white heat of a great inspiration or self-revelation. T.S. Eliot's Prufrock wishes to cross the seas by turning himself into a pair of claws. Here are a pair of blessed feet that descend within easy reach of every swimmer in the ocean of life and he has only to put forth his tired hands and cling to them if he wants to be carried safely to the other shore.

When Baba stands up there on the platform, he is like a snake-charmer, singing as the snake-charmer plays on his *pungi* and even cobras, with venom on their tongues, sway their hoods and forget all about the evil that is in them. This is how Baba wins the hearts of even the most sophisticated individuals.

His appeal to the intellect is unobtrusive and gains on one, not immediately, but by degrees, as one ponders over what he says. He has always said that to be an *acharya*, a teacher, has been his pet idea and with royal ease, he plays the role of a world teacher, a *jagadguru*. His philosophy is cast in the traditional mould, since his mission is one of, as he has said, a revival of the *sanatan* or eternal *dharma* and a resurrection of the Vedas[1] and the establishment of a spiritual era all over the world through India. But the philosophy is as new and this-worldly, as revolutionary in its essence, as that of Sri Aurobindo. *Iha* and *Para*, this world and the next, Matter and spirit, are not divorced from each other. They are like the two legs on which a man stands erect. From *Danavatva* or *Animality*, man has to ascend into *Manavatva* or humanity. He has then to take the next step to *Madhavatva* or divinity. If he does not realise the deity, the *Sivam* in himself, he is no better than *Shavam*—a corpse. It is obvious that the world teacher in Baba loves to work his way through puns, like Shakespeare. But not only did Shakespeare love quibbles. They were, for him, a Cleopatra for 'whom he' lost the world and was content to lose it. But Baba keeps this *maya*, this siren, at a

[1]For the universal teaching that they contain.

30

considerable distance. He makes good use of puns for purposes of instruction. He is not used by them.

A film had to be shown to students. The screen was there before them and the cine projector had been set up in its place. This was too golden an opportunity to be missed. Baba walked up to the screen before the lights were switched off. He pointed to the screen and said that it would soon be covered by a shadow show. The shadows to be projected on the screen were pure illusion. The screen represented the unchanging reality. When it was covered by shadows, it became the world, *mithya*, not just false, but true and untrue at the same time. This was how a point in Sankara's *Advaita* was driven home with the help of very modern visual aids.

But the world is not just an illusion. As Baba often reminds us, there is the other sacred sentence: *Sarvam Khalvidam Brahma* (All this is brahman). This world is divine, for divinity resides in the very heart of it. *Dharma*, as he points out, is a complex concept. It comprises the values of *sanatana* or eternal *dharma*, *Vyakti Dharma* (the laws of individual life), *Sanghika Dharma* or the *dharma* of the collectivity, *Varna Dharma* or the *dharma* of the community and *Yuga Dharma* or *dharma* of the age. The perennial philosophy has to be disengaged from all these other elements, cultivated intensively and infused into the entire composition when one is master of it.

Bhagavan will emphasise this role more and more, but in different ways, probably by organising *yoga* classes, seminars and so on. The discourses that he delivered on the Vedas in Nava Ratra, 1972, would do honour to any intellectual for the rigour and logic of their exposition. I was once startled when I came across a passage in which Coleridge labours at the three-

31

fold distinction of man, a distinction which Baba has rounded off in one of his well-known triplets. He speaks of the three I's,—"The one you think you are, the one others think you are and the one you *really* are." Here is Coleridge's passage in which he makes the first distinction second and the second first. In his *Philosophical Lectures*, Coleridge describes the mind of man, "We find him gifted, as it were, with a three-fold mind. The one belonging to him specifically, arising, I mean, necessarily, out of the peculiar mechanism of his nature and by WHICH he beholds all things perspectively from his relative position as man; the second, in which these views are again modified too often disturbed and falsified—by his particular constitution and position as this or that particular, individual; and the third, which exists in all men *Potentially* and in its germ, though it requires both effort from within and auspicious circumstances from without to evolve it into effect—by this third and higher power he places himself on the same point as nature, and contemplates all objects, himself included, in their permanent and universal being and relations."

Even more significant is Baba's role as an educator of the vital, of the desire-self in man. It may be easy to convince the intellect. But the vital has to be dealt with in the university of hard knocks. It learns only through direct and bitter experience. The *vibhuti* or *prasad* of divine ashes which Baba gives is itself an austere symbol of what he wishes to suggest. Ash Wednesday is the day of a holy christian festival, the first day in Lent, when the priest anoints the forehead of the householder with ashes and says: "Remember, man, that thou art dust and unto dust thou shalt return." As Longfellow pointed in a didactic poem of his, the Bible did not speak this of the soul, only of the body. From this point of view, every day is Ash Wednesday in the eyes of Baba. *Vibhuti*, which is his gesture of recognition to every one, indicates the transitoriness of earthly glory and its reduction to ashes. But, at the same time, *Vibhuti* establishes the white purity and imperishability of all spiritual glory.

Baba is a real *kalpataru*, a wish-fulfilling tree. He showers his love on his devotees, satisfies extraordinary but legitimate demands and drenches each person with the delight of existence. Many are drawn to him and some are chosen to be in closer touch with him. These few who live, as it were, in a dream-paradise are gradually put on probation, on the mat. Eclipse is everywhere and the rest no more. Man—*Manushya Matruru*, as Baba says, is liable to err. Even the chosen naturally nod a number of times. Baba selects one vulnerable point or the other, disapproves of it sternly and rejects firmly any liberty taken by the devotee. All geniality and all smiles at one time, neither smile nor talk now, Baba does not extend even a glance of recognition to the perplexed devotee. The devotee does not know what to do. He is thrown back on himself, in a burning pit for some time. He enters on a period of self-scrutiny and introspection. He may not be seen by Baba for months. I know he said about one: "He has indulged in small talk. I will not see him for a year." Even if he happens to talk to the devotee who is on trial, it will be in a matter-of-fact manner which is more hurtful than soothing. I know a friend who, caught in such a plight, implored Bhagavan, "I pray, do not deny me your smile. You may not talk to me. I promise, I will not seek an interview at any time in life with you. But, for heaven's sake, please don't deny me your smile."

If a devotee makes a serious mistake, Bhagavan first

33

mentions it to him so that he may improve. If there is no reformation, a rebuke is administered when there are other people sitting and this is repeated another time, if necessary. Thereafter, if the devotee does not improve, he is no longer in the fold and Bhagavan will neither see him nor talk to him again. He loses his privilege till he has atoned for it for years and years. I said once to him: "One is afraid to speak to you, Swami. You are so unsparing and you are such a task-master." Immediately came the dispassionate reply: "We also melt."

What is more, Baba is the great exemplar, the model that the seeker needs to keep before him for his own progress and perfection. An ever-flowing fountain of pure love, an amazing intellect, a mind always at peace with itself and a fine sense of humour which is active whenever he is not in one of his explosive moods of sublimity, Baba himself has said that *Sathya* or truth is his *Prachar* or mode of communication, *Dharma* or Right Action is his *Achar* or behaviour, *Shanthi* or peace is his innate disposition and *Prema* or Love is his *Swaroopa* or likeness. His is not the not ochre robe of renunciation but the red, saffron and white of a veritable mastery of the world. There are pretenders who imitate him in his dress without the inner necessity and without that purity that characterises the body carrying divine cargo.

Truth, Beauty, Goodness, Love and Power are abstractions and one does not know where to find them. Great individuals, however eminent, present themselves to us as imperfect versions of these abstract entities. The capital letters, T, B, G, L and P, look like pretentious perpetrations. But one is tempted to say that these capital letters gain in meaning as one begins to know Baba.

His most fascinating phase is his accomplishment as a *Yogishwar*, a great organiser, the master of works. He gives spiritual guidance to each one according to his need. I have known Baba giving to a numerologist a figure that opened up new vistas for him. He created, for a biologist, an image of the Missing Link. He gave exact guidance to a visionary, asking him to disregard the other lights and gaze only on the mystic sun within him, so intimately did he know the occult life of this seeker. He drew into conversation a millionaire who did not drink but was the cause of drink in others by serving them drinks at evening parties and, materialising a jewelled ring for him, slipped it on his finger and said that he should never serve, or have served, drinks to others again. To a student who was extremely fond of film-shows and who could not abstain from seeing at least one picture a day, he materialised and gave a wrist watch and warned him that it would stop if he ever saw a picture again. Indeed, it happened that, jubilant because of his success at a public examination, he went with other friends to an evening film-show, forgetting all about this injunction. What was his dismay when he discovered in the street light, after returning from the cinema-theatre, that the watch had stopped! No watch repairer in Hyderabad or in Bombay could set it right. Crest-fallen, the student went to Bhagavan who set it right by a waive of his hand and warned him against future transgressions!

In Baba's *Durbar*, as in *Chaucer's Canterbury Tales*, there is God's plenty. All types of mind, all categories of being and all classes, castes and professions are represented there. It is a most heterogeneous crowd that collects on his precincts and in his courtyard. Saints, *sanyasins*, poets, philosophers, ministers, officials, musicians, cinema stars, merchants, politicians, police constables and Inspector Generals of Police, lawyers, judges, doctors, surgeons, teachers, professors. It is difficult to say who is *not* there. The orthodox man of religion is there as well as the reformer. Even positively wicked people are there and when asked about them Baba replies: "They have more need of me than you have." The one spiritual bond that joins this motley crowd into a fraternity is Baba's love for them and their equally spontaneous love of Baba. Baba appeals to the innermost heart of each of them, for it is he who resides in those depths.

Having drawn to himself one of the most diverse and colourful concourse of devotees on record, Baba proceeds to educate them in the many Sai institutions that he has got organised, from the *Bal Vikas* or children's centre to the Seva Samitis. A detailed account of these institutions has been given elsewhere. These are training grounds for disciples and centres for dispensation of grace to mankind as a whole.

It is as a prophet and the inaugurator of a new social order in the world that we think of Baba in his overall role. But it is equally true that he is the deity in the bosom of every individual, a presence constantly to be felt in our innermost hearts. It is from that centre that he guides, corrects and protects us. His presence is there because he is one with the World Soul or the Oversoul and the soul of each one of us. As Shelley says, he is made one with Nature and is a "portion of that loveliness". Many have recorded their experiences about the inscrutable but unmistakable presence of Baba in their hearts. Even a half-believer like Mr. Schulman has, in his book on Baba, recorded his dream in which Baba helped him to locate certain important papers which he himself could not trace anywhere in spite of his best efforts. There, in our innermost hearts, the World Soul waits patiently for us, allowing the mind, the vital and the body to discover the presence in their own appointed hour.

As for the inauguration of a new social order, there is the claim that he is a prophet and an *Avatar*. In his discourse at the Shri Sathya Sai World Conference held in Bombay in 1968, Baba spoke in ringing tones of the insoluble mystery of his manifestation, of the mission for which he has come,—the spiritual regeneration of mankind through the all-round regeneration of India and the unequivocal pronouncement that he would leave the world only after completing his mission. He has emphasised the unity of all religions and adopted a symbol which makes the idea of that unity concrete. It is this aspect of Baba's personality that gives it the sense of power, power which is indispensable if a mission is to be fulfilled. As many people know, he went into a deep trance for nearly an hour as his body lay still at a public meeting on Shivaratri day at Prashanthi Nilayam. Everybody was getting anxious when he came out of the trance and casually remarked that he had just taken a trip round the world to know how it was faring. There are tokens of his 'Arrival', as it were, in homes in remote places—Delhi, Madras, Jamnagar, Puri, Chandigarh, Shillong, Colombo, Los Angeles, London—by way of the mysterious profusion of ashes or *vibhuti, kumkum*, turmeric, *Amrit* or ambrosial honey, in photographs and albums and in prominent characters on walls. None can explain this phenomenon. But no one can deny the fact that it indicates the presence of an extraordinary power, —a power that sets at nought all laws of chemistry and physics. An eminent scientist thought, some time back, that setting the laws of physics and chemistry at nought was a lesser achievement than that of transcending them. I suppose it is clear that, if one can defy these laws successfully, that itself is an act of transcendence, unless one loves to quibble. "One day, I shall walk across the sky", said Baba, half jokingly and half in earnest, "so that every one can see it for himself."

Every man possesses this secret of Godhead. Somebody asked Baba once: "How can you say that you are God?" Baba remarked: "You have not heard me out completely. I say that I am God. And I say that you are also God. The only difference is that I know it and you don't know it."

It is only when one grasps this sunbeam—secret of Baba's personality that one is on the right way to experiencing his reality. Its unity can be realised all the better by apprehending its infinite variety.

5. MORE ABOUT BABA

WHO is Sai Baba? Nobody can say. Baba himself has said: "Do not try to understand who I am. You will never succeed. Try and follow me and do what I say should be done for one's soul-awakening." Tennyson wrote about King Arthur: "From the great deep to the great deep he goes." This mystery enwraps every human soul. The mystery is infinitely greater especially when it concerns the advent of an incarnation.

Another fact is that, spiritually, he is self-born, *swayambhoo.* When he announced his advent at the age of fourteen, he knew he was a Master. He said: "My *bhaktas* are waiting for me. I must go."

Baba has no life of his own. His is a life lived for others. He ploughs, sows, plants and reaps for others every hour of his life.

His retentive memory and his fund of knowledge are amazing. He can spot out an acquaintance in the midst of thousands of people. He attends to minor details like the decoration of a pandal, when a function is on, himself. His passion for perfection is insatiable and his industry does not have a minute to spare. A minute wasted, says Baba, is life wasted.

Baba's philosophy, in one sense, is a philosophy of pragmatic transcendentalism. There is no single remedy for all. The remedy differs from person to person, for Baba deals with individuals, not abstractions. He may prescribe the path of Works for one, Meditation for another and so on as the person and occasion demand it. 'Each according to his need': this is the rule.

Baba indulges occasionally in innocent jokes. "If you try to deceive me," he says, "I shall be like Krishna and outwit you in your game." Whenever Baba grants *darshan*, the rule is that the devotee does not bow down and touch Baba's feet unless he is allowed to. Standing beneath one of the trees in the Brindavan garden, when a devotee tried to touch Baba's feet, what Baba did was to point to the branch against which he might have struck his head while rising! A middle-aged person tried to touch Baba's feet when Baba moved near him, immediately after lunch. "It is not good for you to do it now", said Baba, "you have just eaten." Another devotee started asking quite a few philosophic questions, in a group sitting, just to impress on Baba that he, the devotee, was well read in philosophy. After listening to one or two questions, Baba simply remarked: "I know you know." Humour is always ready at hand for Baba, both as a testing device and for pricking vanity balloons.

But the great humorist is also a relentless hammersmith, beating gold, any cosmic substance, into shape for turning it into an ornament. He is the Diamond that cuts rough and uncut diamonds into form.

Baba does not know what anger is. But he can simulate anger when the guilty are to be brought to book and make you feel that you are a crawling worm. He will, on such an occasion, make sublime statements and ask questions which are rooted in truth and therefore unanswerable.

He has considerable powers of persuasiveness. When he desires to win over the listener to his point of view, his very tone is different. He pronounces the name of the listener very sweetly and trippingly on the tongue and even the word *bangaru* (dear one, 'goldie') is uttered with great charm. At the world conference in Bombay, he promised to be photographed with each group the next day. Every one went away satisfied. But the next day never arrived. It was always the 'next'. But who knows, the recollection of the time spent with him would be printed indelibly on the memory of each delegate.

But his sublime affirmations, like the affirmation of his own advent made at the first Sathya Sai World Conference in 1968, are uttered in a tone that carries conviction with it. The golden eloquence of those memorable moments is like a chain-reaction, one sublime explosion following another.

Using utterance to great purpose, Baba also knows how to make use of silence. Two of his devotees had a pitched quarrel once. Baba was deeply hurt by it. He just went upstairs and sat quietly in his room. He refused to talk to any one or to come downstairs for any purpose at all. The devotees repented in their hearts that they should have been the cause of this isolation on the part of Baba. They made it up between themselves and then went upstairs together and reported to Baba that there was, now, perfect understanding and harmony between them. It was only then that Baba came down to grant *darshan* to the hundreds that had been waiting for hours.

It is on the bedrock of Peace that his oceanic and colourful personality stands and shows its many-coloured magnificence.

It is his divine love for man, animal and plant that has made him the god of millions of homes. He loves one and all for, in each loved object, he sees himself. He feels one with the whole of creation. It is a total love untainted by any consideration for self. When the roof

41

was laid on the original Prashanthi Nilayam in Puttaparti, Baba was graciously having fun with the engineers and other devotees who had worked for this day. It was a dark night and no parapet wall had been built around the roof. In the midst of jokes and repartees, Baba suddenly got up and started to run, exclaiming: "I'm coming! I'm coming!" He almost went over to the edge of the roof and would surely have toppled down had not a few of those present hastened to throw a cordon round him and bring him back. He lay down unconscious for some minutes and, when consciousness returned to the body, he narrated the whole episode. A devotee in a village in coastal Andhra was a wealthy landlord. Some dare-devils wanted to loot all his property. A hundred strong, they were marching towards the village with knives and spears. The landlord came to know about this as they approached the village. But all that he could do at that hour was to pray for help. The dacoits would have carried out their intention fully but for the timely arrival of a policeman on the scene. This led the dacoits to believe that the landlord had been forewarned and that he had secured the help of a police force and got it to camp nearby. They ran away, leaving the landlord undisturbed. Needless to say, the policeman was Baba himself!

When asked about this incident and the rashness of the love or altruism implicit in it, Baba said: "This was an incident which happened in the early days. But what does it matter? All that would have happened if I dropped dead from the roof is that the eleventh would have gone with the tenth!"

Baba loves all, even those who regard themselves as his enemies. He plays the host to men who have deceived him and worked against him. None can be a better adviser or friend. His love itself cures and heals all manner of ills provided it is reciprocated. Apart from this, numberless people have been helped with food, shelter and money, frequently without their asking, according to their need. It is a love which floods and inundates your whole being. As Baba himself says, it is much more than the love of a thousand mothers. He once gave sixty thousand rupees to a foreign devotee who was in business, facing liquidation. But Baba's love is not blind. He is critical and mindful of the faults of devotees and yet full of love for them. It is a love that is diamond-hard and jasmine-soft. Its main aim is to make the loved one evolve spiritually.

Who is Baba? He is one whose words come true for they are immediately followed by deeds. His miracles are his visiting cards and his presence is felt everywhere, whether he is present in the flesh there or not. He can dismiss cancer and the evidence of X-ray photographs with a gesture of his hand and a little *vibhuti*. After paying a visit to Dwaraka he remarked that he had gone to Dwaraka, his 'old home'. He himself has said: "See me in every saint and sage. Worship me in any name or form. All religions are one." Though he has pitched his tents in Time, he comes from the heart of Eternity.

He knows what goes on in each mind and heart. A primary school teacher in one of the Karnataka districts had a dumb daughter. She attended Sai *bhajans* or singings in a neighbour's house. The father had no particular regard for Baba and he instructed the girl not to attend the *bhajans*. But her devotion was great and she used to go there on the sly. The father noticed this once. He was angry and he raised his hand to slap her in the face. Then it was that his daughter spoke her first sentence: "I'll tell Baba."

Another person positively disliked Baba though his wife was a great devotee. He used to ask: "How can that shaggy-haired bear be God?" But the wife finally persuaded him to go to Puttaparti on a festival day, after accepting his condition that he would not bow down to Baba or touch his feet. Sitting in the auditorium as Baba was distributing sweets to the thousands of devotees there, he was impressed by the fact that each one was disposed to regard it as a supreme fulfilment if he touched Baba's feet. When Baba passed by his line, the husband, who was a critic of Baba, also wanted to touch Baba's feet. Baba drew back and exclaimed: "Why do you wish to touch my feet? Can a shaggy-haired bear be God?" The man felt like collapsing on the spot. He has been an ardent devotee ever since.

Baba is the dispenser of what I may call 'omnifelicity'. His mere presence is a delight. It is, in fact, a fountain of peace. We go to him with a hundred questions humming in our heads. And we fail to ask him even one of them when we get there. We feel in his presence that all our questions are resolved, that there is nothing to ask and that the only thing we can do is to taste the peace and delight that flow from him imperceptibly all the time.

The Hindu sees Divinity in every type and scale of creation: the *Kaustubha* or *Chintamani* in the stone kind, the *Parijata* among trees, the Eagle or *Garuda* among birds, *Matsya* among fish, the *Kamadhenu* among cattle, *Maruti* among apes, the *Varaha* or Boar among other animals, Nrisimha or the Man-Lion and Vamana or the Dwarf. This vision would be incomplete without seeing the Divine in man. So we have Rama, the satwic avatar, and Krishna, the over-mental man. The claim is that Baba also is an advent in this illustrious line.

What can we do for Baba and what does he do for us? All that he asks of us is our love. In return, he will do everything for us. He is the *bhava roga vaidya*, the heavenly physician who has a sovereign remedy for this disease called mundane life. He expects us to surrender ourselves to the shaping will of the Master. His is the giving hand, like a waterfall and not a receiving hand. A surrender of this kind is necessary for the infinite enrichment of one's own personality,—for the replacement of the ego by the soul. I wrote in *Narahari* regarding this problem:

"There is a notion current in certain circles that to be a disciple is to lose one's own individuality. The one possession which modern man values is his own personality. A person moulds his character, nourishes his intellect, refines his emotions and awakens his intuitions by experiencing deeply the beauty of Art, Life and Nature. He is intensely aware of his own unicity in the scale of creation. To surrender to another man what one has fashioned for oneself with so much labour and to be ironed with others as the disciple of this individual or that is worse than primitive animal sacrifice, for what is sacrificed is infinitely more precious. To be a master's echo is to be a gramophone record."

"But persons arguing in this fashion hardly look at the other side of the medal. It is true that in some cases, discipleship might lead to mental dependence and lack of originality. But conformity to a known discipline may be better than mere waywardness and eccentricity or originality without substance or form. Again, a true disciple is not a mere shrub growing under the shadow of a banian tree. He is himself a banian sapling. He grows and fulfils himself in his own way. Sri Ramakrishna did not swallow up Vivekananda. On the other

45

hand, Sri Ramakrishna enabled Vivekananda to be himself, more truly and nobly than he would otherwise have been. A true disciple accepts the teachings of his master, not because of intellectual servitude or his own incapacity to think but because he finds in those teachings a philosophy towards which he himself has been spontaneously evolving. He does not surrender his personality to his master. On the other hand, he finds that his own personality is essentially like that of his master. The only difference lies in the fact that, in the master, it is raised to the *nth* degree. What the disciple is striving after is what the master has already achieved."

As Baba has explained, "All that the master does for the disciple is to enable him to discover himself. You have misplaced a hundred rupee note when you were reading a book. You can't remember now where you have kept that currency note. The master is your friend who turns over the pages of the book of your heart and shows you where exactly you have slipped in this currency note amid the pages of your book."

This currency note is drawn upon again for another beautiful example. We go through life burdened with so many anxieties. The Master says: "Transfer all your worries and anxieties to me,—bags full of them! My shoulders are broad enough to bear them. In return for this small change, I'll give you a currency note which you can easily carry in your purse or pocket. The currency note stands for only one condition: Think only of me."

Baba is not a pawn in a game of chess. He is one of the champion chess players. And his histrionic abilities, which are great, make this role colourful. You also feel, when you are at Puttaparti, that you are a

46

player and champion along with Baba. You will not feel that way even in the midst of ruling circles in Delhi, Moscow, Washington or Peking,—you are still a pawn there, trying to checkmate other pawns.

6. SOME MORE GLIMPSES OF BABA

I WAS in the United States in September-October 1974, visiting Sathya Sai Centres. The California newspaper, named "The Movement", devoted to an exposition of the spiritual life, interviewed me regarding Baba in Tustin, California. As the interviewer asked very interesting questions, I was made spontaneously to comment on aspects of Baba's personality on which I do not always dwell. I have included the interview in this chapter.

Movement Newspaper : I have the feeling, Dr. Gokak, that being with you is like being with Baba, in a vicarious way, of course.

Dr. Gokak : Well, he asked me to go to America, and he said, "I'll take care of you in every way." My prayer to him is that I should be worthy of him; whatever I say or do should not be unworthy of a man representing Baba. He said, "I'll help you in every little way." So far I have nothing to regret.

M.N. : Does Baba ever speak through you? Do you sometimes hear his voice?

D.G. : In dreams, yes.

M.N. : How about during the day when you're involved in doing something, or contemplating doing something?

D.G. : I don't hear him, but suddenly there is guidance. There is no doubt about that! As long as I'm going right, I am guided. The moment I go wrong, I know that I am going wrong, and I correct myself. That moment of knowledge, self-knowledge, is where he steps in. I can't say that I hear this, but it is there in the system.

M.N. : Like an alarm clock.

D.G. : It has been like that all these days. I very clearly see what he is doing for me.

M.N. : Is this your first trip to the United States?

D.G. : No, I was here fifteen years ago on an academic
assignment. I was the head of a delegation to report on
reforms in examinations of higher education in universities.

M.N. : Have you been surprised by anything that
you've seen here this time?

D.G. : This time I am in a different kind of company.
For the greater part of each day I have been with Sai
devotees. Wherever I've gone there has been so much
love. I have been spoiled! I have been so well looked
after. There has been so much love showered on me that
I cannot tell India from America.

Looking to the young people, because on my last trip
I spoke with many of them, I find a very significant
change. At that time, they were asking questions about
India, about what happens there, exotic questions; but
now they ask me about time, about eternity, and things
like that. They are greatly interested. This is a very significant change.

M.N. : I've heard you say that living so close to Baba
you sometimes can get "burned". To what does this refer?

D.G. : It means that he is all perfection. In that Light
around him, no iota of untruth can survive. No insin-
cerity can have any place around him. No double standards. But we are imperfect; this is why we are human.
In our dealings with him we will sometimes try to impose
this imperfection on him without our knowledge. He is
very sorry for us because he knows that we are going to
get "burned". He can't help it; he, himself, can't help

us when we are getting burned because this is a very natural thing. But if one understands what is happening, that it is the impurity within one that is being burned, then one can stand it all right. Plus, there is Baba's grace. While this is happening, his love is still there. It still flows to the person. This is what saves and heals him. This is what I referred to. You are on top of a volcano; this is perfection.

The moment you go slightly wrong in what you do you are blown up. This is a critical moment in one's life; one may or may not survive it.

In a fit of ego a person may go away. He is hurt; he is deeply hurt. If he goes, he goes, it's his loss. There is no compromise. As Baba has been saying, "The nearer and dearer you are, the greater are your chances of getting burnt." In becoming worthy of him, you have to burn a great deal. This is what happens to everyone around him.

M.N. : The "burning" then is purification?

D.G. : Yes, it is all the same.

M.N. : What is an Avatar?

D.G. : An avatar is one who is a physical projection of a ray from the Transcendental Plane, that aspect of God that is above the Universe; the third aspect. From that aspect there is a ray which is not subject to cosmic laws. The human being who is a God-man, an avatar, derives from the Transcendental Plane. He is Spirit in all its glory, transcending cosmic laws. The God-man represents man in the highest awareness.

M.N. : It must be strange at times relating to Baba, being so close to him and knowing him. How do you relate to him, as a close friend or as a vehicle for God to come through this shell called Sai Baba? How do you relate to that situation?

D.G. : He's the friend I love, the God I fear, and Krishna at whose enigmatic hands I love to be slain, making myself immortal. This is how I relate to him. I am prepared for everything. For my doing, for my undoing, for all that. And I am also prepared for the human relationship. In the morning, when I am in the next room and the Avatar walks in and says, "Do you have a shaving brush?" I give him mine because he has forgotten his own. I relate to him in this way also. He is so intensely human. He can be so divine.

M.N. : Does this seem like a paradox to you?

D.G. : No. Even when I am aware of all that he stands for, when I am near him and he cuts jokes with me, I forget all that he is and I begin to talk as a friend. It is only when I get away from him, and come to America, for example, and see what is happening to him in all these homes, all these photographs everywhere that I say, "Is this Baba with whom I'm staying?" I begin to experience a sense of awe.

Once I said to him, "When will you show me your cosmic form?" He said, "Wait, wait, I will show you." He said, "Why do you think I have taken you so close to me? For that reason I have taken you close." But actually, I don't know what else he is going to show, but what I have seen already (laughter). When I am near him, I still forget that he is Baba. I think of him as very great and all that and near to me. I can take liberties and joke now and then, when he smiles, not otherwise (laughter). But then I forget the rest of it. When I go to other places and see Bibbuthi (sacred ash) showering in photographs and images appearing from nowhere and people going into ecstasy repeating his name, then I say, "Yes, this is the cosmic form."

M.N. : What do you think of astrology, palmistry, psychic readings and other such things?

D.G. : I'm an amateur palmist. One morning I was sitting in my room looking at a particular point in my own palm which refused to grow; Baba happened to come in at that moment. He asked me what I was doing. I couldn't explain, I was rather shy. But he knew and he asked me, "Do you know palmistry?" I said, "Several years ago I read some books on palmistry." He said, "Come on, read my palm!"

When he held out his hand, it was not for me to say, "No." So I spent some time looking at his palm. In fact, I was quite interested as it was the palm of an Avatar. I only know Western palmistry. There is Indian palmistry in which signs of discs and conches reveal if a person is an Avatar. Unfortunately, I had not studied this, so I was unable to apply these tests to his palm. I used all I knew from Western palmistry and I said, "This palm reveals no traces of Avatarhood." Then he said, "Good, proceed. After all, how can the physical body bear on it traces of the Avatar; it doesn't." So I was quite satisfied that I was a good palmist. But, he probably said this to satisfy me. Then I proceeded to look for the signs of the supreme power that he exercises among us. Being an amateur I was unable to locate many of the signs. But, I did find some of them. He saw that I was fumbling, and seeing another young man near, he said, "Look at his palm. Tell me whether he is going to marry or not."

I tried all of my palmistry cleverness and spent some time reading his palm. I thought he was going to marry, but I didn't want to be dogmatic in the presence of Baba. He might change anything. If I said, "Yes, he is going to marry." Then he might see to it that he would never marry at all and falsify this prediction. So I said, "There are tendencies towards marriage on this palm, and if Baba will, he may marry." As it turned out, he married after two or three years, making my prediction right. But he went into this marriage with full permission from Swami.

Palmistry and astrology can anticipate certain possibilities in human life. Something, of course, depends on the science of astrology and palmistry, but much more depends upon the astrologer and palmist. One must have something of a psychic attunement with the object whose fortune one is going to read. If this is there, then everything comes out correct.

There is an English story about an astrologer who told a subject that he was going to kill someone at eight clock the next evening. The whole day this person kept himself indoors. The time was 7:30, 7:45, 7:50; he still kept himself indoors. He didn't want to take any chances. If he stayed in his room, who could he kill except himself? He knew he was not going to commit suicide. At 7:50 he came out of his room. He left for an evening walk, greatly relieved that he had falsified this prophecy. As he was walking along he met this astrologer and he said, "Such a false prophecy came from you! You don't know your own job!!!" And he hit him in the face. The man fell dead on the spot! So the astrologer was killed and the prophecy came true.

There are these possibilities both in palmistry and astrology, but Baba has also told us that the moment that a man has realised his soul, he ceases to be a creature of circumstance. He ceases to be swayed by his own destiny. What rules him is not the stars, but his own soul. He consciously shapes his own life as he chooses. At this point, astrology and palmistry lose their meaning.

M.N. : You've mentioned prior to this interview the "Hour of God". You said that this hour will be brought to us sometime during the 1980s. Will this come about by the development of man, or will this be an act of the God force itself?

D.G. : The development of man's technological forces has been going on for years. There is a possibility that there is going to be a world crisis around the 1980s, after which there will be a definite turn towards what we call the Golden Age. At this time, it will be clear to man that any more entering into world power games will end in disaster for the whole world; and this will not be done. Simultaneously with this realization, there will be a descent of Grace. This descent of Grace is what will really bring forward the "Hour of God". This "Hour of God" is different from the prediction regarding the collapse of California.

The "Hour of God" is the hour of the unexpected; there will be different patterns in things. We may find that all elections that take place will place good men into positions of power. It is the good men that will begin to lead the industries. It will be the good men that will serve the people. Then there will be a great change in the very atmosphere. This will be one of the signs of the coming of the Golden Age.

This spiritual awareness will assert itself in small gnostic groups, a group here, a group there. These groups will have lived this kind of gnostic lifetime. And meanwhile, there will have been a change in the pattern of circumstances and there will be signs of the coming Golden Age.

Sai Baba hinted that the person who was to come in a red robe, with a shock of hair on his head, is already here. If you like, this is the coming of Christ. You may or may not accept this, but this is what Sai Baba said.

M.N. : What is the importance of being with one's Master, one's Teacher, physically?

D.G. : It has very great importance. One cannot consummate a relationship if his work takes him away. One cannot then draw all the love and all the delight that he can receive by being near. Suppose I have Rama Krishna for my Master. He is no longer in the flesh. It is quite possible that I could get in touch with my Master in my own meditative musings and moments. But there is a particular delight in the physical presence of one's Master right with us as a human being. One relates to him as a human being and still he is the Divine in the human. This brings in a certain sense of fulfilment and a certain experience that has been spoken of in all the ancient Indian texts. They say that even the gods hunger for this relationship.

In this evolution, when God comes down and is represented in human flesh, he brings something of the Divine himself in human flesh and is part of the evolutionary term, "existence". There is a peculiar joy in this relationship of the human-divine, which you don't get even in the Divine by Himself.

M.N. : If God wanted man to hear His voice, why does man have difficulty in hearing Him?

D.G. : As long as man loves to hear his own voice, how can he hear the voice of God? It's only when he shuts his own ears to his own voice that he is able to hear the voice of God. It's very difficult. The voice of God has to penetrate through the many layers with which we have surrounded ourselves. The purer we are, the nearer we are to His voice.

M.N. : How has your spiritual development changed since working with Baba? Have you noticed the change?

D.G. : Yes, there has been a great deal of change. The first change was that he made me conscious of what divine love stands for. I was an intellectual. I compared my emotions to water that jets out from a rock. It is very difficult for this water to come out. It's like penetrating the heart of a rock. This was my emotional life for a long, long time until I met him. I don't know what he did, but he cut down some of this rock. He made it possible for this spring to gush forth. This is only one of the great things that he has done for me.

Another thing that he did for me was to correct me, in so many small, even trifling, matters, to which I never gave any thought. In India, an intellectual is a lazy person. There is so much labour available that one never has to do anything. This creates an imbalance in one's personality. Baba does everything. He never allows anyone to do his things. He must do his own packing. If there is a public meeting, he must put up the buntings. He does that. All of this enabled me to get back this balance that was lost.

M.N. : Would you encourage any spiritual students to attend the Sai Universities in India?

D.G. : Not unless an American student joins the College for Indian History, Sanskrit, or learning a modern Indian language. If he joins everything like Chemistry or Engineering, he will find that he is doing something which is useless for his purpose. The Chemistry or Physics required in a developing country like India is different from the kind of Physics or Chemistry which is required here in America. One can join these universities for study in Indian disciplines, Indian Philosophy, and so on. And even better, he can join our summer courses where we admit others along with our own students. However, it may be difficult for them.

Their diet has to change, their habits have to change. They have to get up at four o'clock in the morning, chant OM, meditate and go about singing songs of God throughout various villages in the early hours of the morning.

M.N.: I've heard that you were visiting with Dr. Benito Reyes of the University of Avasthology in Ojai. What was your impression of what was happening there?

D.G. : I have great faith in and a deep appreciation for what Dr. Reyes represents. I believe that he is a very genuine person who doesn't mince matters, who calls a spade a spade; he never compromises. When it comes to giving up advantages he might have, he will never compromise his Truth. This is a spiritual college interested in spiritual things. The entire management is interested in building a spiritual institution. Thus, there may be a great deal of strength in its success because this has been assured by Baba. Dr. Reyes told me that his own Master, who has synchronized with Baba, has told him that between the year 1976 and 1980 a great World Teacher will visit the institution. Dr. Reyes is sure that Sai Baba will come there during this period of time. For all of your readers who want to know when Baba will come to America, here is a prophecy. Between 1976 and 1980 he is going to come here.

M.N. : Would you encourage people to come to India to see Baba?

D.G. : Oh, yes. Particularly because he has set a limit about it. He says he is not going into retirement until all those people that were destined to see him in this lifetime have seen him. Apparently, there are a certain number of people who still have to see him. Until then, he is open and accessible to everyone. I don't know when this will be completed, when the statistics will be over. Therefore, the sooner one goes to him the better.

M.N. : What does Baba require of people, if anything, so that he would wish to come to America? What should the people do here so that he would be satisfied?

D.G. : He would be very happy to come here and to see seekers of Truth, steadily pursuing their goal. Nothing pleases him better than the sight of a man who is sincere to himself and loyal to Truth. Those who have been Sai devotees in this country, if they have pursued the Sai way of life, which really means right doing, right thinking, right feeling, and the pouring forth of love to those who are around them; if this is done, if the Sai way of life is adopted by them and practised by them, nothing would be dearer to his heart. It's not that he wants big receptions. He really would be very happy to go to the homes of people who have lived this kind of life and spend his time with them. He has ideas of coming over here and speaking directly, without an intermediary. But when, I am unable to say. Probably in two or three years. Next year he won't be able to come here because that is the year of his 50th birthday and the year of festivities for us in India.

M.N. : What does Baba say of the different religions?

D.G. : The first thing he says is that there is only one religion, the religion of Love. There is only one language and this is the language of the Heart. There is only one caste and this is the caste of Humanity. There is only one God and He is omnipresent. I'm quoting Baba's own words. He stands for this universality of outlook; his ashram flag contains the symbols of all the great religions of the world. Those people that want to believe in their own religions should never be disturbed. They should practise their religion spontaneously, but with proper understanding; they should not practise it in a blind manner. One should be guided by one's studies.

There are people who don't want many rituals to bind them on their way. They want to feel free. They want to live a life of psychological awareness. They don't want to be bound down by any particular rituals. Their hearts prompt them to turn their whole life into a pilgrimage. If one wants to turn one's life into a ritual and be a free person, not profess any religion but be speaking only of the Divine, then this also is welcome. Just as Baba doesn't want rituals to be discarded, he doesn't want rituals to be adopted either. It depends on a person's needs in his life. If one needs a religion, then one takes it with understanding. If one needs the other life style then one takes that with understanding

M.N. : Is there a reason why Baba is always seen in crowds?

D.G. : This is his role. The twentyfour hours of every day are directed towards liberating the common man, setting him free from his bondage, wherever he may be from. All the methods, techniques, and exposition of his philosophy are directed towards this particular purpose.

His methods are those for redeeming the common man. His bhajans, which are sung with concentration on their rhythm, music, meaning, and imagery, can liberate the heart and release these springs of life. He has transformed the lives of millions of Indian people and thousands from all parts of the world.

M.N. : Does Baba ever manifest large objects like a house or an airplane? I've seen some of the small objects that he has manifested—rings, necklaces, and statues.

D.G. : I have not seen anything like this done; but from what I know of him, a thing like this is possible. If a man can bring back the life of the dead, which has happened in two or three cases, or be in two places at the same time, this also can happen. It has not happened because it has not been necessary. These materializations do not take place for fun. They take place when the need is there, when the circumstances require them, then they are done.

M.N. : Has Baba explained his ability to do the miracles that we hear about, and his manifestations?

D.G. : Yes. He has said, "I don't perform miracles, these miracles flow from me; how can I help it? It's my love that expresses itself in this form. I see a person who is dear to me, such a beautiful soul and a ring comes out and I give it to him. Here is somebody else; he needs to be healed. He is such a fine person; and some medicine comes out or some healing Vibhuthi and I give it to him!" This is love, nothing else but love. Somebody asked him, "How is it that you cure so many incurable diseases?" Baba answered, "It's not always done. It's my experience that I am in the heart of every living being; I am seated there whether he acknowledges me or not. I am in the heart of every living creature. I therefore love everyone, for in a sense, I love myself. If I do this and if the other person also responds to me and loves me, then the negative and the positive meet and my love and his love flow into each other; there is a conjunction. And then there is a cure. Where there is no response in love, there is no cure."

"If I am to satisfy the legitimate worldly desires of my devotees, later I want them to want spiritual gifts. I want them to ask for God Himself. In order to train them toward this desire for God, I satisfy their worldly desires now. I do this so that they might come to me for something greater."

These are techniques required of a redeemer who deals with the common man.

7. SHIRDI SAI AND SATHYA SAI

SRI Sai Baba of Shirdi was the third child of a boat-man, Ganga Bhavadia, who lived in Patri, a village near Manmad, on the banks of a river there. His (Sri Sai Baba's) mother's name was Devagiriamma. On a certain night when the river was in flood, the boat-dealer Ganga Bhavadia, who had all his boats moored to the bank, was afraid that they might be swept away by the swirling waters. He went to the riverside leaving his wife alone at home. At that time, an old man came and asked Devagiriamma to give him food. She served him food in the verandah. He then asked for permission to sleep there as he had nowhere else to go. She permitted him to sleep in the verandah. After a little while, she heard somebody tap at the door. It was the old man again. He said that he could not sleep. He desired that a lady should 'malish' or massage his legs. Devagiriamma went at that hour of the night by the back-door to the houses of one or two courtesans, but could not find any one of them at home. She was bewildered and did not know what to do. She was a devotee of Goddess Parvathi, even as her husband was a devotee of Eeswara. She sat in her worship-room and prayed and cried bitterly. At that moment, she heard a knock on the back-door. As she opened the door, she saw standing there a woman who said that she was from one of those houses that Devagiriamma had visited and she wanted to know what she could do for her. Devagiriamma was overcome with joy and she took

61

the woman to the old man in the verandah and closed the door on both of them. After a while, she heard another tap on the verandah door. She thought that the woman probably wanted to return home and she opened the door. What did she see there? Lord Siva and Goddess Parvathi were themselves standing there, ready to bless her.

Goddess Parvathi said to Siva, "Let us together bless her." Siva replied: "Since I came here to test her, I will speak to her separately." Devagiriamma was childless till then. Goddess Parvathi blessed her and said, "Be the mother of two children." Devagiriamma bowed down to Siva, who said to her, "I will be born as your third child, a son." By the time Devagiriamma looked up, the Divine Pair had vanished.

When the husband (Ganga Bhavadia) came home in the early hours of the morning, Devagiriamma narrated all her strange experiences to him. He was incredulous. He thought that those were the result of an over-heated brain, as she had been left alone at home on a stormy night. But the events that followed did prove the veracity of her experience. Devagiriamma became the mother of two children. And it was soon clear that she would become the mother of a third child also.

But an unusual situation developed on the domestic front. The husband gradually lost all his interest in mundane things. He was pining to see GOD face to face. When his wife reminded him that all that the Divine Couple had told her had come true and that SIVA himself would now be born as their child, he said, "Even if it be so, it will not satisfy me. There will be the mask of a human child between me and GOD. I want to gaze on that unmitigated primordial splendour." And he set out on his quest. Torn between her husband and her children,

Devagiriamma decided that it was her duty to follow in the footsteps of her husband, sent her two children to her mother's house and accompanied her husband into the forest.

After they had covered some distance, Devagiriamma felt that she was soon going to be in child-bed. Birth-pangs had set in. She implored her husband to wait for a while. But he went his way. As soon as she was delivered of the child, a son, beneath the shade of a banyan tree, she placed her child on the ground, covered it with banyan leaves and hastened after her husband, for her duty lay in that direction. Blood-stains were still visible on the child's tender body. One could see that it was born a few minutes ago.

This is how DESTINY works. A person named Mr. Patil from a neighbouring village was fetching his wife from her mother's hamlet, in a tonga (one-horse carriage). At this very spot, his wife felt like answering a short call. Mr. Patil asked the tonga-driver to stop for a while. Sreemati Patil alighted from the tonga and went to the very spot where the child had been made to lie by Devagiriamma. She heard the child's cry, removed the banyan leaves and found that it was a new-born child. Excited, she called her husband to the spot and showed him the child. They were a childless couple. And it was their feeling that GOD had given them this child to look after and to play with. They took the child home. They brought it up as their own son.

The child grew up in the Patil household. Patil died when the child was growing into boyhood. The mother was the only one left to take care of him. She was unable to cope with his activities. The boy used to go into Hindu temples and recite the Quran there. He installed a stone Lingam in a mosque and worshipped it there.

Enraged Hindu and Muslim neighbours came to the foster-mother and complained bitterly about the boy. She was puzzled.

One day, the boy was playing at marbles with the son of a neighbouring sahukar or wealthy man. The sahukar's son lost all his marbles, to Babu (Shirdi Sai Baba as a boy). Tempted by the game, the sahukar's son went to his mother's worship-room, seized a saligram or a black globular stone kept there for worship and played with it as a marble. The sahukar's son lost that saligram also to Babu; but he thought that Babu had played foul and that the saligram should be returned to him. Babu refused to part with it. He kept it in his mouth. The sahukar's son went to his mother, told her how he had taken the saligram away from her worship-room and played with it as a marble and that Babu had taken it away from him through foul play. Babu had kept it in his mouth and he was not prepared to return it. Horrified, the sahukar's wife rushed to her worship-room and found that the saligram was missing. She ran to Babu standing with her son outside and importuned him to return the saligram. Babu sat tight-lipped and refused to return it. She then compelled Babu to open his mouth and saw in it what Yashoda had seen in Sri Krishna's—the Viswarupa, worlds rolling on worlds. But there was no saligram there. Babu laughingly said that the saligram was in the worship-room. She ran back there and found the saligram in its place. She came back to Babu and prostrated herself before him. She had now realised that he was divine. Thereafter, she went to Babu's house every day to touch his feet. It was only when people criticised her for it that she turned this homage into a mental act.

But Babu's disturbing acts—his Hindu worship in mosques and Muslim chanting in temples—continued to irritate the people. Unable to control the boy, Sreemati Patil, the foster-mother, came to know of an 'ashram' started some miles away by a sadhu named Venkusa. There were, in the 'ashram', some orphan boys and waifs. She decided to take Babu away and leave him there.

Venkusa had a dream on the night previous to the coming of the foster-mother with Babu. In this dream, Lord Siva told Venkusa that he, Siva, would go to Venkusa the next morning at about 10 A.M. And, sure enough, Sreemati Patil went there at about that time, with Babu. She told Venkusa about the boy's disturbing activities and prayed to Venkusa to take Babu as an inmate of the ashram. Venkusa did so with great delight and reverence.

Venkusa was extremely fond of Babu. He showered all his affection on Babu. Babu became an object of jealousy for the other boys and they were bent on persecuting him. They got an opportunity when, one morning, Venkusa sent Babu to bring some Bilva leaves for worship. As Babu went into the woods, he was overtaken by a group of the other boys. They beat him and threw a brick at him. It hit him on the forehead. He bled profusely. Babu did not say a word. He picked up the brick, which had some blood on it and returned to Venkusa. Venkusa was deeply grieved to see Babu in this plight. He tore a dhoti and dressed the forehead wound, bandaging it with a piece of cloth tied round the forehead. He shed tears over the brick that had been thrown at Babu. He kept it with himself for it was stained with the blood of Eeswara Himself. There is in Sri Sai Baba's biography a reference to the brick and to the tomb of Venkusa, on which spot he was seen sitting at Shirdi before settling down there.

The incidents noted above can fill a real gap in any

biography of Shirdi Sai Baba. Very little is known about his early years. Venkusa has been called a 'guru' of Shirdi Sai Baba. I had my doubts about this. One morning, when I was reading the typescript of this biography in Brindavan, it came to Bhagavan Sathya Sai Baba's notice. The same evening, when college teachers and hostel students were assembled to hear him, he turned round and wanted to know whether any one had a question to ask. I wanted to know whether it would be permissible to ask a question relating to Shirdi Sai Baba. On being permitted, I wanted to know whether Venkusa was Shirdi Sai Baba's Guru. Then, Bhagavan narrated all that I have set forth above. The next evening, when he was requested to continue the narration, he was not prepared to do so, saying: "It is not very pleasant to be talking about oneself. I will talk about some other saint."

It does not occur to any devotee of Bhagavan Sathya Sai Baba to question his identity with Shirdi Baba. The fact of identity is too intimately woven into the very texture of the ashram-life at Puttaparthi Prashanthi Nilayam to be questioned by any one there. On Guru Pournima Day, the silver statue of Shirdi Baba in his usual cross-legged posture sitting on an impressive silver Adisesha is brought out and 'abhishekam' is performed with vibhuti coming out in a profuse shower from an empty pot. In the meditation hall of Prashanthi Nilayam is a fascinating statue of Sri Krishna. HE has just stopped playing on his flute. His fingers are poised in mid-air, and there is an expression of concern on his face, listening to the cry of agony that springs from the heart of humanity. That expression of Sri Krishna explains the very genesis of avatarhood. On that central platform, flanking Sri Krishna's statue, are the two life-size portraits of Shirdi

Sai Baba and Bhagavan Sathya Sai Baba.

When Bhagavan Sathya Sai Baba materialises lockets for devotees, they very often bear the images of both the Babas. Rings are frequently materialised, bearing Shirdi Baba's image. The other day, giving to a young devotee a locket with both the images on it, Bhagavan explained, "This is myself. That is your Thata, the grandfather."

Bhagavan has said that his "avataric design" is one of three incarnations. As Shirdi Baba, he laid the foundation for his spiritual mission, bringing about Hindu-Muslim Unity. That edifice is being raised now, in his role as Sathya Sai Baba. He will live for 96 years, fulfilling this role. As Prema Sai Baba, he will be born in Mandya District, Karnataka State. On the structure raised by Sathya Sai Baba, Prema Sai Baba will set the Kalasa or spire soaring to heaven.

His Mission is all so clear, precise and outspoken. Bhagavan's statements take one's breath away. Does a human being have a cycle of many births? The question does not arise. The answer is implicit in this statement and in the Gita. Is it possible to limit one's incarnations to a definite number? An Avatar can do anything. Is it possible for God to incarnate as a human being? Yes. Here are proofs.

How, after all, can it be established that Shirdi Baba and Bhagavan Sathya Sai Baba are ONE? The answer is, "Ascertain it in any manner you like." Shri Kasturi records an incident relating to the Rani Saheb of Chincholi. Years ago, she went to Puttaparthi to see Bhagavan. Even as she was entering the gate, Bhagavan told one of the close devotees standing there: "Ask her to bring the brass lota that I left at her house years ago." The Rani Saheb herself did not know much about it. But, on a thorough search of heirlooms in the house, it turned out that the brass lota of Shirdi Baba, who had visited the house years ago, had been carefully preserved by elders among other things. Shri Dixit, the nephew of Kakasaheb Dixit, who was a close disciple of Shirdi Baba, went to Puttaparthi to put to an acid test the identity of Sathya Sai Baba with Shirdi Baba. He always carried a small photo of his uncle in his pocket. The first thing that Bhagavan asked Dixit to do was to take out the photograph of 'My Kaka' from the pocket! There is also the thrilling story of the old lady, who had seen Shirdi Baba and who found the promise given to her by Shirdi Baba fulfilled by Sathya Sai.

There are numerous other incidents that bear out the identity. Several devotees are visited by dreams in which Shirdi Baba and Sathya Sai Baba move indistinguishably. I once dreamed that an old man was pursuing me with two pretty girls by his side, and he was persuading me to marry one of them. In my dream, I did not wish to marry either of them. But the old man was running after me, nimbler than myself and pleading that I should choose at least one of them. I was so annoyed with him that I lost my patience and said to him, "Who are you? Why are you pursuing me and persecuting me in this fashion? Where do you come from?" "I come from Ahmadnagar District", said the old man with a smile. This did not mean anything to me in my dream. Out of sheer fatigue and in order to get rid of the old man, I said that I would marry the younger one of the two. It was only when I woke up in the morning and remembered the dream that I realised that it was Shirdi Baba that had come to me, for Shirdi is in Ahmadnagar District, in Maharashtra. The purport of the dream had something to do with what Bhagavan Sathya Sai Baba was planning for me by way of a government job. It was registered in a striking manner when the dream took a symbolic turn, bringing Shirdi Baba into the dream instead of Sathya Sai.

But we have to remember that this is a question of identity on the spiritual plane. Many ask me the question: "Why does the Shirdi Samsthan go on, not showing the least interest when Shirdi Baba himself has been re-born here as Sathya Sai Baba?" We expect that Shirdi and Puttaparthi should be merged in each other. We are keen that the whole world should know of this identity.

But how does it matter, speaking even spiritually, if the Shirdi identity is generally understood as being different from the Puttaparthi one? We have it on record that Shirdi Baba said he would be reborn eight years after his death in 1918 and, sure enough, in 1926, Sathya Sai was born. The same love of 'udi', though there is no 'dhuni' now; the same love of the unity of religions indicated on the enlarged Prashanthi Wheel; the same overwhelming love for devotees coupled with the utmost detachment; miracles intensely dramatic in a similar fashion, revealing omniscience and omnipresence; the same utter disregard for personal safety, comfort or fame; the unaccountable moods of utter self-forgetfulness: to know the identity that persists in these matters is to add a new dimension to our understanding of either Shirdi Baba or Sathya Sai. Even then, how does it matter if the two prophetic roles are regarded as different from each other? It is the same Divine Existence-Consciousness-Bliss that works in them and in the other Great ones as well. In a special sense, through certain common characteristics, the same Divinity works in a more intimate way through Shirdi and Sathya Sai manifestations. I once saw Sathya Sai Baba looking at a large portrait of Shirdi Baba, sitting in the famous cross-legged pose, the right leg thrown across the left lap and the left hand

69

resting on the right foot. Sathya Sai looked at it amused for a while and said in Kannada with a smile, moving his head a little: "Aha, Enu Jambha" (Aha, what vanity!). He seemed to say: "You deliberately wear these ragged clothes. You have chosen a dilapidated musjid to live in. You live in a village dead to the world. You do this, so that your supreme self-confidence may shine through them all the more and the world be put to greater difficulty to find out that you are the King of Kings." These can be regarded as Sathya Sai's comments on himself through perceived identity. They can be regarded as comments on the other role that the same DIVINITY was acting. A new dimension is added to our understanding of either of them both ways,—realising their actual identity as well as their apparent difference.

I was once approached by some local Shirdi Sai devotees to be chairman of their organisation. Since the two were one, they said that I could be head of their society too. I told them that I would consult Bhagavan Sathya Sai Baba and let them know. When I put the matter before Bhagavan, he suggested that it would be wise on my part not to accept such a chairmanship. It was true that Shirdi Sai Baba and Sathya Sai Baba were identical. But as two legal entities, they were different. In the world of practical affairs and in the sphere of organisational activities, one's limited time and energy could be used better by focussing on one entity rather than two. One has to accept 'entity' as well as its essential identity with another object or person.

8. BABA'S POWER

POWER creates, sustains or destroys. If it is exercised on the side of Good, it is divine power; on the side of evil, demoniac power. The earth oscillates like a spinning top, this side and that. It reveals its dark half and its bright half through space and time.

This is true of human potency. But when there is a descent of superhuman power, power which stems directly from the Divine, it contributes, not to the mere oscillation of earth, but to a new dawn, the world's great age, a new step in human evolution.

Baba's power is the power of spirit. Temporal power may not heed it for a while, blinded by its own glory. But it bends its head low before Spirit at the end. It proves to the hilt the truth of the poet's utterance:

" 'Tis the eternal law.
That first in beauty should be first in might."

Here 'beauty' means sheer innocence and purity of being and becoming. It is the power of truth that knows no compromise, justice undimmed by any frailty of heart or head, love that washes all the human shores of earth, whether they be black or yellow, white, red or brown. This power is a white radiance, a transcendental sunbeam.

What exactly does it consist in? It is a dewdrop that descends from the thousand-petalled lotus, the elemental exercise of a will that is omniscient and omnipotent. It is the will that sees and acts simultaneously. What it wills fills and fulfils itself in space and time. But it bides its time, unwarped by slushy sentiment, unbiassed by impatient hurry. And when it strikes, it is there for all to see, like a column of light that unites the earth and sky.

Baba's power is not the display of a *siddhi* attained after prodigious labour. It scatters its silver and gold with a rare prodigality, giving people what they want till they begin to aspire for what Baba likes them to want. It is the cascade of *vibhuti* or holy ashes, endless, exhaustless. It is the crystallisation of *lingam* after *lingam*—spheroids of alabaster or jade—from the silk-soft lotus leaves in the abdomen. It is the ceaseless oozing of honey from the heart of granite itself. It is the descent of a succession of golden images of gods and goddesses,—from nowhere. It is the transformation of stray particles of sand on a seashore into the divine image of Sri Krishna, the reconstitution of water into petrol. It is the profuse inpouring of *vibhuti* and the massing in of *kumkum* behind the glass framed on the photograph, the footprints in holy ashes leading to the worship-room in a house and out of it. It is the flower moving marvellously from the top of a photograph to its base, or whole garlands aflutter, as if shaken by the wind. It is the tyrannical teacher glued to his chair in the class, unable to rise unless he rises with it. It is the rain that suddenly stops raining or the electric bulb that blazes with light when the whole area is plunged in darkness. It is the shaft of light that hits you in the eye from a photograph. All this is not magic. It is the magic of magic ,—creation itself, for there is no hand of the magician there anywhere to be found. No wonder a hippie said that he knew, now that he had met Baba, that the world was safe from atom and hydrogen bombs. The atomic stock-piles of great powers might, at a strategic moment, lie defused in their vaults, with no hand touching them at all.

This is Baba's elemental power over Nature, which is incredible and yet as clear as daylight. It becomes even more staggering when you remember that these phenomena occur in thousands of homes simultaneously, though removed thousands of miles from each other. It happened years ago, it happens today with unabating vigour and it will continue to happen more miraculously than ever.

There is another dimension to this power. Baba can appear in an operation theatre, behind closed and guarded doors. He can be here and there in another place a thousand miles away at the same time. His image can stamp itself, as in the heart of crystal, on the stone *lingam* in a village temple. He can appear in dream before numberless devotees and recount them their dream-experience when he meets them individually. In a chat over the breakfast table speaking to the devotees who were there at the time, regarding all such miracles, he once said: "This is happening in millions of homes. The time has not come as yet to assess it publicly. I am waiting so that all the devotees who have yet to come to me may do so."

An American devotee who was present at the time when this remark was made, asked: "Baba, have I your permission to tell my friends in America about this pronouncement?"

Straight came the answer: "It's not my business. It may be your duty."

Baba is what he is. It is not for him to proclaim from the housetops what he is. But it becomes the duty of the devotee who has come to know him and to experience his effulgence to tell the world what Baba is, if the devotee is convinced that what he has experienced is the truth.

It is well known that Baba takes on critical attacks of illness by which his devotees are afflicted. This has happened in a striking manner once when he took on paralysis at Puttaparthi and, again, when, in Goa, he took on acute appendix resulting in peritinitis. To put it more precisely, these diseases come on him, rather than being taken on by him. His body, like an aeolian harp, trembles in response to the call of those who love him with a pure and intense love. It is a matter of sympathetic vibrations, for he is Love itself. What saves his body from these fatal attacks is the immortal and unconquerable power of this very Love.

There is another facet to Baba's power. As an American disciple said, Baba can change the human heart. It is not merely a question of teaching one yogic or meditative practices. He brings about a transformation in a man's character and personality. Thousands have been changed in this way by his compelling sweetness, his ineffable love, a casual word or look. His compassion can put on the mask of harshness when that becomes necessary.

What is much more difficult to understand is Baba's power to change human destiny. He is endowed with that power of Grace which can alter the characters writ in the stars or on one's forehead. That he can do this, I have no doubt whatsoever. If it sounds incredible, it has to be experienced in order to be believed. Here, again, it is a divine love that is at work for its own inscrutable purposes.

Baba has declared that he is here in the flesh to restore India to her former spiritual glory and to carry the message of spirituality to the whole of humanity through her. He has said in categorical terms that his labours in this manifestation will not cease till his mission is over. I am one of those who believe in him and in the surety of his pledge. The question may be asked: Why? On what grounds? My one answer to that question is: I believe in Baba and in the surety of his pledge, not because I am what I am but because Baba is what he is.

9. BABA'S LOVE

AT an informal gathering, one of the group asked Baba: "Swamiji, what is the secret of the cure that many afflicted persons experience in your presence?" Baba said simply and instantly: "It is my experience that I am one with every sentient thing, every human being. My love flows out to every one, for I see every one as myself. If a person reciprocates my love from the depth and purity of his heart, my love and his meet in unison and he is cured of his affliction. Where there is no reciprocation, there is no cure."

Baba's love knows no frontiers. It overflows all boundaries. Like the universal sun, it shines on all and bathes them in its radiance, whether they be sun-worshippers or owls.

But his love has eyes, a million eyes like stars. It cuts through falsehood like a blade of the ice-brook temper. It draws close to itself a heart that is pure. While it melts and turns into compassion at the sight of dire suffering, it blinds and confuses the man of pretence and the creature of cunning. To the man who loves but is infected with worldly desires, it is bitter to the taste but a healing balm to the soul. Like the surgeon's knife, it heals where it wounds.

Baba's love is love but not attachment. It is divine love precisely because of its supreme detachment. It may tolerate sentimentality; but is itself the least sentimental, though it is the quintessence of all sentiment. There is an anecdote about Shirdi Baba. He had great affection for a cook who had served him devotedly for many years. When the cook died, tears trickled down the eyes of Shirdi Baba. But he exclaimed the very next moment: "Where have you gone, after all? You have become a part of Me."

Baba's love floods the vast spaces of the soul and irrigates the arid heart that it may burst into bloom. It is beatitude itself:

Human love is a wickered light,
A tiny flame that flickers in the heart's niche.
You feed it with your own blood for oil
And do all you can to shelter it for a while
From storms within and without.
But Divine Love
Is the naked majesty of midnight stars.
It is an infinite and luminous downpour
That fills all your being
To the very cells of the body.
Human love is a little laughter heard amid tears.
To mentalise it is not to transform it.
It wells out of the body
And loses itself in earth.
But Divine Love descends on you
As from the Milky Way
And more and more, the more open you are.
It upholds your sail on its ocean of being
And is the chart(er) of uncharted seas.
Human love is the fire of the body
That creates man in the image of man.
It is a sallying out of self to self.
But Divine Love is the light of heaven
That recreates man in the image of God.

It is the rallying point of his self to the Divine.
Open yourself, my friend!
Let your earthly sojourn
Prepare you for the divine pilgrimage.
Let human love,
Which is but a track in the forest of being
Lead you to divine love
And make you labour loyally
For the paradise of Tomorrow
In the forest of Today.

10. BABA'S WISDOM

FOR all mortal men, knowledge comes, as Tennyson said, but wisdom lingers. Man pays a heavy price for every particle of wisdom he acquires. He drops his blood into drachmas for it.

But Baba is full of wisdom from the foot to the summit of his being. Whether it is *practical wisdom* which is common sense, *psychological wisdom* which is a sympathetic apprehension of the angularities and infirmities, the obsessions and aversions, the predilections and preferences of men, *philosophic wisdom* which is an uncanny insight into the heights and reaches and the pitfalls and aberrations of the intellect, *occult wisdom* which is a profound identification of the subconscient and inconscient ailments of man, or *transcendental wisdom* which is a precise visualisation of the spiritual evolution of a human being and the problems that confront him on the path, Baba overbrims and overflows with it. It comes as naturally to him as leaves to a tree.

What is the primordial source of the wisdom with which he is instinct? The source of his wisdom is the source of all light. It is an integral and divine perception, the very fragrance of the thousand-petalled lotus that blossoms over the crown of his head. It springs from a divine consciousness which identifies itself with each created thing in the cosmos and which regards creation itself as part of its own unfoldment. It moves with royal ease from the highest heights to the lowest

79

depths of the human personality; for there is nothing that is a stranger to its vision; for even the undivine is an obscure emanation of the Divine.

This wisdom is supported by an incredible and easy access to all knowledge. No one knows when he studied the Vedas. But he can correct the most accomplished Vedic scholars, while reciting Vedic hymns, with reference to the proper accent on a recondite word. He can contradict noted zoologists and show them what exactly is the link missing in the evolutionary chain. He can tell a numerologist, who has delved deep into the mystic significance of numbers, about the import of the numbers that he has failed to grasp. He can discourse eloquently on poetry to poets and come out with startling perceptions. He can tell a businessman how to run his business or what his next business enterprise should be. He can do this because wisdom is the quintessence of all knowledge. If wisdom is a divine countenance, knowledge is the aura around it. The divine ray can penetrate any part of this aura and wear it as its garment.

This wisdom encompasses not only the present but the past and the future. To look before and after is child's play to it. It can say what was the shape and size of the *linga* that was installed in the innermost shrine when the Someshwara Temple was built for the first time. It can dip into the future farther than human eye can see and spell out the destinies of men and nations. It can read a human being like an open book, not only the sequence of events in his present life but in lives past and yet to come.

Shelley imagines a time when Nature, confronted with the question: "Hast thou any secrets?", returns the answer: "Man unveils me. I have none." This is the millennium to come that Shelley describes in his *Prome-*

theus Unbound. But here in our midst is this Prometheus who makes this millennium a living reality every moment of his life. Neither time nor space can stand in his way.

And the wonder of wonders is that this depository of divine wisdom is simple and innocent as a child and as accessible as your own dear friend, cracking jokes with you even as he cracks a piece of betel nut.

11. DARSHAN

HAVE you seen Baba
Who sets cities aflame with longing
And drenches them with the delight of existence?
You've missed the very meaning of your life
If you haven't seen him and been spoken to by him.

Baba is a lawn of blue light
With a may-flower on top of his hair
And a golden lily on his cranium.

He is the healer of a world in pain,
The blue-throated god
That drinks the poison of its suffering
To make it happy and whole.

He is the patriarch of each family
That gathers around his knee
And drinks the golden honey of his love.

He's the eternal child playing in his garden
Winning back the adults of an erring world
Through sheer simplicity and innocence of heart.

Baba's aura of hair
Sends forth incessant arrows
To destroy the evil in the world.

He defies the laws of physics and chemistry
That he might assert the higher Law of Spirit.

82

A lingam materialises
That a million souls may be born.

Matter and Spirit are Siamese twins
That have an identical body but a different face.
Only the androgynous god—
Ardhanarishwara—
Purusha and Sakti in one—
Can solve the riddle of their birth and growth.

Have you seen Baba
Who sets cities aflame with longing
And drenches them with the delight of existence?
You've missed the very meaning of your life
If you haven't seen him and been spoken to by him.

12. SCION OF THE SUN

GREATER than this cannot happen to any man that he be accepted by his master and bathed and anointed in the holy waters of his love.

He feels the breath of the Infinite Person in the very air he breathes.

His pulse has felt the impulse that moves the primum mobile.

A creeper of lightening springs in his heart and sends its shoots and tendrils over the lattice-work of his body.

He floats on an ocean of the milk of paradise. His voyage knows no beginning and no end.

In a brief hour of mortality, he enjoys the integer of immortality.

He sits in the sun in his meridian hour of exceeding glory. And the sun is mellow to his eyes and limbs.

The scion of the sun becomes a sun-crystal.

He receives the quintessential ray and concentrates it on the world that it may be purged of its dross.

And in the moment of Apocalypse, that sun-crystal melts into the sun.

13. THE WORLD REDEEMER

WHO is this Narada, this world redeemer,
The singer of three worlds whose voice awakens
Souls that sleep, earth that forgets to live
And heaven all unwilling to descend?
He is the voice that builds, sustains, unbuilds,
Making all things divine, as he keeps singing.

Who is this world-teacher, master supreme,
Whose skilled hands fashion souls unnumber'd, who
Unravels the riddle of the Siamese twins
Of Spirit and Matter, two faces with one heart
And makes me live in the subtle and the gross,
The archetypal and eternal light?
He's the prophet that rings in a new age,
The poet who *makes* with souls, ev'n as with words.

Who's this great task-master, makes each day
Ash Wednesday? Turns all splendour into dust
And dust into the blossoming of soul?
He is the wishing tree, the infinite love
That gives each child the instant boon it asks.
He's the knife that cuts, the fire that burns,
The path of the razor-edge that makes me bleed
Even as I walk. He's Beauty and Terror.
He is the friend I love, the god I fear
And Krishna at whose enigmatic hands
I love to be slain, making myself immortal.

Who is this exemplar in the rose-red robe
Of love, the saffron of wide mastery?
He is a bark on the high seas of life
Lad'n with rich cargo and divine.
A luminous intellect that is truth itself,
A heart that is incarnate peace, a will
Flawless in doing, a soul that rolls like the sea,
Breaking into myriad waves of love.

Who is this master of yoga that unites
All creeds into a religion of love?
Here in his presence criminal and king,
Poet and politician, sinner and saint
Live in close friendliness like lion and lamb
And help to change the earth from hell to heaven.
He is the seer that knows life at its roots
And makes it branch into many graceful bends.
He is the fountain of pure love that pours,
Turning the desert sand into paradise.

Who is this being or god of mystery
That dwells within the heart of man and beast,
Of elephant and child? He is the flame
That burns in a million hearts and burns for ever.
He's but man in the company of men,
None other than woman amid women,
A mere child among children playing,
But God Himself when he is all alone.
An Avatar whose obverse and reverse
Are man and God, a divine path-finder,
Sai who has come to save the world
From its own utter ruin.

See you not rose-red footprints in your heart?
The eternal child has made your heart his home.

Songs sweeter than the music of the spheres
He sings to you in moments of dream-sleep.
He sits upon the peacock-throne you made
In your sleep and waking, for the god of victory.

14. A PRAYER

O Fullness of LOVE!
O Effulgence of SPIRIT!
O TRUTH itself!
O SAI!
O Surpassing ONE!

You are mine.
I know you belong to a million others.
But so far as you live in me
You are mine.

I am thine.
I know thou ownest millions of others.
But so far as I live in thee,
I am thine.

O SAI!
Hear my prayer.
Here's my prayer:
Guide my footsteps towards my Being!
Guide my darkness to its light!
Lead my mortality
To Immortality!
This is my prayer.
Grant that it be fulfilled.
AUM! Shanthih, Shanthih, Shanthih!

15. ON REMEMBERING THE MASTERS

THESE the saviours, these the masters
That shield the world both night and day
Ri ding on storms and clouds and moving
With constellations on their way.
These the great whose love illumines
Paths that very few have trod.
These the wise whose mercy beckons
Every son of earth to God.

These the shining ones celestial
Living in the world's deep core.
These the fullness overbrimming
Pouring life through every pore.
Theirs the quiet and the splendour
That the seven worlds sustain.
Theirs the one Primaeval Will
That rules the sun, moon, wind and rain.

These the wisdom of the ages,
The high lights of the universe.
These are of three worlds the masters
And. kings of light; the rhythm that stirs
All that is and yet to be:
Creation, evolution, doom;
Incarnations of infinite
Splendour in a little room.

Where the tongue that, not descanting
On their names, is eloquent?
Where the eyes that, not beholding
Their form, decipher heaven's intent?
Where the arms that, not enfolding
Them, have loveliness embraced?
Where the mind that, untransfigured
By them, with equipoise is graced?

These the ancients, the eternal
In Life's Temple; those who know
The secret springs of life; the makers
Of revolutions as they go
Moving from age to age; the Presence
That the world aspires to view.
These the changing and unchanging
Souls for ever old and new.

In the winds they blow for ever.
In the seven seas they seethe.
Ever burning in the fire
In the seraphim they breathe.
Beneath the foaming, milk-white ocean
They make the python-bed, unseen,
For Life who lights the path of splendour
For her Lord as His loved queen.

It is they who furl the flower
And unfurl the timorous bud.
And their word dries up the oceans
Or swells the rivers in their flood.
It is they who cast forth Maya's
Net and catch us even like fish.
They can lead us gently, kindly
Out of error, if they wish.

May my living be as the lotus
Dedicated to Life's pleasure
With the gentle benediction
Of the Masters as my treasure,
Blossoming near the holy shrine.
For pilgrims, at the Ancients' will,
May my song be as the honey
For them, bee-wise, to drink their fill.

May the earth, at the Ancients' bidding
Be as the caravanserai
On the way to peaks empyrean;
Or else, beneath a boundless sky,
A seminary of supermen
Who, bent on their eternal quest,
Will make this earth a paradise
And man divine, before they rest.

II. Philosophy

16. BABA AND THE INTELLECTUAL

THE problem that confronts a man of faith is whether he can be fair to those who do not share his faith and even to those who actively resist it. In predicaments of this kind, a great deal of tolerance is necessary. My reason and faith are mine; his reason and faith, his. But a good and interesting dialogue is possible between the two if each one is keen on understanding the other man's point of view. If we stoop to violence in facing such situations, as happens sometimes in politics, we will lose whatever nobility there may be in our stance. We have to realise that all wrong developments are ultimately traceable to our own error in the initial stages.

A number of philosophies and ideologies are clashing with each other in the world of today. Existentialism *versus* Essentialism; Rationalism *versus* Irrationalism: Humanism *versus* Nihilism; Mysticism *versus* Marxism: these and many others hold the field and one has to be wary in treading it.

Coming to Mysticism, one has to remember Pascal's remark that the Heart has its own reasons as Reason has. Goethe said that the heart has its own dialectic. For example, Swami Vivekananda had somehow an intuition that he had to attend the World Congress of Religions in Chicago even when he had no invitation and when he hardly knew any details about it.

Faculty psychology speaks of mind, heart, intellect, will, memory, imagination and other faculties. But Coleridge has pointed out that it is only when these faculties have been illumined by the soul or intuition that any higher cultural development is possible in the individual.

Science answers questions beginning with *how* but not with *why*. To the question how the element of water comes into being, science points to the formula: H_2O. But it is unable to say *why* the observance of this formula results in the formation of water. The *why* questions give the scientists a rude shock till we come to the big hurdle,—the indeterminism of modern physics which gives us the reason why metaphysics holds itself together as a subject.

Of the three cardinal principles, *Sat*, *Chit* and *Ananda* (Existence, Consciousness and Delight), science has clearly visualised the first one by resolving all Matter into pure Energy. Parapsychology has recognised the second principle. Even a psychologist like Jeung speaks of the Collective Unconscious and W.B. Yeats, the Irish poet, of the Earth Memory. It is only the universality of the third principle, that of Delight, which remains to be affirmed by a section at least of vanguard intellectuals.

Then there is the question of the correspondence between the macrocosm and the microcosm. Man contains the entire universe within himself in miniature and the Divine is involved in both. That is why T.S. Eliot says in The Four Quartets:

"The dance of limps along the arteries
Is figured in the drift of stars."

The One splits itself partly into the Many and the Many are enfolded in the One.

Mysticism underlines the importance of the Guru or spiritual Master. Baba eulogises the Guru, saying that the Guru is a creator like Brahma, sowing the seed of spirit; that he is a sustainer like Vishnu, tending the seed into a sapling; and that he is a destroyer like Maheshwara, removing the weeds in the garden of the disciple's heart. Sri Aurobindo has observed that the Guru promotes, not knowings, but Knowledge, not willings but Will; and makes you experience, one may add, not feelings but the Feel of Reality. He gives to his disciple, not world-knowledge, but soul-knowledge, and God-knowledge.

An intellectual once asked Baba: "Since you are an Avatar, why not liquidate the poverty of the nation at one stroke? Every one will be happy." Baba said: "I will give you the power to do so. But do you have the capacity to accept it and contain it?" The person had no answer to give to this question.

Reality is many-sided. Liquidating poverty in a phenomenal way may lead to other dangerous results. A premium has to be put, besides, on human endeavour for, after all, man is here to learn in this vale of soul-making. It is this fact which explains the human aspect of the Avatar. The Avatar is here to teach man how to suffer, strive and achieve.

Baba is not learned or highly educated. He is a non-matriculate playing with undergraduates in the Sathya Sai College . But Colleges have been, and Universities will be, named after him. He who holds the secret of the universe in the palm of his hand does not have to worry about the acquisition of university degrees.

Academicians everywhere are baffled by Baba. Because he does not fit into their academic frame   , they declare that he, the picture, is non-existent. But he laughs, like the cloud, at his own cenotaph. The physical scientists, with all their elaborate theories, cannot explain the origin of the universe better than he does, for he has known the universe from Alpha to Omega.

The scientist generates power by discovering the laws of steam or electricity and by applying them in certain ways. Baba produces power by defying these laws: he uses water as petrol and turns particles of sand into a beautiful golden image of Krishna. Similarly, sacred ashes, red powder or kumkum and turmeric fall in great quantities from within and without photographs (not only his but of various gods and saints) and a very delicious and fragrant honey oozes from them.

This much about the chemists and physicists. Nor can the biologists explain the origin of life better than he does. Even the *Bhagavata*, the king of Puranas, describes the growth of an embryo in the womb of the mother so marvellously, that no gynaecologist can improve on it. All Sai devotees know the *Kalpataru* or wish-fulfilling tree at Puttaparthi. Baba took out all manner of fruit from this tree and gave them to his devotees to the utter chagrin of the cycle of seasons: apples and custard-apples, berries and mangoes, any fruit that you could ever think of. Shri N. Kasturi has narrated, in his biography of Baba, how, while discussing the missing link speculated upon by zoologists, Baba filled in the gap by materialising it and showing what it looked like.

As for the environmental sciences like ecology and meteorology, devotees have testified to the fact that Baba can stop or bring rain at any time. As for complex sciences like medicine, engineering and agriculture, the marvellous powers of Baba as a diagnostician and as a curer of incurable diseases are well-known. Speaking to agricultural experts some months ago, Baba was pointing out how tube-wells, multiplied indefinitely, lead to water-famine.

I may now offer a few comments on Baba in relation to the social sciences. A critic pointed out, a year ago, that the payment of Customs Duty is evaded under the Law, when Baba materialises gold rings, gold images and so on. This is a good example how one is blinded by the very sciences that one is trying to build. To prove that Baba has brought in gold on which Duty is to be paid, we will have to measure all the quantity of gold in the Kolar and other gold-mines. Even when we have done this, we shall realise that these materialisations are not economic goods. The devotees who have been given these rings and images will part with their life rather than with them. They are, in that sense, invaluable.

Baba has spelt out his own version of the social sciences. His version is not the socialism of under-payment,—going to Ashoka Hotel for coffee and *idli* and, after refreshments, refusing to pay more than fifty paise for coffee and twenty paise for each *idli*. It is, rather, an economics based on love—putting the rich man on his guard and making him realise, in his bones, that he is the trustee, and not the owner, of his wealth. A trusteeship based on love is the foundation on which the science of economics should be reared. Similarly, the science of sociology should be rooted in co-operation, love and brotherhood and not competition and diplomacy. Anthropology should be so oriented that, in all its analysis, it never loses sight of the one 'caste' of humanity, the one 'religion' of love and the one 'language' of the heart. Political science is the science of power. But the political scientist has to realise that the only true power that is there, flows from truth and love. As for Law, we should have a humane law-giver like Manu, revised and brought up-to-date, with all the spiritual foundations of Law properly preserved.

Baba never indulges in making hair-splitting metaphysical distinctions, though he can do so as well as any

99

pundit, alive or dead, if only he is required to go in for them. He is the saviour of the common man and he has formulated his philosophy for the common man. Its central message is one of transformation. What the individual requires is, not information, but transformation. He has often said: "My life is my message." We don't have to ask questions about the hereafter but live the life given to us as well as we possibly can. Like the two legs of man, the two-legged creature, we have to reckon with both this world and the next, not merely one of them. His philosophy is a simple and universal formulation based on the psychology of man,—the philosophy of Truth, Right Action, Peace, Love and Non-Violence. He is a prophet by virtue of this new formulation and an Avatar because he lives it himself and has the power to persuade the individual and the collectivity to live in the light of this philosophy.

The intellectual has to realise the enormity of the crisis that confronts India and the world today in order to explore possibilities that can meet the crisis. The scientific and the intellectual approaches are, it is well known by now, unable to meet it by themselves.

In India, on the physical plane, there is such frightful poverty and such an utter lack of discipline after twenty-five years of Independence. On the vital plane, adverse forces like greed, jealousy and pride have been let loose so that linguism, casteism and factionalism are tearing our society to pieces. On the mental plane, we find that men with public standing are mostly worshippers of Mammon rather than of the Divine. On the spiritual plane, there has been a drying up of the current of spirituality in society at large. The great religions have been trying to uplift individuals and make men masters of themselves. But religions themselves have become

100

merely formalistic and lost their spirituality. This is the atmosphere in which we live in this great country today.

In the world, of which India is only a part, we are faced by similar obstacles. The world is already in the midst of an electronic civilization and it has shrunk a great deal. But we are going farther and farther away from each other, the nearer the various parts of the world come together. A strong country browbeats the weak one. One Power Bloc tries desperately to exploit the other. In the frosty atmosphere of a cold war, our hearts are chilled and each big country struggles to dominate the world. So the planetary civilization, of which we have been dreaming and which might make all mankind socially and politically one, is as remote from us as ever. In fact, nationwide hostilities, based on race, religion or nationalism, are as rampant today in some parts of the world as they were some centuries ago. Both physically and vitally, the world is in a very bad shape.

On the mental world-plane, there are a number of ideologies conflicting with each other. As W.B. Yeats said: "Things fall apart; the Centre does not hold." The world crisis itself consists in the fact that the Centre does not hold the parts together. The weapons of total destruction are piling up on one side and, on the other, those reserves in man which enable him to face a crisis are fast shrinking.

What ideology can help us in this predicament? Democracy is a noble ideal, with its respect for the 'divine average'. But it most often results in a continuous game of setting up and pulling down governments. And it won't help us when the world is in a melting pot. As for the individual, he is confused between Gandhism and hippism, the East and the West.

Nor does Socialism help. For it makes the individual

101

a screw in the machine in the interest of the collectivity. We dehumanise man in the interest of building up a socialistic republic. Marxism, with its insistence on anger and class-war, is unable to meet the crisis, for no philosophy of hatred can succeed in making the world one.

Under Anarchism, each individual becomes a law unto himself. A truly anarchic society will become possible only when each individual has evolved into a Sri Ramakrishna, Sri Aurobindo or Bhagavan Baba.

Rationalism and humanism, each in its own way, ignore the fundamental basis of Spirit. We build on quicksand without it. A humanism, devoid of love flowing from Spirit, cannot heal the many fissures from which Life suffers on this planet. None of these philosophies filled with the intellect, can control those wanton human desires which are driving the world to the edge of a precipice, or be a substitute for Spirit. No diplomat can save the world unless he practises the diplomacy of vision and love. A different kind of philosophy and a totally different kind of personality are required to meet the world crisis of today.

Sheer sincerity and innocence: this is what is needed today. There is the great Bhagavata image of Doomsday. On the waters of the ocean that have submerged the world and brought about a *Pralaya* or utter dissolution, there is a little Divine Child lying on a banian leaf in the midst of mounting waves, forgetful of everything, masterful of everything, sipping the nectar of delight, of immortality, oozing from it own toe. It is this Child that is going to save the world from the Day of Doom by saying: "Let dry land appear."

This child is the symbol of a divine personality. Statesmen indulge in double-talk, double-think and double-doing. They make life much more complicated than it is in itself. They are pawns in the cosmic game of chess, not chess-players. They continuously speak of equality, liberty and fraternity but do not even observe the elementary decencies of honesty, justice and recognition of merit. Intellectually speaking, the true saviour of the world is going to be one who is unfalteringly and unerringly loyal to Truth. From an ethical point of view, he will never swerve even an inch from right in the continuous swing and movement towards action. Scrutinised emotionally, it will be seen that he stands unshaken, whatever the fury of the storms and waves around him. He becomes himself the Rock of Ages. Again, he is a ceaseless fount of love, the love that makes each one a friend and disarms enemies. It is a personality that stands foursquare in the world. The saviour who answers this description will have infinite patience with things as they are, a clear vision of Truth, the power to implement his vision and universal love.

The saviour of our imagination must also have been endowed with the genius of the four great goddesses,— Maha Saraswati and her perfection in executive skill; Maha Laxmi and her capacity for establishing love, harmony and beauty; Maha Kali and her power to punish the wicked and trample down the foe mercilessly; and Maheshwari and her surpassing wisdom.

The one question that has faced mankind ever since the morning of creation is: When shall right find its appropriate might? I give the question here as AE, the Irish poet, worded it. We live in a world where might is right, where the law of the jungle still prevails. When shall we win the world for God so that we can say: "Thy kingdom come." For achieving this we require a personality endowed with Truth, Right, Peace and Love and all the excellences of Saraswati,

Laxmi, Kali and Maheshwari. But for establishing Right and Beauty as Might, you also require Power exemplified by the other divine qualities,—omnipresence, omniscience, omnipotence and omnifelicity. We cannot expect Presidents and Prime Ministers to be either omnipresent or omniscient, much less omnipotent. Only the Avatar can be the X outside brackets, manipulating circumstances and determining the value of the quantities within them. This X is not only outside the brackets. It is outside metropolitan cities and cabinets and gives to everything its final worth and value. To crown all, the Avatar brings universal delight, shining on all like the sun.

And yet, while in human form, even the Divine suffers like human beings. Otherwise, how can the human become Divine or be lifted to the level of the Divine unless the Divine descends into the flesh, suffers like us and still is conqueror? The Immortal puts on these garments of mortality, to make us feel confident, to realise that we can suffer like mortals and yet be Divine.

Baba said once: "While in the company of men I am a man. In the company of women, I am a woman. In the midst of children, I am a child. When I am alone, I am God." It would be good if intellectuals try to assimilate these steps in their own daily life.

The rationale of the Avatar consists in the fact that he comes down to teach human beings how to make themselves divine. The democratic ideal animating the Sai movement demands that the whole of human society should be, as Keats said, a grand democracy of forest trees, that each tree should be an oak instead of our having a shrub or briar here and there.

At the same time, SAI should not be regarded as a limiting word. The name or the form of SAI, Baba has warned us, should not blind us to the names and forms of other manifestations. We should have the same respect and love for all of them, for the Divine permeates them all equally. Wherever we utter the name of SAI, we should be able to utter all the other great names in the world of spirit.

17. BABA AND THE PATH TO REALITY

THE world, which is too much with us every day, is a denial of the Love, Beauty, Delight, Truth, Goodness and Power of the Divine. This universe has been compared to a *Varuni Vriksha* by the Vedas and then to an inverted *ashwatha* or peepal tree in the Gita, with its roots going up the skies and the branches down to earth. The roots of the tree derive their sap from heaven and it is my fancy that these roots are the six attributes of the Divine mentioned above.

How did evil and imperfection originate in this universe? Its very life is based on violence,—a fierce and eternal destruction. Keats detected this violence even in the ravening of a worm by a robin redbreast. God is Truth. But the world is enveloped in falsehood. God is Beauty itself. But the world is full of crocodiles and other misshapen creatures. God is infinite Love. But the world is full of hatred. God is beatific Power. But the world is full of a power that corrupts.

When God created this world for *lila* or for the joy of it, the paradox of opposites came into being: Being and Non-Being, Mortality and Immortality, Spirit and Matter, Darkness and Light. The principles of Division, Ignorance and Maya or Illusion came into being. The world could not have been created without them.

But this instrumentality itself became a stumbling block in the way of man's own approach to Reality. But a divinely ordered harmony is still the birthright of man if only he surrenders himself to the Divine.

Baba gives a full exposition of his own metaphysics of *Advaita* in *Sandeha Nivarini*. The scholar can immerse himself in it to his heart's content if he desires to. There is also a robust and positive side to his philosophy which reminds us of Sri Aurobindo. For instance, Baba says that this world and the other world, the *Iha* and *Para*, are like the two legs of the two-legged creature, man. Both are equally essential for the fullness of his being.

There have been quite a few revolutions on the face of this earth in recent times,—the French, the Russian and the Gandhian. But the greatest of revolutions—the revolution of revolutions—is the one for which Baba strives incessantly. It is different from other revolutions in its texture as well as structure. It is transformation that Baba insists on,—an integral change in the individual so that his intellect attains the Truth, his heart Peace, his will attains Right Action and his soul overflows with Love. The transformed individual will then gird up his loins to bring about an integral transformation of society. This will be his field of disinterested endeavour as a seeker and his unique adventure as a transformed individual.

Baba has always asked the tremendous question: Why fear when I am here? And our fears are allayed when we come to know who he really is,—an Avatar of Love. It does not mean that he gives us a blank cheque to desire and do what we like when once we accept him. He is not a bank to which we can go for the encashment of all our desires. It means that a transcendental awareness, to which our past, present and future are an open book, has agreed to take care of us and to see that our *sadhana* or period of spiritual preparation is not ill spent, our effort is not wasted and that our suffering does not prove to be sterile. It is really the attributes of God—Love, Beauty, Delight, Truth, Goodness and Power—that take care of us. One may display heroism in suffering by saying with Henley:

"I am the master of my fate,
I am the captain of my soul."

But one turns suffering itself into incense burnt on the altar of God by responding to the question: "Why fear when I am here?"

The Master conducts his disciple to the soul-knowledge within himself. What he expects from the disciple is *love*, which is meat and drink to the Master; a readiness to suffer, the kind of readiness that is required of gold when it is to be hammered into ornaments; purity of feeling, thought, word and deed; and pure and total surrender resulting in the acceptance of the daily round of activities for which organisations like the Samiti and Seva Dal have been created.

What does the Master himself do in return for the disciple? He gives him self-knowledge and self-confidence; a sense of the Presence that wipes out all the sorrows that ever the disciple has felt; his Grace in times of crisis, even service of all kinds and in all capacities, should an occasion arise demanding it; and, finally, the Divine Himself in all His plenitude and glory.

Thus the SAI path is the path that blesses him that takes it. To put it more philosophically, there are six *upasanas* or proximate disciplines, six approaches that Baba speaks of for an experience of integral Reality. The riddle of Man, God and the World is the riddle that faces all religions and philosophies. One is the *Sathyopasana*, the pursuit of Truth. In the ancient world, this meant the study of the Vedas, the Brahmanas, the Aranyakas and the Upanishads. Baba has called the Vedas the milk of human enlightenment, for they contain, in essence, all the wisdom of the ages. The Brahmanas are curds—an altered form of milk, a ritualistic version of the Vedas. The Aranyakas are like butter. They give in a concentrated form the spiritual thought of the Vedas. The Upanishads are like *ghee* or clarified butter. Vedic thought is presented here in all its fullness and clarity. Baba devoted all his discourses at the summer course of 1974 to an exposition of the message of the Vedas.

But the modern world has many other sources of knowledge and wisdom and we ignore them at our own peril. Baba has therefore suggested a comprehensive approach to Truth. For one thing, we should know what the Revealed Word has to say regarding any problem that we wish to tackle. The Revealed Word of each religion is equally valid and is, in substance, the same as the Revealed Word of any other religion. Next, we should find out what the *shastras*—the code of Manu and the codes of other law-givers, have to say regarding the same problem. We shall then see what Law and Usage have to say on these matters. The third approach is that of the Puranas and epics—the legendary angle. What does the Padma Purana, the Bhagavata, the Ramayana or the Mahabharata say about it? What verdict does the *Iliad* or *Beowulf* give? This will reveal another facet of the Truth regarding the problem. The fourth angle is that of History. What does the recorded experience of humanity say about it? A global view of the problem will enable us to see it in the right perspective. We shall be able to ascertain and experience a particle of Truth when we direct this four-pronged attack towards it.

Baba also recommends the kind of fundamental inquiry that Ramana Maharshi stood for. Who am I? Why am I?

Wherefore am I? If we ask ourselves these three questions and find out and experience the answers, we will have solved the cosmic riddle itself.

Baba has not mentioned this approach specifically. In his exposition of these *upasanas*, he gives the five-fold approach, comparing it to the five-faced goddess, Gayatri, the Vedic Rik that celebrates the supramental effulgence and puissance of the Sun of Truth. But this sixth approach, which we have placed first, is implied in his various pronouncements on the subject.

A second *upasana* is that of *Anyavati*, the proximate approach of *Soundarya* or Beauty. It consists in an apprehension of the *Karana* or seed-state of Reality, for that is where Beauty is Truth. We must find our way to Edmund Spenser's Garden of Adonais or Plato's World of Archetypes. It is the world of archetypal and spiritual beauty as distinguished from sensuous and imaginative beauty. It is also the plane on which one meets the Beauty that is terrible,—Time, the Destroyer, of the eleventh canto of the Gita and Pnemosyne, the Goddess of Memory that Keats describes in *Hyperion*: "But for her eyes I would have fled away." One meets all the gods on this plane, Indra who is the Mind of Light, Usha, the goddess of supramental dawn, the Sun of archetypal Truth and Soma or the Moon of Delight and Immortality.

If the approach sketched above, the *Anyavati Upasana*, enables us to realise the Many in the One, the *Angavati Upasana*, or the proximate discipline of Goodness makes us realise the One in the Many. We are made to see that all forms and names are those of the Divine and we must be one with each one of them. The essence of Goodness consists in making the spirit penetrate and permeate the five senses, the five *pranas* or vital breaths and the five

110

elements. It should flash through them as lightning flashes in the midst of a mass of dark-blue rain-clouds. Goodness is really Love applied to daily life, and the life not only of one individual but the life of all.

The fourth is the Savitri *Upasana*, the proximate discipline of Power, the apprehension of Adi Sakti, the primaeval supramental goddess, the splendour or daughter of the Sun. Sage Visvamitra's great Rik or rhythmic utterance, the Gayatri, is really concerned with this Sakti or Power. Everything is visible in sunlight. The mystery of All is similarly resolved in the light of Spirit. The face of Truth, says the Upanishad, is covered as with a golden lid; that thou, O Pushan, remove so that the way of Truth may be visible. It is the lifting of this lid that results in the unveiling of that Knowledge or Wisdom which is Power.

Goodness is the application of Power by the individual for the transformation of his own life. It is a limited private sphere. But the power of Will shines forth at its most resplendent when it is harnessed for the transformation of the collectivity. This is where Power is illumined energy on a lavish scale.

The fifth is the *Pranavopasana* or the proximate discipline of Light, illumined introspection or *dhyana*. It is the cultivation or propitiation of a *mantra*, the esoteric word or utterance, by remembering it intensely and meditating on it deeply. Each *mantra* is efficacious. But the *mantra* of *mantras*, their very crown jewel, is AUM. Through the lights and rhythms of the subtle world, through That (i.e. the Brahman) and *Sat* or the Principle of Being or Existence, the *mantra* leads the seeker to *Parabrahman* or the Transcendental Reality. The *mantropasana* is as much a window on Reality as any of the disciplines mentioned above.

Lastly, we come to the *Nidhanavati Upasana*, the

111

approach to Reality through Love. This love is an illumined and sublimated emotion flowing from a pure heart. It can flow towards the Personal as well as Impersonal Divine. It is the realisation of the Divine by expressing one's devotion through the well-known nine modes: worship; obeisance; remembrance; chanting the praise and glory of the Divine; touching the pair of blessed feet; listening to the songs and stories of the Divine's glory; friendship; service; self-pouring with self-surrender. Or pure love can flow through any one of the five channels of devotion: the serenity of resignation; service; parental love; friendship; and self-pouring with self-surrender.

All these six approaches are illumined by intuition, which is love. The sixth approach in itself is, in fact, love. These approaches represent, if one were to use Coleridge's terms, Reason (Truth) as distinguished from mere unillumined understanding, Imagination (Beauty) as distinguished from Fancy, Will (Goodness; Power) as distinguished from Choice and purified and sublimated Emotion (Love) as distinguished from Passion. Similarly, Introspection is Meditation, not merely Introversion.

It will be seen that this six-fold approach to Reality is as integral, in its own way, as that of Sri Aurobindo's yoga. It does not have in it the idea of ascent and descent and of the Supermind. But it aims at experiencing Reality through the purification and perfection of all the faculties with which man has been endowed.

Baba speaks with great moral fervour especially to the young, for morality is the stepping stone to spirituality. He wants youngsters to be happy warriors, men of action as well as contemplation. As the Gita puts it, "Where Krishna, master of perfected works and Partha, the great bowman, come together, there, in that society, is Wealth,

112

Victory, Splendour, Immutable Morality. This is the Truth."

Baba uses homely parables and interesting catchwords to make his point. A catchword fixes in the memory the point that he desires to make. '*WATCH*', for example, is a word that he employs for this purpose. *W* stands for Word. The words we use should be such that the minimum number of words should give the maximum meaning. Again, words are like dwellers on the threshold. They boomerang on us if we misuse them. We should watch the words we use. Words can also be creative. Meaning ran after the words that sages used in a moment of inspiration. Use words that way.

A is the second letter in *WATCH*. *A* stands for *Action*. Watch your actions. They should always be right, real *dharma*. Think of Sidney dying on the battlefield, lifting a glass of water to his mouth but giving it to the soldier who lay near him thirsty and dying, looking avidly at the water. Watch your actions.

T in *WATCH* stands for *Thoughts*. Watch your thoughts! They should not be the impure and wicked thoughts of a Macbeth. His thoughts made him wade through blood to the throne of Scotland and stay there saying all the while to himself that life is a "tale told by an idiot, full of sound and fury, signifying nothing". On the other hand, think like Kanaka, the great saint of Karnataka. His master gave him and other disciples a plantain each to eat at a place where no one would be able to see them eating it. The others went to several secret spots and ate their plantains. But Kanaka returned, plantain in hand, and told his master: "There is no place where I can eat it unseen. Everywhere God is witness."

C in *WATCH* stands for *Character*. Watch your character. Think of Gandhiji, the father of the nation.

113

In his hour of triumph, when Independence was won, he did not stay in Delhi to form the Government of India. He went into the wilderness, Noukhali and elsewhere, for the people there needed the help of this half-naked fakir. Character is the 'crown and glory' of life. Keep it undimmed.

H in *WATCH* stands for *Heart*. Watch your heart. Keep it selfless and pure. Think of Dadhichi, the ancient sage. The gods were told that Vritra, the great demon, could be killed if the backbone of Dadhichi were to be made the shaft of Indra's bow. The gods approached Dadhichi hesitantly for this gift. But Dadhichi did not hesitate even for a moment. "There can't be a better use for my backbone",—he said. He cast off his body by going into a yogic trance and the gods took the backbone from the body and made a bow with it for Indra. The demon was destroyed.

Whether it is metaphysical discussion, spiritual illumination or moral exhortation, Baba lays his finger unerringly on one thing essential for man: a change in his behaviour patterns and a step forward in his evolution towards divinisation. This is what ultimately matters. Philosophy is justified only if it leads to this consummation. Keats exclaimed that all charms fly at the mere touch of cold philosophy, i.e., the natural sciences. But even 'warm' philosophy— philosophy proper—is no better. It may wander in the void, ending up in a blind alley. It is only when we regard Experience as primary and prove a principle on our pulses that the morning "breaks like the pomegranate, in a shining crack of red".

18. BABA'S VIEWS ON EDUCATION—I

THE educational system of a country, says Baba, "is the bank on which the nation draws a cheque whenever it requires strong, reliable, skilled workers. If it goes bankrupt, as ours has very nearly gone today, it is a national disaster. If the system is overhauled and lubricated, the next generation is assured of good leaders and, what is equally essential, good followers."[1]

That our educational system has gone bankrupt is evident from the headlines and column-headings that keep on appearing in our newspapers on educational matters. Our syllabuses are antiquated, our teaching methods are outmoded. Our examinations have lost all meaning. Our students and teachers alike have been disillusioned with the system.

What is now required is a new kind of manpower. Baba says to students: "You must learn to become a new type of leaders, leaders who have passed through the crucible of *Seva* as *Sadhana*, leaders who have passed through school and college and mastered the problems of the present and the future, in the light of the past, leaders who appreciate the traditions and culture of this country." (p. 209)

Seva turns into *Sadhana* when any public duty is undertaken and discharged, not only with a sense of self-involve-

[1] P. 203. *Sathya Sai Speaks*. Vol. VII. All the page references that follow are made to this very book and volume.

ment but with complete self-effacement. It should be gone through as service to the Divine, for the sheer joy of it and for no personal motive whatsoever.

He refers to arrangements made by students themselves for their College Day: "Boys are really good, willing to do their duty and shine well in studies as well as in the field of service. The fault, for their vagaries and waywardness and for their occasional sprees of indiscipline, lies with the elders who set before them poor examples of truth and self-control."

Our colleges today are full of prospective bread-winners and degree-hunters, not genuine seekers of knowledge and truth. "The schools and colleges, once revered by the entire population as temples of Saraswati, the Goddess of Learning, as a means of attaining the supreme state of self-realisation, have degenerated into temples for the Goddess of wealth...the process of education has become a trade." (p. 489)

"Colleges have been infected, at present, by anxiety and perplexity, discontent and indiscipline, irreverence and futility." (p. 490)

What, then, is wrong with our educational system? It does not result in the end-products for which the system was founded. As Baba insists, "Politics without principles, education without character, science without humanity and commerce without morality are not only useless, but positively dangerous." (p. 215) The reason for this grave deficiency of the system is that the main purpose of life—the acquisition of *ananda* or disinterested delight and the sharing of that Ananda with others—has gone under and a number of mundane desires have taken its place. India is being turned into a *bhoga bhoomi*, the land of skyscrapers and tinned foods. A college for women trains its alumni to be 'desirable wives' and not

116

'worthy mothers' so much. One does not have to under-estimate the significance of wealth. But primary objectives should not be mixed up with secondary ones.

One can read or study at home. Why, then, should it be necessary for students to attend schools and colleges? Students have to attend them, says Baba, "in order to cultivate discipline, control emotions and canalise passions. Learning is just a small fraction of what can be gained from schools and colleges. They instil into the pupils the lessons of mutual co-operation, good manners, courtesy, compassion and comradeship, adjustment to limitations and overcoming of obstacles with calm deliberation." (p. 214)

It is a pity that, quite apart from fulfilling these larger objectives, our educational institutions are unable to cope even with the more circumscribed one of intellectual illumination. "It is indeed deplorable that the education of the spirit has been totally neglected, while attention is devoted to the training of skills and for gleaning and garner-ing information." (p. 156) Even the cultivation of skills and the gleaning of knowledge have become antiquated procedures because of our outmoded syllabuses and eva-luation methods. Theory and work experience are not as closely linked together, as they should be, in the teaching of professional courses of study like those in engineering and agriculture. The student's curiosity is lulled to sleep; he hardly picks up effectively any skills connected with his subject of study and his brain is crammed with bits of knowledge for examinations while his intellect lies unused for any analytical or synthetic study.

Baba has his gaze fixed steadily on the renaissance in Indian education. A renaissance will surely come about if the men and women who are associated with the vari-ous aspects of education are themselves transformed. It

117

has been late in coming because the greatest dislocation of our tradition has taken place in this field. The committee for Management should not be, as Baba says, "a come for tea affair"! Its members should be men of public standing genuinely interested in students and ready to make any sacrifice for the sake of a principle. They should be intensely human and above board in their dealings with others. They should not import the agitational methods of the legislatures into committee meetings.

The guardians and parents of students too should take a real interest in the cultural well-being and progress of their children and wards.

A school or college exists in order to make full-fledged the potential humanness present in an individual. The teacher is the most important asset of an educational institution. "He shapes the manners, behaviour, attitudes and even prejudices of the pupils under his care...the teacher dedicates himself to a great *Sadhana* when he enters upon this profession. He has himself to be what he advises his pupils to be.... Any misdemeanour of his becomes the talk of the town, it is discussed during dinner in a hundred homes the same day." (p. 199)

As for students, Baba loves them and pours forth his love and grace on them. "Children's minds are innocent, tender and pure.... The snakegourd is apt to grow crooked, if left alone. So gardeners tie a stone to its end, and the weight pulls it straight as it grows longer and longer. The minds of children and of youth are too apt to grow crooked under the influence of sensuous films, the hollow hypocritical atmosphere created by the elders, the lure of glitter and glamour and of a false sense of adventure and fame .... The stone should not be too heavy lest it snap the gourd in two! Avoid extremes at all times, in all

118

cases. Disciplinary rules have to be well thought out and adapted to the age-group you wish to correct."

Here is a piece of golden advice to students: "When you clamour for rights, you must bend your shoulders to carry the obligations too; finish your studies; develop the skill to distinguish between what is good and what is not, and the means to secure the good and avoid the evil. Instead, if you plunge into the streets behind the leaders who use you for their ends, you are harming your careers and harming politics too." (p. 201)

Side by side with the change in the outlook of individuals connected with higher education, we have entirely to reformulate and restate its objectives. Baba's philosophy of education derives from his general philosophy of life as a whole. Its watchwords are *Satya, Dharma, Shanti* and *Prema*: the fulfilment of the quest of the intellect in Truth and Being, the confirmation of the human will and its doing in right action or *Dharma*, the resolution of all the welter and conflict of human emotions into the basic attitude of peace and the awakening of the soul and the steady flow of intuition or love.

Truth is that which is changeless. *Vibhute*, or ashes, are the Truth of Matter. Truth is becoming reduced to imperishable being. *Dharma* or right action is what is founded on Truth. *Shanti* or Peace, in its lower aspect, is that equal state of mind which remains unaffected either by joy or sorrow or by any other pair of opposites. In its higher and more positive aspect, it is not exactly *ananda* but *madhura ananda*, a sweet pledge of or prelude to delight, when you apprehend the prevalence of God everywhere—the entire manifestation appears as the projection of Divinity. *Prema* or love is nothing other than the flow of soul itself.

These four pillars of Baba's philosophy yield the four

119

ideals of higher education,—Knowledge, Skill, Balance and Insight or Vision. Knowledge as its own end is one of the aims of liberal education. The capacity to think has to be aroused and applied to new life-situations. All knowledge, as Keats said, is a remembrance. It should not be reduced to the state of an encumbrance. The idea of general or great issues in education should, no doubt, be emphasised. The engineering student should have some poetry or music and the student of literature some science,—as living experience and not as a load on the memory.

The next aspect of education consists in imparting certain skills to the student, skills which will enable him to earn a decent livelihood. It is not merely the scientist, engineer or technologist that needs to cultivate skills. The student of poetry has to be familiar with scansion and the student of linguistics with linguistic analysis of various kinds. It is agonising to see arts graduates from our universities who have acquired neither these skills nor ordinary skills like typing and shorthand nor the apprehension of archetypal patterns in poetry.

The university degree has become, in effect, only a begging bowl: give me a job! Graduates cannot stand on their own legs. The mistake, says Baba, lies in the teachers and elders, the leaders and their advisers. As for balance in character and equipoise of being, this is regarded as something extraneous to liberal education which looks upon intellectual illumination as its supreme goal. But it is Baba's desire to provide the youth with an education which, while cultivating their intelligence, "will also purify their impulses and emotions and equip them with the physical and mental disciplines needed for drawing upon the springs of calmness and joy that lie in their own hearts." (p. 157) He desires that students should be happy warriors balancing action and contemplation. The study of psychology and philosophy, the company of the mature and the detached, meditation: all these are necessary to have the three supreme S's mentioned by Tennyson:

"Self-reverence, Self-knowledge, Self-control."

These three alone lead man to sovereign power. Balance is the key to the integrated personality. Vision is the fourth factor. A human being is but purblind without soul-sight.

Referring to students, Baba says, "Their higher natures will have to be fostered and encouraged to blossom, by means of study, prayer and *Sadhana*, contacts with the sages, saints and spiritual heroes and heroines of their land." (p. 157)

It is Baba's view that each student should be guided on the four-fold path of self-confidence, self-satisfaction, self-sacrifice and self-realisation. Self-confidence comes of an intensity and earnestness of aspiration which make a person march towards his goal regardless of all difficulties on the way. Self-satisfaction is born of the fact that he has been able to put his goal first before everything else and pursue it single-mindedly. When he has settled down to the quest, it is a pleasure for him to expend all his energies for its fulfilment, even beyond his normal capacities. In this way the seeker becomes one with his goal, the devotee with God.

This makes it clear that it is the goal of every human being to climb these four steps. "God", says Baba, "is so much intertwined in every word, act and thought of the people. Dams, factories, universities—these too will prosper and attain the targets, only if the men and women involved in them and benefiting by them have the earnestness, the sincerity, the humility and the reverence which bhakthi can build into them." (p. 158) In other words students, teachers and educational administrators have to be *dedicated* persons.

Baba is unsparing in his criticism of the objectives that animate higher education today. He says that "it has hardly done anything to destroy certain illusions that are nourished by the common run of mankind. One of these illusions consists in living under the impression that you are the body and that you are destroyed with the death of the body. The living culture of each people should be enough to show to us that these are brave translunary things of the spirit which go to form a great, if not an imperishable tradition. Another illusion is that happiness consists in accumulating money or knowledge or comforts or reputation. Happiness can be attained only by cultivating a state of mind which is unaffected by fortune, good or bad. Students are not equipped to face the fortunes of life, and to bring the best that is in them and place it at the service of the community... No effort is made to introduce the pupil to the sweet experiences of meditation and yoga, or of the joy of inquiry into one's own reality." (p. 213) Students should be attracted to cultivating *Vignan* or science and *Pragnan* or spirituality, together. If science brings us into close communion with the empirical facts relating to this universe, spirituality takes up where science has come to a stop and it acquaints us with the dialectic of the human heart and the profounder laws and states of consciousness.

Education knows no fruition without intuition or love. Scientists and technologists need it as much as artists do. With the splitting up of the world of knowledge into minor countries of the mind like the earth sciences, life sciences and health sciences, knowledge is losing its unity. It is only through soul-sight that unity can be restored to the world of knowledge.

It is with these objectives in view that Baba has planned to establish a College in every state in India. The Sathya Sai Trust, which runs those colleges (those at Anantapur and Bangalore), is animated by the ideal of yoga and tyaga—of equanimity and detachment. The College for Women at Anantapur will educate generations of women to live in the light of *dharma* and raise heroes full of the spirit of devotion and dedication.

The College for Men, set in the midst of rural surroundings in Whitefield near Bangalore, will train youngsters who will exercise a healthy influence on their kith and kin as well as on the villages simmering with restlessness as a result of the incompetence and intrigues of elders.

Baba has often thought of a programme for training college teachers. The fact that a person has a postgraduate degree in his subject does not mean that he can become a teacher overnight. He has to be familiar with the principles of pedagogy, the psychology of language learning, evaluation procedures and the techniques of classroom presentation for topics in his own subject.

We may draw up a programme for such training. To begin with, we have to consider how best the current syllabuses can be taught. Discussion may have to be organised on these lines:

(1) Doubling the number of periods provided for teaching a subject and using the extra periods as tutorial periods for groups of students.

(2) Using during these tutorial hours self-correction or group-correction exercises.

(3) Devising new syllabuses for the course.

(4) Preparing guidelines for teaching a particular lesson or topic.

(5) Preparing question-papers which do justice to the scope and objectives of a course.

(6) Going practice in a fair and proper evaluation procedure.

Baba has some practical suggestions to make regarding courses of study and teaching methods. Elaborate syllabuses are drawn up which, if taught properly, promote learning and train pupils to think on their own. If teachers are concerned only with the percentage of passes and do not teach the topics in the curriculum fully and well, they deceive the public as well as themselves.

Mini-convocations will be a good feature of college life and they deserve to be encouraged. The convocations organised by universities for all the graduates of the year achieve nothing or very little.

One has to think on these lines and find out in what other respects the present system can be reformed.

The next question to ask concerns spiritual education as not only a desirable but as an essential objective in our college courses and the ways and means of realising it. The aims of spiritual education can be expounded as follows:

(1) To place a student on the path of self-confidence, self-satisfaction, self-sacrifice and self-realisation.

(2) To promote the spirit of dedication in all we do through earnestness, sincerity, humility and reverence.

(3) To remove the illusion that happiness consists in accumulating money, knowledge, comforts or reputation, whereas happiness is a state of mind which can be cultivated and which is unaffected by fortune, good or bad.

(4) To enable students to bring the best in them and place it at the service of the community.

124

(5) To see that a student is attracted to cultivate *Pragnan* along with *Vignan* or science.

(6) To introduce the pupil to the sweet experiences of meditation and yoga or of the joy of inquiry into one's own reality.

The ways and means for achieving these aims may be listed thus:

(1) The teachers themselves should be disinterested seekers of truth, on their way to realising these aims.

(2) There should be regular contacts with the sages, saints and spiritual heroes and heroines of the land through discourses or literary study where a personal contact is not possible.

(3) The student should have his own daily *sadhana*.

(4) There should be an opening prayer each day in the college and all should pray together.

(5) There should be a regular provision in the time-table each week for studying great spiritual classics, the psychology of spiritual development, biographies of saints and books on the essentials of Indian culture.

It would be interesting to discuss and find out how much of this can be fitted into the college curriculum.

Baba tells us about an episode from the *Mahabharata* regarding the slaying of Draupadi's children, that he dramatised for the Sri Sathya Sai College at Whitefield. A Muslim student played the role of Krishna in this play and two Christian students played the roles of Arjun and Bheema. Ancient Indian culture is the heritage of the Indian people as a whole irrespective of their faith or creed. Similarly, students have to be taught the equality

125

of all faiths by being made familiar with the great personalities and sayings connected with each one of them.

"We are also giving in this College", says Baba, "instruction in the fundamental principles of all faiths, from
the sacred books like the Gita, the Quran, the Bible,
the Dhammapada." (p. 206)

In another context he says that the Ramayana and the
Mahabharta are reservoirs of knowledge for the seekers
of peace. They are replete with examples and precepts
which are inspiring and timely. By taking the teachings
to heart, purity can be attained. These and other great
scriptural texts can be taught with profit. "There is only
one God, one Goal, one Law, one Religion and one
Reason." (p. 208) The various religions are only so
many roads to God.

Baba does not hesitate to trace the social, political
and economic ills in our country to our faulty educational system which has made no arrangements to ins-
truct the young men and women of India in the principles
of Indian culture. "When man is not trained to lead
the good life, the godly life, teaching him various skills
and tricks only make him a danger to himself and the
others." (p. 213)

It would be worthwhile inquiring how the cultural
activities in a college can be utilised for promoting this
sense of unity and the equality of all faiths. Instruction
in the fundamental principles of all faiths will promote
the attainment of this objective in a great measure.
Again, there should be a course in the essentials of
Indian culture for first year students.

As important as spiritual and religio-cultural education in a college is moral education. We are faced today
with the collapse of moral values in every segment of
society. Special emphasis has, therefore, been rightly laid

in the Sathya Sai Colleges on the fostering of character.

Baba thinks it is essential that each school or college should function as a *gurukul*, a tutorial hermitage as in ancient days, if the right kind of education is to be imparted to students. In these institutions and in hostels attached to them, the atmosphere must be so charged that discipline comes automatically, with full heart. "Such discipline", says Baba, "will shape good soldiers for the nation. Unlike the present generation of leaders, these can inspire and guide the people along right lines. They have also to be good followers; fine soldiers make fine generals." (p. 200) This becomes possible only if the teaching, clerical and menial staff in a college help to maintain this atmosphere under the supervision of a dedicated principal.

Secondly, Baba would like the food habits of children at school (and possibly even in higher secondary schools) to be regulated: "Food determines to a large extent health and intelligence, emotion and impulse. Set limits to the quality and quantity of food, as well as to the number of times it is consumed and the timings." (p. 200) Food does not just refer to the intake of calories, *satwic* or otherwise. It also includes sights and sounds and tactile impressions, the entire environment and the vibrations that the food is charged with, due to the thought processes of those who handle it, prepare it and serve it.

Thirdly, Baba would like recreation also to be moral and elevating, in the company of the righteous and God-fearing. This means that a visit to crowded cinema houses in which sexy films are shown, would be quite a disaster to students. It would always be better to select pictures which you would like them to see and show them in the school auditorium.

Prayer is a good item to be included in the time-table. Silence is invaluable and pupils can be asked to practise it. In this connection, Baba narrates an incident that happened in Bangalore Sathya Sai College: "You can picture the kind of change I welcome. At the public examinations held at the College, which is one of the Centres, the moment the candidates got the question papers, all the examinees stood up together. The invigilators were surprised and some of them were struck with fear that, perhaps, they were trying to create a scene and protest against the paper and the paper setter! But they stood up only for a minute of silent prayer." (pp. 203-4)

Students should be encouraged to write to their parents about the school and their progress... This will help to correct defects in time and to the full.

One should also see to it that the young are not kept idle and unoccupied. Time well used is like food well digested.

There should be clean and comfortable clothes for the body, not clothes that attract attention. "I like dress that will not discourage people from approaching you for a kind word, a bit of service, a helping hand." Similarly, you must have clean, consoling exercises for the mind like *japam* and *dhyanam*. "Do not use the eye to vulgarise your brain, the feet to stand in queue for deleterious films."

Character is the most precious gift of education. Baba tells the students on a Prize Distribution Day: "When your parents hear that you are honest, serviceable, leading useful, honourable lives, they are full of joy. That joy is the prize *you* give your college." (p. 211)

Why should students attend schools and colleges, spending large amount of money? They could as well read and study at home. They attend them, says Baba, in order to cultivate discipline, control emotions and canalise passions. They learn there the lessons of mutual co-operation, good manners, courtesy, compassion and comradeship. If there is no proper atmosphere for learning these things in a college, it would be in the national interest to close it down.

We must learn to cultivate unselfish love without fear or suspicion. "Teachers must lead lives based on upright conduct, moral grandeur and spiritual *sadhana.*" (p. 215)

Speaking at the inauguration of the permanent buildings of the Sri Sathya Sai Arts and Science College for Women, Anantapur, Baba said: "This will be a Gurukul, a place where the teachers and taught will grow together in love and wisdom, as close to the ideals of the hermitages of the past, as is possible under present conditions." (p. 491)

Baba has a suggestion to make regarding the taking of attendance in classes. When the teacher has the attendance register before him, he calls out numbers and students respond to them, as if they are prisoners or policemen known only by their numbers. Numbers conceal the individualities of students and mould them into dead uniformity. The teacher should call out the names of students.

It would be interesting for college teachers to weigh and consider these suggestions in their own minds and see how far these can be translated into action. Needless to say, there emerges from Baba's teachings a philosophy of education which, like that of Mahatma Gandhi, Rabindranath Tagore and Sri Aurobindo, insists on the need for an all-round education of which spiritual education is an essential part. We will ignore these arguments of the great only at our own peril.

19. BABA'S VIEWS ON EDUCATION—II

A SHORT figure in a flowing silken robe stands on the rostrum before the gathering which is a hundred thousand strong and speaks in a ringing voice that carries conviction into the very depths of the heart. That is Baba's voice and the voice has been heard by now from one end of India to the other. Millions have been moved by the magic in that voice and by the stream of love that flows from it. It is a voice that sounds the clarion call to humanity to transform itself and to live a nobler and a fuller life. It is truly amazing to think how a school boy from the wilderness of Puttaparti has grown marvellously into a prophet and transformed Puttaparti itself into a paradise. His voice is also the clarion call to all Indians to realise the glory of their ancient heritage and to build a great, modern and renascent India.

One should see Baba move with students. He has the greatest love for them because he knows that these are the builders of tomorrow. He talks to them like a friend and an equal and lives with them in their room. I was present at a hostel dinner which some students gave him. One could see him diving into the very hearts of students. Thousands of young men and women have been warmed by the flow of affection that they have felt from his heart and have dedicated their lives to his service.

What is his message to students? It is a universal

message, the message meant for all. He would like students to live disciplined lives and dedicate their energies to the Divine. He would like them to be true warriors of the Divine in the station that Life has placed them in and with the status which it has given them. An uprightness and righteousness in behaviour which does not deflect even by a needle's length from Truth as they see it; a pure and chastened heart which is the abode of peace, unaffected by the gusts of passion or prejudice and a spring of love welling out of their hearts towards all: this is the ideal that Baba holds before them all the time. He would like them to preserve whatever is noble in their heritage and also to know all that is to be known by way of knowledge in the modern world. Thousands of students have been thrilled by his call. They have responded to him magnificently by enrolling themselves as volunteers in the service of the great cause for which Baba stands,—the regeneration of India and all humanity.

The power that commands this loyalty is love. Baba is incarnate Love. But this incarnation of Love has also the irresistible drive of the warrior, the analytical grasp of the seeker, the puissance of the strong and the humility of the meek. Love can be itself only when it is endowed with all these qualities.

Baba educates, not merely the pupils in the college but also the teachers and the management. He is their friend, philosopher and guide. If a poll were to be taken to ascertain the teacher most popular with the hostel students in Whitefield, a 100% vote will mention only Baba. He permeates their life, corrects their errors at all levels,—from brooding to meditation and befriends them in their moments of distress. His precepts, his example, his informal talks and his gifts win their

131

hearts for ever. He even spends hours with them in guiding them in their rehearsals of the play to be staged on Annual Day.

The average student is full of animal spirits. He is like the fruit of the *peepal* tree,—a handsome exterior, but a hundred worms or worm-like desires beneath the skin. He is incapable of understanding divine love. He takes it to be human love and gets burnt like the moth courting a flame. He puts his own construction on Baba, without apprehending his reality. In Sathya Sai colleges, students have a free access to Baba while thousands of grown-up devotees, dying to touch his feet, can hardly catch a glimpse of him. Students have to realise the uniqueness of the privilege which they enjoy in Sathya Sai colleges and summer courses and derive the fullest benefit from their opportunity.

In discussing the provision for moral and spiritual education at the school level, the Kothari Commission Report points out that the absence of provision for such an education is a serious defect in our school curriculum. Every one knows that, in the life of the majority of the Indian people, religion is a great motivating force. It has a great impact on the formation of character and the inculcation of ethical values. The Commission, therefore, recommends that a conscious and organised attempt should be made for spiritual education at school.

The child will develop a sense of values at school if the school atmosphere is good and healthy and the personality and the behaviour of the teachers are what they should be. Every teacher, whatever the subject, has to be held responsible for building the character of his pupils because, all that he does and says leaves an enduring impact on the child's mind. The teacher has to teach his subject in a manner that will bring out fundamental values such as integrity and social responsibility. It is not as though he is driving at the underlying moral of a lesson all the time. If he himself is aware of values and has given some thought to them, the values will pass into his teaching imperceptibly and inspire his pupils. The school assembly, the co-curricular activities, the celebration of religious festivals, work-experience, team games and sports, subject clubs, the social service programme—all these should contribute towards building up the values of co-operation and mutual regard, honesty and integrity and discipline and social responsibility.

We should not forget the fact that this indefinable atmosphere in the school, which we have tried to describe above, goes a long way towards establishing a good centre for moral and spiritual education. Moral and spiritual education cannot flourish where there is no such atmosphere in school, even when we provide for moral and religious instruction in the time-table.

A point that the Sri Prakasha Committee makes in this connection is that the home of the child must be influenced first. The education of the parents should be regarded as a very important factor in the educational scheme. The Committee suggests that this should be achieved through lectures, leaflets and pamphlets, the radio and the cinema and through voluntary organisations. Good manners are a very important part of moral education and we have been fast ignoring them. They have to be inculcated both by example and by precept. Parents should be told in an impersonal manner how the drawback in their homes, both in the matter of physical orderliness and of the right psychological atmosphere, comes in the way of children.

Since moral and spiritual instruction should have its

own place in the school curriculum, what specific provision can be made for it? The Kothari Commission Report suggests that one or two periods a week should be set aside for it in the school time-table. At the primary stage, such instruction should be imparted through interesting stories including stories drawn from the great religions of the world. As the report says, all religions stress certain fundamental qualities of character such as honesty and truthfulness, consideration for others, reverence for old age, compassion for the needy and suffering and kindness to animals. In the literature of each religion, parables are used for inculcating ethical values in the followers. If the teachers narrate such stories at the right moment, they will be most effective. The ethical teaching of the great religions should be broadly explained and dogmas and rituals excluded. Simple and interesting stories about the lives and teachings of prophets, saints and religious leaders should be included in the syllabus for language teaching.

Thirdly, the Committee suggests that audio-visual material should be used such as good quality photographs, film-strips and coloured reprints showing great works of art and architecture, closely connected with the main living religions of the world. Such material could be used in the teaching of Geography.

Fourthly, the school assembly should be held for a few minutes in the morning for group meetings.

Fifthly, through the school programme, the attitude of service and the realisation that work is worship should be developed in the child.

Lastly, all forms of physical education and all forms of play in the school should contribute to the building up of character and the inculcation of the spirit of true sportsmanship.

What programmes of moral and spiritual instruction do the Kothari Commission and the Sri Prakasha Committee envisage at the secondary stage? The Commission suggests that moral instruction should not be divorced from the rest of the curriculum. Nor should it be confined to a single period. If the values are to become a part of the student's character, an all-embracing treatment of the moral way of life is needed.

The Commission makes the suggestion that there should be frequent discussions between the teacher and the pupils on the values which are sought to be inculcated. The hour a week that is assigned to moral instruction may be utilised for this purpose.

The Sri Prakasha Committee makes the following suggestions (modified or amplified by me slightly):

(a) The morning assembly should observe two minutes' silence. This should be followed by readings from the scriptures or the great literature of the world or an appropriate address.

(b) Community singing should also be encouraged.

(c) The lives (and not merely stories about the lives) of great religious and spiritual leaders should be studied. They could be included in the History or Literature curriculum.

(d) The essential teachings of the great world religions should be studied as a part of the curriculum pertaining to Social Studies and History during the last two years of the secondary school.

(e) Simple texts and stories concerning different religions may be included in the teaching of languages and general reading.

(f) Suitable speakers may be invited to address the students on moral and spiritual values.

(g) Joint celebrations may be organised on the occasion of important festivals of all religions.

(h) Knowledge and appreciation of religions other than one's own and respect for their founders, should be encouraged in various ways including essay competitions and declamations.

(i) Organised social service during holidays and outside class hours should be an essential part of extra-curricular activities. Such service should teach the dignity of manual labour, love of humanity, patriotism and self-discipline. Participation in Sports and Games should be compulsory and physical education, including sex-hygiene, should be a normal part of the school programme.

(j) Qualities of character and the behaviour of students should form an essential part of the overall assessment of a student's performance at school.

The first All India Conference of Bal Vikas Teachers was held in Bombay in the year 1971. Over four hundred delegates from all over India attended the Conference. There were three items on the agenda: (1) Why Sathya Sai Bal Vikas? (2) The Course for Bal Vikas. (3) Rules and Regulations for conducting Bal Vikas classes. Baba gave the lead to the Conference, in his address on the discussion on these subjects. It divided the concerned children into three age-groups: (a) 6-10, (b) 11-14, (c) 14-17. What Baba said on the subject bears a startling resemblance to what experts have to say on several aspects of the problem.

First regarding the Bal Vikas teachers themselves. Taking his cue from the 'Guru Brahma' verse recited by children in the beginning Baba told the teachers that they could be called *gurus* or teachers only if they played all the three roles of Brahma, Vishnu and Maheshwara well vis-a-vis the child: sowing the seed, creating the proper environment for it to sprout and removing strangling weeds and shrubs. He said that they would be able to be in tune with *Para Brahman* or the Transcendental Reality if only they played their three roles well; for the Bal Vikas was meant for them as a *sadhana*, a programme intended mainly for cleansing and purifying the teachers' own minds and hearts.

Again, he reminded them how the teaching in the schools began and ended now with memorisation. But this will not do. Much less will this do when we think of moral and spiritual instruction. It is no use hammering these ideas into the heads of children; they should be so taught that they are imprinted on their hearts and become part and parcel of their lives.

Teachers will have also to recognise the fact that Dhruva and Prahlad are no mere creatures of legend and that children have great potentialities in them. They will be mistaken if they think that children know very little and that they can be taught through the methods evolved by the teachers themselves. On the other hand, the teachers have to adopt such methods as children themselves indicate by what they seem to be saying or doing.

Baba points out that the home is a great influence on the child. Parents go to clubs, play cards, smoke, drink and quarrel. How, then, can they ever guide their children to desist from these and other evil habits? Baba therefore tells teachers that they should occasionally go to the homes of the children under their care, and tell the parents that it is not possible for their children to improve unless they themselves mend their ways. And if teachers have to do this for children and their parents, they will have to mend their own ways and set their homes in order.

Most of the teachers in Bal Vikas centres are women. Womanhood in India has always been greatly respected. It is women who have been the custodians of Indian culture for centuries. Savithri, Chandramati, Sita and the names of other great Indian women shine like stars. In collocations like ⌐SitaRama, Laxmi Narayana, and Parvati Parameshwara, it is the name of the goddess that comes first. Every household should become a Bal Vikas centre and every mother a Bal Vikas teacher. This is how the glory of India can be revived. "How can you, women", asks Baba, "how can you, in the name of the motherhood of this land, tolerate obscene cinema posters in the streets and the objectionable type of dressing seen there?"

He tells the teachers that they should take a vow to make a success of Bal Vikas. They should not feel that it is thrust on them by somebody. They should take to it as a process of *sadhana* for their own purification and enlightenment.

Again, women are inclined to be tender and to handle children gently. But they should not overdo this, for a child that is fondled is also a spoilt child most often. Misplaced tenderness undermines discipline and does damage to the child. The love that heals should also be the love that punishes, for the child has finally to be made to turn to the Divine Self. A fish that has been thrown up on the shore by the sea waves has to be put back into its original home, the sea, to put it on a luxury bed and give it coffee means only killing it.

Baba further tells the teachers that they should regard themselves as blessed with Bal Vikas teaching. How many women get such an opportunity to serve the Divine? They should regard Bal Vikas children as their own. It is their personality that is going to influence the children. They should go steadily forward, act with decision and in a spirit of sacrifice.

When a child enters the Bal Vikas class, what is his plan that we have in mind for the child? We expect that, in the first place, its behaviour patterns will change. The child is expected to start rejecting a few things that it used to do before, and to cultivate a few other habits that it did not have. For example, the child is expected to get up early in the morning, practise Omkar, prayer and a little meditation, bow down to its parents, show respect to its teachers and behave with other children in a friendly spirit. These will be now behaviour patterns. for several children coming to the Bal Vikas classes. In this way the child will reach a higher level of character or moral behaviour or right action. Our schools do not spend much time in aiming at this kind of achievement. But the Bal Vikas plan attaches the highest importance to these new patterns of conduct.

Secondly, the child will be expected to speak the truth. In other words, the thoughts and words of the child will spontaneously be true just as its deeds or behaviour patterns will invariably be on the side of good. The words and thoughts of the child will always be illumined by truth. The parents and teachers have themselves to set the right example for the child. How shall we measure the element of truthfulness in the thoughts of the child? This can be achieved in the following manner:

(a) Questions can be asked of the child to narrate the thoughts that were running through its mind a few moments before.

(b) Questions can also be asked, expecting the child to react to a certain imaginary situation that might lead in the direction of truth or falsehood. This will be a test of the intention, the imaginativeness and the creativity of the child.

(c) The child may also be asked to narrate what impressions it has formed of certain persons that it is expected to like or dislike. This will give us a peep into the thought-processes of the child.

Another aim in the Sathya Sai Plan is to so train the child that its habitual temper will be one either of natural serenity or of spontaneous delight. This is the emotional purity that the Bal Vikas Plan expects the child to achieve. It may be that the child has its moments and fits of anger, gloom, depression, envy, pride, greed and so on. The six enemies of man's poise are busy at work right from the days of childhood. One has therefore to see whether these moments and fits get reduced once the child is being trained according to the Bal Vikas Plan. This is only negative evidence. One has also to be on the watch for positive results. For example, at the end of an excellent bhajan session, one can find out whether the child is unconcerned, absent-minded, partially responsive or in a mood completely to surrender to the beauty and grandeur of the bhajan. When the child recites a prayer aloud, one can see whether it is being repeated in a routine fashion or whether there is any accent of sincerity in the recitation. When the child goes into meditation, it is possible to find out whether the child is practising an artificial closing of the eyes and an aimless wandering of the mind or whether the child is really diving into the depths of such consciousness as has been awakened in it. When a bhajan is going on, the teacher or researcher can also find out whether the child is reciting the bhajan feelingly or only in an absent-minded fashion. When little dialogues or plays are staged, the extent to which the child identifies itself with a given role, can also throw some light on this aspect of its achievement.

Lastly, the Bal Vikas Plan exects that the child will have an active intuition. Intuition, according to a certain system of philosophy, is nothing but love. If the soul of the child has been stirred in some way, its love will flow spontaneously towards others, even towards those whom the child has not liked. It is easier to awaken the soul in a child than in an adult. Once the soul is awakened in a child, there is every chance of its psyche remaining in the front of the child's personality. How is one to know whether the child's love has been made active in this way? It should be possible to know this by using the following methods of enquiry:

(a) Does the child, left to itself, recite feelingly any bhajans that it has heard or croon to itself devotional songs and snatches?

(b) Is the child fond of reciting with real enthusiasm the lives of saints, devotees, etc.?

(c) What are the child's reactions when it sees other children or other people in distress?

(d) While playing games or participating in group activities, is the child's behaviour likely to promote quarrels, or bring about group understanding?

It is the realisation of these four aims that has to be evaluated while assessing the results of the Sathya Sai educational plan. Prayer, meditation, bhajans, story telling, reading the lives of saints, etc., are included in the syllabus. One has to see how far these prescriptions have been useful in promoting the four-fold aim mentioned above.

141

An annual summer course in Indian culture and spirituality is being organised by Baba ever since May 1972. These courses have been a blessing to university students from all over India. About 15 students were selected from each State in India and admitted to the Summer Course in May 1972. They stayed in Brindavan for a month and Sri Sathya Sai Trust was responsible for their boarding and lodging. About 35 eminent scholars were invited from all over India to lecture at the Summer Course. Bhagavan himself was the moving spirit. He was practically with the students and the faculty from morning to evening, serving them and cutting jokes with them and he delivered an inspiring discourse every evening during the Course. The lives of many of the students who attended the Course were changed during the month. As Bhagavan himself expressed it, cars were brought to the workshop, repaired where repair was necessary and put on the road again practically as new cars. I have met several students who attended the Course months after the course was over and I know how profoundly they have been influenced by it. They get up at 4.30 A.M. even now and have their *OMKAR* every morning. Some cinemagoers, who saw at least two or three films a day, have never walked into a cinema-house after they attended the Course. I am only mentioning instances of radical change. Almost everyone who was on the Course has felt its life-giving impact one way or the other.

A volume containing an account of the Course, its educational significance and the summaries of the lectures delivered at the Course was published in May 1973. What prospects does the Summer Course hold for students?

For one thing, the Course will broaden the mental horizons of students. The Course consists of a series of lectures on the characteristics of Indian Culture, the sacred texts of Hinduism, the main tenets of the great religions of the world, the lives of Indian saints, the six systems of Indian Philosophy and the notion of values with reference to the physical and social sciences. It is a sad fact that the average Indian student hardly knows anything about his culture and heritage. Nor is he enabled to develop the world-view in the light of which he has to cultivate the various intellectual disciplines that he selects for study. The Course helps him to do this and to realise the value and dignity of the life of a worthy citizen of India.

The second thing the Course does for him is to help him to realise the dignity of labour. It is a great experience to move with Bhagavan on Sunday mornings and do some manual work, clean up the garden, mend the road, etc. and be rewarded with fruit from Bhagavan's own hand. The students also listen to the inspiring discourses from Bhagavan before they start their manual work. It is well known that our students are hardly enabled to cultivate any skills during their career. Science students hardly find any apparatus in the laboratories for their own experiments. Students of poetry cannot scan. Students of botany have hardly any first-hand experience of the wonders of the world of botany. Work experience on this Course helps participants to be aware of this important aspect of education.

There is another aspect of education which is greatly neglected in our colleges. In addition to intellectual illumination and the cultivation of skills, the student has to acquire a certain amount of balance or equipoise in life. Today the student is entirely thrown back on himself in this matter. He can sink or swim in the process and nobody is there to help him. The present-day teacher thinks that he has done his work for the day if he has delivered two or three lectures in the course of the day, though the lectures themselves may be no better than tutorial instruction on a mass scale. The students run their election campaigns in the way as politicians do. This fact and the fact that there is hardly anyone to help students to face their various problems from day to day, leaves them helpless and at the mercy of many evil forces that are generally active in society. But the participants of the Summer Course live with their teachers. Students from all over India live together in the same rooms and observe the same discipline. A new spirit of accommodation is seen to develop day by day. As Bhagavan himself told the first Course at its inaugural session, the difficulties about food (since there is no all-India menu as yet) and several other inconveniences are digested and ironed out during the Course. Students develop a toughness and tenderness of character which is remarkable indeed.

Last of all, there is Bhagavan's love flooding the Course and overwhelming the teachers and participants. This, in fact, is the most distinguishing feature of the Course. Who can awaken the love that is hidden in our hearts and the intuition that lies dormant in us excepting Bhagavan and saints who belong to a similar tradition? This is the highlight of the Summer Course in Brindavan.

The Course helps young men and women to be themselves the *India of tomorrow*.

What is the new turn that the Sathya Sai colleges in India are expected to give to Indian education? Education should not be based on a compulsive pattern as in socialist countries. It should not be exclusive as it tended to be in ancient India, or merely colonial as in our own times. Nor should it be merely competitive as in a permissive society and predominantly intellectual as in ancient Greece and Rome and in modern Europe. A national system of education in India should be mainly rooted in Spirit, in accordance with the genius of this country. It should envisage a society built on love and co-operation. Even the physical and social sciences should, in such a system, be taught from the angle of their essential value and spiritual significance. This is what is being done in the Summer Course in Indian Culture and Spirituality.

An educational system of this kind aims at a two-fold transformation. It aspires to train the individual in the process of creative self-sculpture and to promote his creative contribution to the building up of a society based on co-operation and love.

III. Work

20. THE PHILOSOPHICAL BASIS OF SATHYA SAI ORGANISATIONS

ONE can study Sathya Sai Organisations, going to them after getting familiar with a biographical and psychological account of Baba's personality. In the alternative, we can study the organisations themselves and form an idea of Baba's personality through them.

Two outstanding facts emerge from a study of these organisations. One is that Baba is a supreme organiser. In his *durbar* are to be found talented men and women belonging to diverse spheres of life: poets and philosophers, kings, princes and ambassadors, merchant princes, ministers and members of parliament, soldiers and generals, clerks and officers and social workers, *sadhus* and *sanyasis*. Baba uses the services of this heterogeneous group for building various institutions and for bringing about a total revolution in society.

The second fact is that Baba's philosophy is not just rooted narrowly in the spiritual life of the individual. Individual and collective awareness are both taken into account as part of the same integral consciousness in all that he says and does.

How is one to account for this note of modernness in Baba's philosophy and practice? For example, though Baba is a lover of tradition, performing the week-long sacrifice at Dussera time and celebrating Sivaratri, he is unorthodox in allowing women to recite the Vedas and resisting the recitation at pilgrim centres ("I am a creature of sin", etc. This modernness springs from the comprehensiveness of his aim; which is not merely the liberation of the individual but the spiritual regeneration of India and, through India, of the whole world.

It is this very comprehensive philosophy that is reflected in the institutions he has built up. The complex of institutions at Prashanti Nilayam, including the Iswaramba High School and the spiritual colony growing at Whitefield, are indeed unique, for these have grown and are growing around the intimate presence of Baba. So are the *sanctum sanctorum*,—the Mandir with three domes and its fascinating sculpture at Prashanti Nilayam and the places of residence for Baba in Bombay, Hyderabad and Madras,—Sathyadeep, Sivam and Sundaram.

The Sai institutions reflect the composite light of the five light pillars of Sai philosophy,—Truth, Righteousness, Peace, Love and Non-Violence. The Sathya Sai Study Circle, the Prashanthi Academy of the learned, under whose auspices scholarly men of vision discourse on the spiritual life, the running of the monthly journal, *Sanatan Sarathi*, in many languages for disseminating the Sai approach to Truth and the translation of Sai literature into all the Indian and European languages (translations are coming out even in Italian and Scandinavian),—all these activities are organised around the scintillating light of Truth. Thousands of devotees and hundreds of devoted scholars are contributing their mite in the service of Truth.

Training is imparted in *dharma* or right action at various age-levels by the *Sathya Sai Seva Dal* till one is thirty, when one becomes a Samithi member and continues his *dharmic* work as an adult. Volunteers are taught

150

to tread the right path only when they are recruited for managing certain functions and ceremonies. But the junior and senior Seva Dal are a dedicated band. They receive regular training and practice in the service of *dharma*. They guide the children who have lost their way, tend the sick in mental and other hospitals, serve splendidly as food-distributing agencies in times of famine and help families in distress. They organise Narayana Seva Camps for feeding the poor frequently. This is the Sai path that makes members realise that Work is Worship and that Duty is God.

A third type of organisation specialises in the cultivation of Peace,—peace within and calm around. The *bhajan* groups which function once a week all over the world and often every day, chanting the name of the Divine in repetitive rapture; the *Nagar Sankirtan* or itinerant singing groups that chant the name of God in the streets, carrying God into the lives of common man; the recitation of AUM at 4 A.M. in the morning, followed by *dhyana* or meditation; and the practice of the special form of meditation known as *Jyoti Upasana* or the propitiation of Light,—imagining a flame, to begin with, in the centre of the eyebrows, carrying it in meditation into all the chakras in the body, seeing it in near and dear ones, friends and foes and, in fact, the entire universe: all these procedures are directed towards the achievement of Peace.

Non-Violence is the ideal in whose service other activities are promoted, such as the regeneration of what is vital in the national culture. The establishment of schools in which students are taught to recite the Vedas in the traditional manner, the performance of Vedic sacrifices and the celebration of festival days like *Guru Pournima* (the full-moon night dedicated to remembering the

Master) *Sivaratri, Dussera* (the tenth day of the ten-day festival), Krishna Ashtami (the birthday anniversary of Sri Krishna): all these activities illustrate the point. An extension of this activity on universal lines is seen in the celebration of Christmas Day and in the flying of the Prashanti flag which carries on it the emblems of the great religions of the world.

As for Love. Baba is an institution in himself. Nowhere can Love be taught except by and through love. His own lightning tours give him opportunities to fill every one with love. The love that flows forth to millions in public gatherings; the evening sittings when he talks to close disciples sitting in a crescent around him; the sessions with students, playful, hortative or stern; the interviews which register great changes in the lives of people; the unsolicited smile that brings salutations even from critics and enemies; and the loving response to Baba's love that results in breath-taking cures and healings: these are only a few manifestations of Baba's divine love.

Other institutions started by Baba are indeed the training-ground for the five-fold *sadhana* or preparation outlined above. These institutions have been designed for different age-groups. Even the Seva Samitis and the *Mahila Vibhags* or women's wings are training centres in spirituality for adults. One sometimes hears the complaint that human nature is the same everywhere, even in an *asram* and that members and seekers quarrel frequently with each other. But we should not forget the other side. Each *samiti* or *vibhag* becomes a magic circle, as it were, in which members can experiment with themselves and deal openly, uncompromisingly and in a forthright manner with other members since the field is ready for the cultivation of harmony. A person who is in service, government or otherwise, has to compromise. He has to carry out the orders of his superiors, whether his conscience approves of them or not, assuming that sins arising out of those orders, if any, will be visited on the heads of the superiors. But in these magic circles, Truth itself is the sovereign head. Peace is the disposition prescribed and Love, Righteousness and Non-Violence are expected to be the substance of each one's behaviour. Each *Samiti* or *Vibhag*, therefore, is a design deliberately created for the five-fold realisation. If a Samiti has some quarrelsome members in it, it also has a few others who are shock-absorbers. And Bhagavan himself is there at the top for giving guidance and advice.

The Central Sathya Sai Trust, the State Sathya Sai Trusts, the Education and Publication Foundation, the various development committees and the Prashanti Nilayam township and other committees are there for this very purpose. They are not there to carry on routine management in the way of the world. What is expected is self-control as much as control of affairs entrusted to their care.

Even annual conferences of Samitis and Seva Dal or Bal Vikas centres serve the same purpose. In a certain State Conference, members were permitted by Bhagavan to break into four zonal groups and elect their own convener. An hour was set apart for the purpose and members were told that Baba would intervene if the matter was not settled within an hour. One of the groups was involved in a vehement discussion and it exceeded the time-limit. Baba appeared on the scene. Three candidates were contesting the election. One of them had the majority of votes, another ten or fifteen and the third one only three or four. The third candidate then began to contend that voting should be by ballot since a show

153

of hands was awkward and exposed the members to vindictiveness. But the voting had been over and the candidate did not raise any objection at that time. When Baba appeared on the scene, the second candidate withdrew his candidature saying that he did not wish to complicate matters. Baba immediately appreciated the self-denial of the candidate and told him that he had been selected by him—Baba—as zonal convener.

As for children, the thousands of Bal Vikas classes scattered all over India and found also in some other parts of the world teach them how to pray, respect their parents, meditate, chant *bhajans* and speak and sing on spiritual themes and act in Miracles and Moralities. The one or two periods of Bal Vikas teaching supplement the 'secular' instruction given in kindergartens and primary schools.

As for secondary education, the Sai practice has been to start schools with an agricultural or technical bias so that the products—usually children coming from poor or middle class families—can find employment easily. The moral and spiritual programme for these children is the same as for other secondary pupils. In Ishwaramba High School, at Puttaparti, the syllabus prescribed by the Secondary Board is taught, as it has to be. But this is supplemented by additional teaching in Indian culture and spirituality.

Sathya Sai colleges for women have been started in Anantapur, Bhopal and Jaipur. A college for men has been functioning in Whitefield, Bangalore. Baba has an idea to start a college in each state in India, for the rising generation has to be trained in the right kind of discipline. In addition to training students in higher knowledge, Baba thinks that students should be trained in 'general knowledge' or common sense and practical skills and in spirituality. In the Whitefield College hostel, students are given free access to Baba. His company is the greatest educative influence on these students. Separate hostels for students have also been planned in order to influence the growth of their character and personality. One such hostel is functioning in Poona.

The summer course in Indian culture and spirituality shows what supplementary instruction is necessary for college students today, since our universities have not provided for such instruction.

A Research Institute has been started in Bombay to revise the Bal Vikas and school and college syllabuses from time to time, in the light of experience. It may also include the phenomena of the spiritual life within its range in due course.

Bhagavan's fiftieth birthday is going to be celebrated in November 1975. This may be an occasion for starting a Sathya Sai University for women in Anantapur and another for men in Bangalore. Instead of having to supplement instruction in important areas which our universities have consistently ignored, it may be desirable to have Sai universities and evolve and implement integrated syllabuses.

It should be clear by now how the Sathya Sai Organisations are a complete blueprint for a total regeneration of Indian society. The public institutions in India generally live an aenemic and unproductive life, for the workers in charge of these institutions are not chosen and dedicated spirits. The selflessness, enthusiasm and sense of dedication of the Sathya Sai worker are required today in all fields of our national life. In a society in which democracy has not evolved, as yet, its own spontaneous discipline, what is required is guided democracy. Baba is a great democrat himself and he gives autonomy in work to each one, from the child to the adult. It is only when the autonomy goes wrong that he steps on the scene.

One can imagine what a revolution will be there when the youngsters trained in Sathya Sai ways and institutions will man the public posts and offices and the Sathya Sai discipline and enthusiasm will animate the wider sphere of our national life.

All this boils down to the fact that each one of us has to practise more and more of the religion of Spirit or *atmadharma* and less and less of the gospel of Nature or the demands of *prakritidharma*. We should know how to receive the God-man and be his conch or flute, his disc of right vision or his lotus of purity so that he can use us as instruments for his great work.

21. AN INTERVIEW AND A TESTAMENT

OF the millions that have changed their life for the better through the impact of Bhagavan's personality, here is an account of one who has authenticated all the details given below. I have known this eminent person and his family intimately and I am happy to narrate his story. The details have been taken from a notebook maintained by a common and esteemed well-wisher.

My friend had been down with a serious heart-attack. When the well-wisher called on him, it was found that his health was causing anxiety. The well-wisher asked the family whether it might not be desirable to take the friend to Bhagavan Baba. The well-wisher was a devotee of Baba. The family were very insistent that this should be done. In fact, the friend began to feel better within five or ten minutes of Baba's *vibhuti* being applied to his body. He was keen on being taken to Baba. But it was impossible, in that state of health, to take him to Puttaparthi.

In the meanwhile, the well-wisher had to go to Puttaparthi for Baba's birthday anniversary in November 1973. She did so. She should have proceeded to some other destination after the birthday. But the car was out of order and she had to return to Bangalore.

Baba was gracious enough to speak to the well-wisher on 25th November 1973. When the friend's condition of health was mentioned to him, Baba said that he knew all about it. He gave some special *vibhuti* to be passed on to the friend. Baba further instructed that the friend should be brought to Brindavan, Whitefield on 9th December 1973. The well-wisher felt that the car had been ordained to be out of order to compel her to return to Bangalore so that she could give the special *vibhuti* to the family friend.

The friend was delighted, especially when he was told, that Baba had asked him to be brought to Brindavan.

The well-wisher took the friend to Brindavan, twelve miles away from Bangalore, on the afternoon of 9th December '73. The friend's doctor was not prepared to take the responsibility for this long drive. Some of the family members were in two minds about it. But the well-wisher took the responsibility. She knew that nothing untoward would happen because Baba had instructed that he should be brought to Brindavan.

The car stopped in the Brindavan garden. The well-wisher asked the friend to be seated in the car and went towards Brindavan to contact Baba. Baba had come out for granting *darshan* and he saw the friend walking towards Brindavan, gasping a little for breath. He administered a mild rebuke to the persons that made the friend walk. He said that the friend should be taken there in the car. Once inside, Baba made the friend sit on a chair and gave him a little *vibhuti*. Baba put it into his mouth and wiped the friend's hand with his (Baba's) own handkerchief. The friend felt, as Baba's hand touched his, that a live current entered his body. Baba told him: "I am with you. I am within you. Have no fear."

A doctor had told the friend that a nerve adjacent to the heart had been damaged; that a major operation would be necessary; and that this would have to be done abroad and it might cost him two or three lakhs of rupees. The friend was thinking of going abroad for this

158

purpose. But he had not even told his family members about it as yet. Baba referred to this and further assured the friend that no operation was necessary. He would be all right. The friend was greatly astonished that Baba should have known what the doctor had told him confidentially.

The friend's family had come to Brindavan with him, excepting his little son. The boy wanted to come. But they had left him at home. Baba asked the friend: "Why didn't you bring your little son? He wanted to come. Well, it doesn't matter. I shall give him *darshan* when I come to your house."

The friend was supremely happy while returning from Brindavan. Every one thought that he should take a little coffee and rest after coming home. But he chatted away till midnight. He even had a dream that night. Baba appeared to him in dream and told him: "You'll be all right in two days." The friend believed intensely in this dream and, in fact, drove himself in his car to the well-wisher's house after two days to prove that he was all right now.

The friend used to apply all over his body, like rose-powder, the *vibhuti* that Baba had materialised for him. It was exhausted only after the friend had completely recovered from his illness.

Things moved next on 5th February 1974. The friend telephoned the well-wisher saying that he would like to go to Brindavan and have Baba's *darshan*. The well-wisher said that she would go to Brindavan and ask Baba whether she could bring the family friend for *darshan*. She went to Brindavan on two successive days. But she could succeed only in touching Baba's feet. By the time she could ask him, he had quietly moved away from her. It seemed as though he was deliberately avoiding her. The well-wisher then thought to herself: "Our family friend is now in good health, thanks to Baba's grace. Why should I ask Baba now whether I should bring him or not? Let the friend come and sit along with the others to have *darshan*. If Baba calls us, we'll go in. Otherwise we'll go away like others." So she rang up the friend and told him accordingly. The friend gladly agreed to go with her. But the next morning he excused himself. He had some urgent work and he could make it only on 8th February 1974, not the seventh. And so the well-wisher went alone on the 7th and sat amid the gathering on the women's side. While giving *darshan*, Baba came and stood before her and asked: "Mother, what news?" The well-wisher replied: "Shall I bring the family friend for *darshan* today?" Baba said that there would be a big crowd, the day being Thursday. He said that she might bring him the next day. The well-wisher called in person on the friend to tell him the good news. There she learnt about the strange things that had happened in the course of those two days.

The friend was completely disgusted with life because of a chronic family dispute that had erupted violently during those two days. His doctor had told him that drinks were like poison to him in his present state of health and that he should find out another doctor for himself if he insisted on drinking. Completely fed up, the friend wanted to die and he thought he would make his exit if he drank a whole bottle of whisky. He took the bottle, poured whisky into the glass and was about to drink it when he happened to look at the wall opposite. There on the wall he saw Baba's face, laughing at him. He then put the glass down, bowed down to Baba and moved quietly into his bedroom and slept there. This was how he was saved from death. The well-wisher felt that, because of all these things happening during those two days, Baba had deliberately refrained from speaking to her.

The next morning, when the well-wisher went with the friend for Baba's *darshan*, Baba told the friend all that had happened to him till then. He gave him *vibhuti* and asked him not to worry. "I'll protect you", he said.

The friend went to Brindavan again on 10th February 1974 because he wished to consult Baba on one or two other matters. Baba asked them to come the next day, which was a Sunday, and spent forty minutes speaking to him. Baba cleared all his doubts and allayed all his fears. He further told him that he would visit his house the next evening. One can only imagine the friend's delight at that assurance.

The next day, 11th February 1974, was a busy day in the friend's bungalow. A gorgeous cushioned seat had been arranged for Baba and incense sticks were emitting fragrance all around. A rose-garland was kept ready for Baba and the friend's wife had prepared *kheer*, a sweet dish, for Baba, herself. Baba had forbidden the friend to come for fetching Baba home, since it might excite him too much. At Baba's suggestion, another devotee did this duty. Baba was there at 6 P.M. After refreshments, Baba spoke to the friend and his family for nearly an hour, blessed them and materialised a Sulemani stone ring for the friend and a locket to be worn by the son for protection.

The friend's little daughter had a lady tutor coming to her. The tutor complained that a little child in her family, three months old, could not swallow even a few drops of milk for the last four days. Doctors had frightened her with naming terrible diseases. Baba told her that there was no cause for fear and that it was simple tonsilitis. He materialised a little *vibhuti* for the child. She gave a little of it to the child and the child was able to drink five ounces of milk the same evening. Baba told the lady that the child's tonsils should be removed after he grew up.

This was a memorable visit.

The well-wisher was away for a few weeks. On her return, the family friend told her that the Sulemani stone had fallen away from the ring and that the precious stone had been found in the car two days later. The friend fought shy of approaching Baba for this 'repair' and went to a goldsmith instead. The goldsmith said that he had fixed the stone in the ring so firmly that it would stay there for the next twenty years at least. But the stone got loose even before twenty days were over and the friend took the ring to the well-wisher. The precious stone could not be found anywhere. The well-wisher assured the friend that there was no cause for alarm. The disappearance of the stone did not predict any calamity since Baba's full grace was on him. Only, the friend must have committed some mistake or the other. That's why the precious stone had returned to Baba.

The friend confessed his mistake. He had tasted a little of the bottle again. How was he to go to Baba now? He was afraid. The well-wisher said that Baba was full of pity and forgiveness. Baba was sure to forgive him. But the friend should improve his ways.

On 27th March 1974, the friend went to Brindavan for *darshan* himself. Before the friend spoke to Baba, Baba told him that he had lost the Sulemani stone in his ring and went away inside Brindavan without any further comments. This frightened the friend all the more. So the well-wisher took the friend the next day, the 28th, to Brindavan. Baba did not speak to the friend though he saw him and stood before the well-wisher, saying: "Mother, what news?" The well-wisher also was somewhat afraid. She finally said that the friend had lost the stone in the ring given by Baba. It could not be traced these twenty days. Baba simply said: "Bring him the next morning."

So both the well-wisher and the friend went to Brindavan the next morning. Baba took the ring from the friend. Holding it in his hand, Baba asked the friend: "Where has the stone gone from the ring?" The friend said: "It has come to you."

Baba laughed. He said: "These are not your words. This is what the well-wisher has told you." And he looked amusedly at her. What he wished to suggest was that the stone had disappeared, for the friend had started drinking again. At this, the friend was mightily afraid. After some time Baba asked him: "Will you wear a Shirdi Baba ring if it's given to you? Or will it go against your faith?"

The friend folded his hands and said: "I'll wear whatever you give."

Baba took the old ring in both his hands and blew on it gently with his mouth once or twice. There emerged a gold ring with the picture of Shirdi Baba on it. Baba placed it on the friend's finger and blessed him to go, giving him a little *vibhuti*.

[*Note*: Since I wrote this chapter, I have been permitted by persons concerned to reveal their identity. The 'friend' is Meherban Nabob Saheb of Savanur. I should not have called him a 'friend'. He is rather the ex-prince of the then Savanur State to which I had the honour to belong. The well-wishers are Shrimant Rajasaheb and Shrimant Ranisaheb of Sandur whom Nabob Saheb respects as he would his own parents.]

22. THE SATHYA SAI FESTIVALS OF SPIRIT

THE use of group techniques and mass media is inevitable when the common man has to be converted to spirituality. *Bhajans* and *Nagar Sankirtans* are, therefore, natural adjuncts to the Sai Path. So is the celebration of various festivals. Prashanti Nilayam resounds with festivals all the year round. *Guru Pournima*, the Master's Day, when a silver image of Shirdi Baba is bathed in a profuse shower of *vibhuti* falling from an inverted empty pot into which Baba moves his hand in a circular motion; Krishnashtami, observing the birthday anniversary of Sri Krishna; the Navaratra or the Nine Nights' festival culminating in Dussera, the day of victory over Evil, with its adumbration of a Vedic sacrifice for a week; the birthday anniversary of Bhagavan himself; Christmas and New Year Day; Vaikuntha Ekadasi, Heaven's Fasting Day, when Baba materialises· a small goblet full of fragrant elixir (honey-like), distributing it to the thousands from that small vessel; Makar Sankrant or Summer Solstice Day; Sivaratri, the Siva Night, on the evening of which Bhagavan produces a crystal *lingam* from the pit of his stomach, signifying the awakening of Spirit in man; and the celebration of Ugadi, the Telugu and Kannada New Year Day: these and other festivals are observed at Prashanti Nilayam, the minor ones sometimes at Whitefield or other places and thousands from all parts of the country and abroad flock each year to witness, the number present at Navaratra and Sivaratri rising to thirty or forty thousand strong. Songsters and musicians with a national or international repute deem it an honour to be permitted to perform on these occasions. College students stage some of Baba's plays, Baba himself being the producer. Groups of little children coming from various parts of India exhibit their skill, in dance or in staging scenes from the lives of saints. Bhagavan is, of course, there in the midst of all from morning to night and his presence is a delight and an inspiration.

When New Year Day comes, we think of Janus, the two-faced god, after whom January is named. He looks back and forth, standing at the point of intersection of the two years. Just as Baba tells us on the occasion of his birthday that he has no birth and that we should strive for our second birth, there is nothing new about the New Year. Only the seasons pass by, as part of the cosmic movement. Making fun of Partridge's almanac, Swift, predicted for the ensuing year that some people would be born, some die and that every thing would be very much the same, but for different names. A New Year Resolution may take us out of this vicious circle, leading us to the point of intersection of Time with the Timeless which, as T.S. Eliot says, is occupation for a saint. Let us understand Bhagavan's message and feel his love:

Duty without love is deplorable.
Duty with love is desirable.
Love without duty is divine.

The sun moves north on Makar Sankrant or Summer Solstice Day. According to Indian scriptures, that is where the gods are. Make the sun, says Baba, the postman carrying your letter to the gods and bringing back Grace from them. Let your letter have the stamp of sincerity and the envelope of resolution. Let your eye be on the Summer

Solstice of 'God', *Uttarayana* and not the Winter Solstice of the 'world'. Time should be calculated, not by the revolution of the earth round the sun but by the work we have been able to accomplish.

The Summer Solstice moves away from darkness to increasing light. On the occasion of Sivaratri, says Baba, the materialisation of a crystal lingam signifies the advent of the Avatar. We struggle to secure a few feet of ground on earth in order to build a house for ourselves. As Dr. Johnson says, we should also struggle to wrest a few moments at least out of a crowded day, for prayer. A bird pecks at the fruit on the tree to see whether they are ripe. A monkey plucks and destroys many unripe fruit in its search for the ripe one. It is the ant that goes straight to a sugar particle. The ant knows what it wants. One should have the steadiness of an ant in one's devotion.

Sivaratri is the fourteenth night of the dark half of the month. The moon is almost invisible on that night. The moon is a symbol of the human mind. Night-long meditation on the fourteenth night will liquidate the mind which is already invisible and make the soul prevail.

166

23. THE SUMMER COURSE IN INDIAN CULTURE AND SPIRITUALITY

I

THE Summer Course has, by now, been an annual feature of Baba's educational programme. The session lasts for a month and the Course covers eight units besides other equally important activities: the texts of Hinduism; the unity of world religions; Indian Culture; the systems of Indian philosophy; sciences and human values; the saints of India; Indian Ethics and Law; and world classics.

An account is given here of the summer course held in 1973. This is fairly representative of the work done in the field.

The second Summer Course in Indian culture and spirituality was a more thrilling success than the first one. It began on 21st May 1973. The number had mounted up to six hundred students this time, admitted from all parts of India. More than a hundred college teachers participated in the course. More than forty scholars from different parts of India gave instruction at the Course. Two more course units were added to the syllabus this year, one in the Saints of India and another in classics of World Literature. A more spacious pandal had been put up for classes, in addition to the one which constituted the dining hall of the course as before. All this was, of course,

167

done on the premises of Brindavan, Whitefield, Bangalore, which was the venue for the first Summer Course.

The procedure adopted for selecting students for the Summer Course was modified this year in some ways. Since pre-University students or students in the first or second year of college were not quite able to follow the Course closely, it was thought that students who have taken their penultimate public examination or will study presently in the final year class, should be selected, whatever the course of their choice might have been. The number was raised to twentyfive students from each state this year, with the result that, including students from Anantapur and Whitefield, the number went up to six hundred this year.

Bhagavan also thought that some college teachers from various States should be taken as observers on the Course this year, in addition to the men and women teachers accompanying the groups. There were nearly a hundred teachers participating in the Course this year.[1]

Many distinguished visitors were received at the Course and they also spoke to the gathering.

An elocution programme was held and names were invited from students intending to take part in it. More than forty students volunteered to speak and their speeches were distributed on Sunday afternoons during the Course. The speeches were extempore and they were given topics from the following list:

(1) Bhagavan Sathya Sai Baba's views on higher education.
(2) What is Yoga?
(3) How to secure World Peace?
(4) Bhagavan Sathya Sai Baba's idea of Divine Love.

[1]There were about ten American participants and two American faculty members on the summer course for 1974.

(5) The synthesising ability is a distinctive feature of Indian Culture.

(6) Not competition but co-operation should be the law of human civilization.

(7) The urgency of Baba's message for the modern world.

(8) How can the fatherhood of God and the brotherhood of man be made possible on earth?

(9) The India of our dreams.

(10) Baba's four-fold path to perfection.

(11) There is only one religion and that is the religion of love.

(12) Science and Spirituality: A contradiction?

(13) Secularism: Its excellences and shortcomings.

(14) Commerce without morality is useless and dangerous.

A selection was made, by judges, of participants who were eligible to take part in the final competition and students were selected for the first six places and given prizes by Bhagavan on Convocation Day. They were also permitted to make short speeches on the occasion.

Summaries of the lectures delivered by members of the Faculty were prepared by an undergraduate and undergraduette selected from among the participants from a particular State each day under the guidance of a few teacher-participants and presented in the evening to the general audience that would assemble each evening to listen to Bhagavan's discourse.

Students from a particular State led the *bhajans* in the evening each day and did the *Arati* so that each state would have its turn.

Participants got up at 4.30 A.M. and did the Omkar. They joined the itinerant *bhajan*-singing or Nagar Sankirtan at 5.30 A.M. for an hour, visiting different villages each morning. After that, they had an hour of *yogasanas* and meditation. The routine of the day followed after breakfast, with three lectures in the morning and two in the afternoon and then the evening discourse by Bhagavan, after tea-break. Films which had a spiritual interest were shown occasionally in the evenings. Students from each state sang *bhajans* before Bhagavan began his discourse.

A test was administered at the end of the course. As there were some postgraduate students, they were treated as a separate group for the test. The participants who won the first four places were given prizes.

All the participants had their hours of social work on Sunday mornings, when they worked in groups in the garden or in the printing press. The women participants worked in the two pandals and cleaned them. Bhagavan addressed them before the groups broke up for the work and his words are sure to be ringing in the ears of all of them. The speech on the last Sunday morning was so moving that there were tears in the eyes of many of the listeners.

Some of the teacher-participants offered to read poems on the impact of Bhagavan's personality on them. This was taken up on a few evenings, prior to Bhagavan's discourse, and it developed into a poets' conference in most of the modern Indian languages and in English.

Medical aid on the campus could be better organised this year. There were separate first-aid rooms for men and for women and a number of devoted doctors gave unstinted service round the clock to the participants. Food was served by Sathya Sai Seva Dal members from Hyderabad and other places and many student-participants them-

selves served their fellow-participants with great earnestness and devotion. What was remarkable was the utter
change of outlook which distinguished these young men
and women in all that they said and did on the premises
of Brindavan. It was clear that they themselves were
inspired by the divine love that flowed towards them
from Baba.

II

The annual Summer Course in Indian Culture and
Spirituality began with chantings from the Vedas. The Vice
Chancellor of Bangalore University Dr. H. Narasimhaiah
inaugurated the Course.

In his welcome address to the large assembly of
students, guests and devotees, Professor V.K. Gokak
described the gathering as a cross-section of educated
India. The main aim of the Summer Course, said
Professor Gokak, was to give a new orientation to education in our country. He traced the genesis of the
Course to Bhagavan Baba's perennial philosophy, of
which *Sathya, Dharma, Shanti, Prema* and *Ahimsa* are the
five pillars. Baba's philosophy of education is based on
truth, righteousness, peace, love and non-violence. Right
thoughts, right words and right actions develop equipoise. Students today are suffering from disordered minds.
They have lost their mental equilibrium and spiritual
balance. Education should aim at the harmonious development of the human personality, an effective integration
of the heart, the spirit, the intellect and the body. In other
words education should promote the physical, mental,
emotional and spiritual growth of a student. The cultivation of some skills and the acquisition of knowledge
alone are not enough. We must produce integrated

personalities. The spiritual lacuna in modern education should be filled.

Bhagavan Sathya Sai Baba's philosophy of education is eminently practical. The hundreds of Bal Vikas Centres, Samitis and Seva Dals all over the country are trying to put into practice the ideals of Baba. The two colleges at Kadugodi and Anantapur do this in the sphere of higher education. The ancient *gurukula* system of education is being adapted to modern conditions. A research institute has been started in Bombay for evolving a suitable curriculum for Bal Vikas children.

One of the purposes of the Summer Course is to arrest the anarchy in education and to prevent the further devaluation of spirituality in India and abroad. The only panacea for the increasing unrest among students is the spiritualization of education. A wrong implementation of the secular idea in education, eschewing a world-view and moral and spiritual values, has done great harm. The moral rearmament of the world will be possible only when spirituality becomes an integral part of education.

Subjects in schools and colleges, said Professor Gokak, are being studied in an atomic fashion. The atomization of knowledge has led to the fragmentation of personality and to emotional conflicts. Students are bewildered by overloaded curricula. Knowledge without Wisdom has produced a generation of educated imbeciles. Students do not know what they have to do with the crumbs of knowledge dispensed to them in schools and colleges. The universe inside us is more mysterious than the external universe. We have yet to explore this. Self-introspection and meditation are as important as experimentation and ratiocination. We have been so much enthralled by modern scientific knowledge that we have forgotten our ancient spiritual tradition. True education must help the student to formulate for himself a comprehensive world-view.

Professor Gokak made a passing reference to three philosophies of education. There is scientific humanism functioning in a setting of either capitalism or socialism. The scientific humanist lays stress on truth and the greatest happiness of the greatest number. But these cannot be had only through a cultivation of the intellect. The marxist's weapons in his ideological warfare are regimentation and indoctrination. This gives a twist to his vivid experience of pity and righteous indignation. Thirdly, there is the mystic's approach. The Catholic Universities in America follow the path of religious education. The Summer Course in Spirituality, Professor Gokak said, will serve as an antidote to the atomization of modern education. It will also develop a well-defined, wholesome attitude to the world and life.

The mystical approach to education will emphasize, not the form, but the substance of religion, the truly spiritual vision. The student should be enabled to grasp the metaphysics and innate meaning of one particular religion, usually his own. But he should also be introduced in unmistakable terms to the unity underlying all the great religions of the world. Giving to the students a background of Indian culture, which itself is composed of diverse elements, will be very helpful in this respect. One remembers Baba's statement in this respect: "There is only one religion, the religion of love. There is only one caste,—the caste of humanity. There is only one language, the language of the heart." The emblem of Prashanthi Nilayam holds together the symbols of all the great religions of the world.

Professor Gokak also gave an outline of the subjects taught in the Summer Course.

Dr. Narasimhaiah said that he believed in the perfectibility and refinement of human nature. All barriers between man and man based on caste, colour, creed and religion should be removed. The essence of religion is spirituality. In spite of his scientific background, Dr. Narasimhaiah said that he believed in God. His scientific training did not prevent him from believing in God. We cannot demonstrate the existence of God through pure reason, but our intuition demands the postulates of God, Soul and Immortality.

The Vice Chancellor concluded his speech with the hope that the Summer Course would have a lasting impact on the students.

In his presidential remarks, Bhagavan Baba expounded the true relation between master and disciple. He laid emphasis on character-training. Self-respect and reverence towards elders are of supreme importance. We have condemned ourselves to cultural alienation by playing the sedulous ape to western culture and civilization. Baba compared Indian culture to an elephant that does not know its own strength. We have been tinkering with our educational system, with disastrous results. We should strive towards perfection. Life is a striving for perfection.

Joy is desired by all. But we should remember that there are other aspects of life, like truth and sacrifice. What is joy? We may say that it is a negation of sorrow. What is sorrow? It is a negation of joy. Thus we land ourselves in circular definitions and tautologies. We cannot dismiss this duality at the intellectual level.

However, it is clear that we cannot be happy unless others are happy. Joy and sorrow, life and death and day and night are eternal dualities at the intellectual level. The opposites can be reconciled at a higher level,

174

where it is possible to experience eternal bliss.

(A detailed summary of Bhagavan Baba's discourse, delivered on this occasion, is published separately in *Summer Showers*, 1973.)

The function came to a close with a vote of thanks moved by Dr. S. Bhagavantham.

III

The convocation day was a day full of bright sunshine, in spite of the monsoon that had set in. Devotees had assembled in their thousands in the ampitheatre, filling all the gallery steps and presenting a very colourful appearance. One could see some ten thousand bodies gently swaying to and fro and some twenty thousand hands clapping when Baba chanted the *bhajans* and the audience followed him. The caparisoned elephant, Sai Gita, college students in their uniform playing the band, Bhagavan himself, Dr. D.S. Kothari, Ex-Chairman of the U.G.C., who had delivered the convocation address last year and was fortunately available this year too as our chief guest as he had come for a Science Seminar in the city, the teaching faculty, the women students in their white *saris* and the men students in their white shirts and *dhotis*; all these constituted the convocation procession winding its way through the admiring crowd that had lined up on either side of the way to the ampitheatre. The white *saris*, shirts and *dhotis* were convocation costumes presented by Baba to the students. Every one was delighted with them.

In his opening remarks, Professor Vinayak Krishna Gokak said that an unbalanced and unintegrated generation was growing up in our schools and colleges because there was no moral and spiritual training or stimulus given to them. This Summer Course had been started as a possible way out of this impossible situation.

Nearly six hundred students and a hundred teachers had gathered here from all parts of India, ranging from Meghalaya to Kerala. During the month, a new India had been growing up in our dormitories. About fifty distinguished scholars and guests had addressed the students.

It is true to say that the individual in India has to be rescued and emancipated from a static society. But he has to be enlightened and ushered into a co-operative, and not a competitive, society. He had to be helped to modernise his outlook. But this did not mean that perennial values had to be thrown to the winds. The country had to be industrialised at a quick pace. But this had to be done in an atmosphere of calm and restraint and a reasonable mastery over desires. A nation-state had to be reared up. But its spiritual roots had also to be discovered and nourished.

Professor Gokak expressed the deep gratitude of all to Bhagavan Baba for this inspiring interlude in their lives.

The six students who won elocution prizes shared their Summer Course experience with the audience. Shri Shiv Pandit, Chandigarh, said that another journey began after reaching Brindavan,—an inward seeking for the truth within. He described Baba as that "Ultimate principle of consciousness and truth, which has assumed a form in order to communicate with humanity and lead it back to the road of God-realization. He said that all had undergone subtle changes during their stay in Brindavan. Their effect might not be perceptible immediately. But the years ahead would tell the story.

Shri J. Sundereshwaran, Bombay, said that a spiritual revolution was in the offing, judging by the impact that

Bhagavan's personality had made on the students and teachers at the Summer Course.

Shri Percy Gandhi, Calcutta, said that it was only Baba's personality that had enabled so many young men and women from all over India to live together in peace and harmony for so long. His practical genius alone could design a course in which body, mind and soul are all exercised fully. It was a month packed with activity. "What we have enjoyed the most is Baba's love and affection for us. We have been deeply touched by the pains he has taken to look to every detail of our comfort... We have bathed for a whole month in the spray of thoughts that have gushed from his fountain of omniscience. We have dipped daily in his ocean of love. For one whole month, our lives and activities have revolved round him."

Kumari K. Lakshmi Rao, Maharashtra, spoke of the sudden exposure to the most brilliant of lights after a long period of darkness. She learnt more during this one month than she had during all her school and college years. "The life here has taught us to exert and adapt ourselves to entirely different circumstances. Girls from different States, with different views and ideas and almost different cultures, stayed together and we learnt our weakness... It is only here that we realized how rich our spiritual heritage is and how many wrong opinions we held about our religion and culture."

Kumari R. Srilata, Bangalore, said that the *Upanayanam* or initiation of students had taken place in this *Gurukul.* "Previously my conception of yoga was limited to the physical aspect only. Now we know that all life is yoga. What is more, Bhagavan has taught us that Prema Yoga is the greatest of all yogas... The lectures delivered here have enabled us to expand our consciousness and become more sensitive to Nature and to the people around us... It is not so much the information we gathered that matters as the experience of living close together as one family with Sai, the most loving of all mothers, as the head."

Shri Sainath Chandavarkar also spoke eloquently.

Dr. D.S. Kothari, Ex-Chairman of the University Grants Commission, who delivered the convocation address, was keenly appreciative of the idea and implementation of the Course and he paid a loving tribute to Bhagavan for this nation-building programme. Himself one of the most distinguished scientists in the country, Dr. Kothari cited the views of some world-famous scientists to show how unscientific it was to be limited by science and to reduce science to a dogma. Science and Ahimsa had to go together if the world was to progress. Social justice and social service were great ideals. But the individual had to rise to that point of fineness if these ideals were to be realised. The self-scrutiny, self-improvement and self-renewal of the individual were essential if equality and liberty were to be established in society. He was very happy that students from all parts of the country had the privilege to attend such a Course.

Bhagavan Baba then spoke, translated by Dr. S. Bhagavantham. (The discourse is published in *Summer Showers*, 1973.)

24. THE VISIT TO DELHI
(A NEAR VIEW)

I

A VISIT by Bhagavan Baba to Delhi was due long since. No doubt, he had stopped there for a few days, on his way to Rishikesh and Kashmir once, and to Badrinath, a few years ago. But that was when Delhi had hardly known him. In recent years, when Punjab, Haryana, Himachal Pradesh, Delhi and Uttar Pradesh were resounding with his name, there was a regular stream of visitors from Delhi, waiting on him and praying to him to come and stay at Delhi for some days at least, and confer his Grace on the thousands pining for his Darshan there. Bhagavan had agreed to do so; and the time finally came for it when, on 25th March, 1972, he flew to Delhi.

The Indian Airlines had brought quite a few devotees to Bangalore from Delhi before this, for discussing preliminaries. Shri Sohan Lal, an ex-M.P., and a prominent citizen of Delhi, was to be Bhagavan's host at 16, Golf Link Road, his residence. Shri Sohan Lal made all the arrangements and he flew to Hyderabad, to escort Bhagavan to Delhi.

Bhagavan had said that there should be no crowd at Palam Airport to receive him. In fact, he had got the booking changed from the morning to the evening flight to avoid crowds. Only two or three members of the

179

Samiti were to be there when he landed; the rest were to assemble at 16, Golf Link Road. These instructions were scrupulously observed. But there was a crowd of a different kind awaiting Bhagavan! The police and customs officials were there with their families, surrounding the gangway and all! It was an arduous task to clear the way for Bhagavan from amidst eager devotees. This was done, and Shri K. Hanumanthaiya, the Railway Minister, had the honour of taking Bhagavan in his car to 16, Golf Link Road.

Bhagavan does not like breaches of discipline, even when they proceed from genuine devotion. He did not approve of the inconvenience caused to the authorities of the airport by an excited group of devotees.

On the plane itself, Bhagavan is not so much at ease as on long car journeys. A car journey means the company of a few chosen disciples, sprightly and luminous conversation, anecdotes, singing and *bhajans*. One does not know how time passes. But on an aeroplane, he feels like one, the whom great restraint is imposed. He may seem to thumb the pages of a book or be in reverie, with eyes closed. But there are passengers who come every now and then and touch his feet, eager not to lose this golden opportunity. The captain, the pilot, and the air-hostesses pray for *vibhuti* with genuine devotion. Bhagavan blesses them and they feel happy.

By the time that Bhagavan reached 16, Golf Link Road, a huge crowd consisting of thousands of devotees had assembled in the gorgeous pandal which was beautifully decorated and lighted. The crowd acclaimed Bhagavan's arrival with thunderous delight. The place was a park converted into a pandal. At a rough guess, it could comfortably hold a gathering of some fifteen thousand people. It was nearly 11-30 P.M., before Bhagavan could retire for the night.

II

Next morning, the 'park turned pandal' presented an impossible sight. More than thirty thousand people had crowded together, where about fifteen thousand could sit or stand! The crowd overflowed on the roadside, where restaurants and refreshment stalls had sprung up overnight. Buses were lined up—any number of them—coming from the interior of Uttar Pradesh, Punjab, Haryana and Himachal Pradesh. The Delhi crowd was, of course, there, spearheading all these arrivals.

It was announced on the mike that Bhagavan would move into the crowd and give *darshan* to all, but that there should be no scramble to touch his feet. Each should bow to Bhagavan in his own heart.

Bhagavan moved out accordingly and there was a tremendous ovation. He collected letters and gave *vibhuti* and the love that spoke through his eyes and his countenance thrilled people. Where people could not resist the temptation to move forward to hand over a note to him or to touch his feet, he cut the line short and moved into another lane. This had an immediate educative effect. The devotees realised that a whole line would miss his close *darshan* even if some persons disregarded instructions. Shri Sohan Lal spoke the truth, when he said that they had all despaired of controlling the crowd into orderly behaviour. It was only Bhagavan's love, which overwhelmed each and every devotee that kept them in their places and enabled him to penetrate deep into the heart of the crowd.

Thereafter, for the rest of the day, Bhagavan refused to

grant any individual interviews. He said that his first
concern was to give happiness to the countless number
of devotees that came from far and near to have a
glimpse of him. He accordingly appeared on the first
floor balconies of 16, Golf Link Road, a number of
times, and on the top terrace where he could be seen
from all sides. He waved both his hands blessing them
all, a divine smile beaming on his face. When the crowd
went ecstatic and shouted itself hoarse with joy *Sai
Baba ki Jai Ho!*, he put his hand on his lips and
gestured so as to indicate that they should not be loud
in their delight. And the crowd learnt to experience its
joy silently. A section of the crowd would now and
then raise its voice—*Sai Baba ki...*, thinking that this
was the *key* to persuading Bhagavan to come and give
darshan; but, he made them learn the lesson that he
would give *darshan* when he chose to do so and not in
response to impulsive shouts. And he appeared on the
terrace seven or eight times a day. Each day was a step
forward in education for the crowd. It was only on the
morning of Sunday, 2nd April, that it became difficult
for Bhagavan to move into the crowd. A crowd, estimated to be a hundred and fifty thousand strong, had
overflowed into the roads, a mile deep on either side.
They stormed round the railings of the compound,
which itself was filled to capacity. The iron gates were
broken and people poured in, eager for a glimpse of
Bhagavan. Every one knew that this was the last
morning for *darshan* in Delhi and each was eager to
hand over his letter of prayer to him and touch his feet.
The best that could be done was to give terrace '*darshans*',
and announce that Bhagavan would deliver a discourse
in the evening and sing *bhajans*. It was only then that

the crowd began to diminish in order to come properly reinforced for the evening meet.

III

Bhagavan could not attend to the physically afflicted during the first two days. It was a surging crowd and the best that could be done was to calm it down with *darshan*. But as soon as the crowd settled down, Bhagavan began to choose the physically afflicted and disabled, for interview. Children stricken down with polio; old men with legs like tendrils of creepers, wheeled down in chairs; women in visible agony with some disease or the other; and teenagers with leucodermia on their faces: all these were interviewed, blessed, given *prasad* and hope and courage to live their lives. Some of the disabled men were made to walk, Bhagavan holding them by the arm. They had lost all faith in looking after themselves. He put them on the road to recovery by infusing into them faith, courage and a mysterious force that worked wonders.

His feeling for the common man was so intense that he dropped his visits to the homes of several office-bearers of the Sri Sathya Sai Seva Samiti, Delhi, in order to grant frequent *darshans* to the crowd and attend to the disabled. Some of the office-bearers, women and men as well, were in tears over this misfortune. One of them, a close devotee, said, "My wife and children refuse to take their food till you visit our home. They are crying incessantly." "I am glad", said Bhagavan, "that they are crying and going without food. You will all now understand the agony of thousands of these women and children who stand for hours on end, in the scorching sun, hungry and thirsty, just to catch a far glimpse of me." Nevertheless his compassion was such

183

that he spent all his hours of rest at noon and up to midnight, visiting most of the office-bearers of the *Samiti* and their families in their homes. Those he could not visit were given the privilege of bringing breakfast, lunch or dinner from their homes and serving it to him at 16, Golf Link Road! On such occasions, Bhagavan jokingly made it clear to Shri Sohan Lal and his family that they themselves were guests as much as Bhagavan himself in their own home!

Bhagavan met all the members of the *Samiti* and also members of the Seva Dal who had served as volunteers ceaselessly during the period of his stay in Delhi. The volunteers, the women and the men, had an unenviable task to do. They had to cordon off the crowds surging forward to touch Bhagavan's feet, when he walked right into their midst. They had to be on duty from 3 A.M., maintaining order in the pandal where people sat hours in advance to secure vantage seats for Bhagavan's *darshan* and blessings. They had to keep the storming crowds, desperate for a near view and for blessings, off the railings of the compound and the iron gates which were broken open twice. The volunteers discharged their duty admirably well. The women volunteers took it on themselves to supply drinking water to the thirsty crowd, waiting patiently in the sun. They also maintained order in the women's section in the pandal. The volunteers had a thankless task to do. They had to control a crowd which resented all restrictions. All this was done with patience and good cheer. There were announcements to be made on the microphone from time to time. These were put through by a member whose voice was ideally fitted for the task. As scarfs were being distributed to the volunteers, by the Seva Dal office-bearers, they said that it should be their privilege to receive them from the "hands of Bhagavan Himself". Bhagavan gladdened their hearts, going to them and giving each of them the scarf himself.

The volunteers who waited near Bhagavan's room had, of course, a privileged and glorious task to do. In spite of their best vigil, it happened that an American hippie managed to enter, not only the compound, but the corridor on the first floor, right up to Bhagavan's room. The arrangements were tightened and the volunteers worked with such selfless enthusiasm that Bhagavan became very fond of them. He got to know from them about their family and their career. He was told by one of them that he, the student, desired admission to the postgraduate course, but that his marks were not adequate for the purpose. But Bhagavan blessed him for admission. Another student was due to appear soon for his public examination. Bhagavan told him that he had been rather careless in his studies. He materialised a pen and gave it to the volunteer and said that he should write his answers with that pen, in the examination hall.

It would be invidious to mention names. All the members of the *Samiti* and the *Mahila Vibhag* worked with a great sense of devotion and helped to make Bhagavan's visit to Delhi a memorable success. The members of Shri Sohan Lal's family worked day and night and were always ready to attend to the most trivial details.

IV

The 'park-pandal' near 16, Golf Link Road, proved to be far too small for the mammoth crowd that assembled there on the first day. Since the National Stadium had already been reserved for sports, the organisers thought of making arrangements on the lawns of the

Modern School, New Delhi. This was twice as large as the park and it was estimated to hold an audience of at least forty to fifty thousand! But the meeting held there on the evening of 27th March,'72 exceeded all expectations. A lakh and a half people collected there, without any press bulletin or wall-paper or any other kind of publicity. A sitting mass of humanity was surrounded by a standing mass! A crowd waiting to be as near Bhagavan as possible burst in on all sides of the dais after he came, and it looked as though there would be disorder. But the crowd soon settled down listening to Bhagavan's enchanting 'prema mudita manase kaho', and other *bhajans* and his thrilling speech. He spoke of the nations of the world as a railway train, the railway engine called India leading them on the spiritual path, the engine-driver being the Avatar!

Dr. S. Bhagavantham translated Bhagavan's speech into Hindi. This was the first time Dr. Bhagavantham had anything to do with Hindi from a public platform. Nor had he cultivated the language in any special way. But it was a miracle that he was able to do what he actually did. For the rest, the gestures and intonations of Bhagavan filled the eyes and ears of people.

Mixing with the crowd, one got to know their responses and reactions. Some of them were saying that they could hardly believe till they saw Bhagavan in action that such a phenomenon was at all possible, in the twentieth century. Others were saying that such a vast gathering for a spiritual purpose was unprecedented in Delhi.

One thing is certain. As the metropolis of the country, Delhi is inevitably the touchstone of each social, political or spiritual movement. If any movement has to succeed in India, it has to succeed first in Delhi. The

186

cradle and cemetery of dynasties and empires, Delhi has developed this testing power through the centuries.

If the Modern School lawn meeting roused and satisfied the expectations of the common man in Delhi, the meeting in Kamani Hall was meant to bring the elite in Delhi into contact with Bhagavan. The Hall is designed to hold an audience of seven hundred and fifty people. For the Bal Vikas function which was held there, about fourteen hundred people were present, filling the passage and other spaces. There was a similar audience for Bhagavan's lecture, adding to it the overflow on the stage itself and outside the Hall.

The meeting was presided over by Shri K. Hanumanthaiya, Railway Minister. He was a frequent visitor and Bhagavan had also dinner with him during his stay. He paid a graceful tribute to Bhagavan after Shri Sohan Lal spoke welcoming the guests, on behalf of the organisers. Dr. Vinayak Krishna Gokak then spoke for some minutes interpreting the mission and message of Bhagavan. Bhagavan then made a soul-stirring speech, vindicating spirituality in the modern world. Dr. Bhagavantham translated the speech.

It was a representative audience. The elite of Delhi had been invited. As 'Motherland', a Delhi paper, reported on 30th March, '72, "The guests invited were the city's topdrawer elite; they included cabinet ministers, former governors, ex-royalty, leading industrialists, important bureaucrats, members of the Diplomatic Corps, chic and hippily dressed foreigners and svelte Indian women."

"Some of the VIPs sighted entering the Hall included ministers such as Shri Karan Singh and Shri Hanumanthaiya, ministers' wives such as Shrimati I.K. Gujral, ex-Governors such as Sardar Ujjal Singh and Shri Dharma Vira, Chief of the Navy, Admiral S.M. Nanda, U.S.

187

Ambassador, Shri Kenneth Keating, and Chief Justice
Hon'ble Shri S.M. Sikri."

Let 'Ariel' of the Sunday Standard (April 9th) speak
on the subject: "Last week Delhi was invaded by one
of India's most renowned mystics and seers, Satya Sai
Baba, who received a welcome from the classes and
masses, more rapturous than most welcomes Ariel has
witnessed over the years."

And all this, without the least publicity of any kind!

V

The members of the Sri Sathya Sai Seva Samiti
were anxious that Bhagavan should visit Meerut and
grant *darshan* to thousands of devotees there. Meerut is
hardly forty miles away from Delhi and Bhagavan
agreed to go there, on the afternoon of 31st March 1972,
and just 'be present' at their *bhajan* party. The *Samiti*
arranged for *bhajans* in the Meerut Stadium and a huge
crowd assembled there. But the volunteers were more
anxious to have *darshan* than to arrange for it for
others. In the scramble that followed the microphone
arrangements broke down. It was with great difficulty
that Bhagavan had to find his way back to the Stadium
Porch, where the car was waiting for him.

But there were pleasant surprises on the way, which gave
us a glimpse of the common man's reverence for Bhagavan.
The people in the Modi Industrial Township on the way
had put up a beautiful arch to welcome Bhagavan
and a big crowd had assembled to catch a glimpse
of him and, if possible, to touch his feet. The crowd made
way, as Bhagavan blessed them and made them realise
that the party would be late for the visit at Meerut. The
motorist, the motor-cyclist and the rickshaw-wallah were
excited as they saw the fleet of cars passing through;

188

their joy knew no bounds when they recognised Bhagavan in one of the cars and they pointed him out to each other. Bhagavan had now ceased to be a mere name to the people in the North. They knew and felt his presence in the flesh and responded rapturously to it.

The visit to Kurukshetra, an important centre in the Punjab-Haryana area, turned out to be a memorable event. Shri Gulzarilal Nanda, who functioned as a minister in the composite Bombay State, and at the Centre as Prime Minister for a short period, had invited Bhagavan to bless the many institutions that Shri Nanda is building there for preserving and interpreting ancient Indian culture. Bhagavan agreed to go there. The devotees in Punjab and Himachal Pradesh felt that Bhagavan should have visited strong Sai centres, like Chandigarh, Ludhiana, Jullundur and Simla. But the visit to Kurukshetra justified itself in an ample measure for, devotees from all the three States and Union Territories flocked to Kurukshetra and an eager crowd, a lakh and fifty thousand strong, had to be managed. Excellent arrangements had been made, and hundreds of policemen had been posted to enable the crowd to see and hear its beloved Baba, without any discomfort. The meeting was held in the Kurukshetra University Stadium; Shri Nanda, the Governor, the Vice-Chancellor, the Chief Minister, the Finance Minister and others were present, to welcome Bhagavan. It was a great and memorable meeting. Mr. Richard Bock, the devotee from America, who filmed it, said that he had never dealt so far with such a vast mass of humanity, with the tiny figure of Bhagavan on the dais, seen against this setting.

VI

During the eight days that he was in Delhi, there was a continuous pressure on Bhagavan from many of the top men and women in Delhi for interviews. Men and women from various walks of life wanted to have the benefit of his insight and wisdom, and it was impossible to meet all these demands during the limited time that Bhagavan had at his disposal. But he did meet a number of them.

Bhagavan had dinner with Shri G.S. Pathak, Vice-President of India. He met here some of the most prominent persons among Delhi's elite.

Shri Yeshvantrao Chavan, Finance Minister; Shri Jagjivan Ram, Defence Minister; Dr. Karan Singh, Minister for Aviation and Tourism; Shri Khadilkar, Minister for Labour; and Shri L.N. Mishra, Minister for Foreign Trade, called on Bhagavan and spent some time with him. Bhagavan had also been to Shri Chavan's house. Members of the family of Mrs. Indira Gandhi called on Bhagavan at 16, Golf Link Road, a few times and spent quite some time with him. Shri Jitendriya, who teaches yoga to Smt. Indira Gandhi, also spent some time with Bhagavan.

Shri and Shrimati Jaya Prakash Narayan, the Sarvodaya leader, spent some happy time with Bhagavan. So did Smt. Vijayalakshmi Pandit and Shrimati Hiren Mukherji.

Bhagavan also met Mr. Kenneth Keating, the Ambassador for U.S.A. and the Ambassadors for Spain, Netherlands, Iraq and Afghanistan, as well as the High Commissioner for Canada. He had tea with Mr. Kenneth Keating, for whom he materialised a ring. The ring was a little loose on the finger and Bhagavan mentioned it himself, when he went there for tea. "It will be tightened. You may ask how it will be tightened; just as it came from nowhere, the ring will be tightened from nowhere", said Bhagavan, smiling. Mr. Keating admitted that it fitted him well by the time the tea was over. General Manekshaw, Chief of the Army Staff and Air Chief Marshal Lal met Bhagavan at dinner at Admiral Nanda's house; General Khanna also had some time with Bhagavan. Bhagavan also met Shri S.M. Sikri, Chief Justice of the Supreme Court, and Shrimati Sikri. He also met the Chief Justice of Uttar Pradesh and Justice Vaidyalingam. The Lieutenant Governor of Delhi spent some time with him.

Shri Swaminathan, Cabinet Secretary, Shri T.P. Singh, Secretary for Agriculture, Government of India, Shri Sunderarajan, Financial Adviser, Shri Khanna, Deputy Auditor-General, and Shrimati Khanna had some time with Bhagavan.

Dr. D.S. Kothari, Chairman, University Grants Commission and Shrimati Kothari and Shri Chitkara, Deputy Educational Adviser to the Government of India also spent some happy time with Bhagavan. Among those that met Bhagavan, film artistes were represented by Shri M. Sunil Dutt and Shrimati Nargis.

Prominent among the journalists that met Bhagavan was Mr. Frank Moraes, Editor, Indian Express. He had a fairly long interview with Bhagavan. He wrote in the Sunday Standard, on 9th April, '72, "Ariel is no respecter of holy men, and indeed approached Sai Baba with scepticism. In the course of a fairly protracted conversation with him, he was first interested and then impressed by the perceptive views and reactions of this truly remarkable man... He presented Ariel with a materialised ring and a stone Cross. What however impressed

Ariel more was the psychic quality of his mind, conversation and thinking."

This is by no means an exhaustive list. There were many others who received comfort and happiness from Bhagavan, during personal interviews. Delhi, as Ariel wrote, was 'invaded' by Bhagavan and Bhagavan let himself be 'invaded' in return by top dignitaries from all walks of life for blessings and for interviews. The common folk received in ample measure healing grace and comfort from Bhagavan, all the days he stayed in Delhi.

VII

On the morning of 3rd April, '72, a strange look of forlornness had come over Golf Link Road. A number of devotees turned up for leave-taking, even in the small hours before dawn. For over a week, 16, Golf Link Road had been shifted as on a magic carpet to the sea-margin, where it had learned to live with the multitudinous roar of the ever-lasting ocean! It was now to be brought back again, to live its wonted life. It was difficult to imagine how Golf Link Road would digest this contrast. Amidst touching farewells and tear-compelling scenes, Bhagavan drove to Palam Airport. Waving his hand to the devotees assembled near the gangway, Bhagavan boarded the plane, and was promptly surrounded there by passengers and by the air staff... An *Avatar* has no rest!

25. A TOUR OF NORTHERN AND WESTERN INDIA (A PANORAMIC VIEW)

I

CIVILIZATION tomorrow is going to be four-faceted. It will be global, electronic, unitive and spiritual at the same time. India will play a prominent role in contributing to the unitive and spiritual side of world civilization.

However, as we think about it today, we see that liberty, equality and fraternity are still a dream in the morden world. What Bhagavan calls the fatherhood of God and the brotherhood of man are as far away from us as ever.

The Master who would lead his country and the world further towards this goal requires a four-fold equipment. He has to have an infinite patience with things as they are, universal love, a clear vision of Truth and the power to implement his vision. This is what we have in Bhagavan. As he himself has said, Truth is his advocacy, Right Action his doing from day to day, Peace his habitual disposition and Love the full manifestation of his being. Further, the Master who would change the world has to be interested in rebuilding the individual as well as the collective consciousness.

II

The tour that Bhagavan undertook in northern and western India is significant because it highlights some of

193

these very aspects of his personality. He left Bangalore on 14th March 1973 by air and returned to Hyderabad on 4th April 1973. During these twentytwo days he covered the Union Territory of Delhi, The Punjab, Himachal Pradesh, Haryana, Rajasthan, Saurashtra in Gujarat and Andhra Pradesh. The climate varied from the freezing cold in Simla to the desert heat of Rajasthan and Saurashtra and the humid and oppressive heat of Bombay. It was mostly by chartered planes that the distances were covered except some regular flights and a few car journeys, as from Mogha to Simla.

Bhagavan flew from Bangalore to Delhi on 14th April 1973 and the next morning to Amritsar, where there was a big crowd at the airport waiting for *darshan* in the chilly air of the morning. A few thousand had gathered at Delhi around midnight for *darshan* and blessings. In fact, as he motored down to Mogha, people had assembled at the threshold of their houses or shops, scanning the cars eagerly as they passed by and joining their palms with great devotion when they spotted him out. The car had to be stopped in one or two places on the way for *darshan* to the crowd, that had assembled there.

Shri Jindal had built a charity hospital in Mogha and named it after Bhagavan. This had to be inaugurated. This took place on 15th morning and more than a lakh of people had assembled for the *darshan*, *bhajan* and message. This number swelled to more than two lakhs for the discourse on 16th afternoon. As one looked on, it was a sea of human faces all around for two or three miles. The sons and daughters of the Punjab had come out in their lakhs to see and hear Bhagavan.

The journey was made to Simla on 17th morning. There were arches put up in Solan and a band was waiting to take Bhagavan in procession through the town. As

194

he arrived in Simla, people were lining along the road and some thirty thousand people had assembled on the Ridge for the meeting announced to be held at 3 P.M. Bhagavan gave *darshan* at the meeting and it was announced that there would be *bhajan* and discourse the next morning at 11 A.M. The next day was bright and there was glorious sunshine. People clambered up on the tops of trees and covered every imaginable inch of space to see and listen to Bhagavan. It was a most inspiring discourse and the *bhajans* were simply enchanting. The crowd was visibly moved and Bhagavan himself felt impelled to say: "This will spread."

There were thousands who sat on the lawns the next day at Woodville for *darshan*. And they were there for the whole day. They gathered round to listen to the talk that Bhagavan gave to the elite in another part of the garden.

Shri Sohan Lal, Bhagavan's host, both at Delhi and at Simla, took the party to Kufri and Phagi for an hour or so on the 17th and again on the next morning. There was knee-deep snow lying on the way. Bhagavan gave an ear-ring and a ring with the Lingam symbol on it to some visitors there. A ring which flashed with light had been given to the D.S.P. at the public meeting on 18th morning.

Bhagavan left for Delhi in the early hours of 20th morning. The devotees at Solan were very keen that he should stop there on the way. They were there even in the small hours of the morning to bow down to him. In Delhi, there were always hundreds around 16, Golf Links, where Bhagavan stayed. In the special pandal that was put up at Talkatora Gardens, there were some fifty thousand people sitting, morning and afternoon, for *bhajan* and *darshan*. A first-aid tent had been put up near this pandal and also an annexe for the sick and ailing who were to be seen by Bhagavan.

During his stay in Delhi till the afternoon of 26th March 1973, Bhagavan spent some time at interview with notables like the Vice-President of India and his family, Smt. Vijayalaxmi Pandit and Sarvashri Jai Prakash Narayan, Atal Behari Vajpayee, Gulzarilal Nanda and Goenka. He also saw Chief Justice Sikri, Shri L.N. Mishra, Minister for Foreign Trade, Shri Chaturvedi, Chief Secretary, Delhi, the Lieut. Governor of Delhi, High Court Judges and other government officials. He dined with Shri T.A. Pai, Union Minister for Heavy Industries, Air Marshal O.P. Mehra, Shri Nakul Sen and other devotees. At Rajkot he granted an interview to Mrs. Morarji of the Scindia Navigation Company.

On the days when Bhagavan gave a discourse in the Talkatora Gardens, the crowd swelled to more than a lakh. It was a thrilling experience for them to listen to Bhagavan's *bhajans* and discourses. While talking to such big crowds, Bhagavan's discourses were translated into Hindi, mainly by Dr. S. Bhagavantham, during the tour. The discourses for the elite were translated by him into English. Arrangements had been made in Vigyan Bhavan for a discourse to the elite. It was packed to capacity and a number of notables came, including the Ambassador for Afghanistan. Professor V.K. Gokak also spoke on this occasion, offering an interpretation of Bhagavan Baba's divine personality.

A member of Parliament who attended the meeting was so inspired by Bhagavan's discourse and *bhajans* that he went into a trance, saw Bhagavan as Siva and uttered loudly: "Aum Namah Sivaya" several times at the end of the meeting.

The Delhi Bal Vikas put up a beautiful programme

one evening at Sapru House Hall. All the children who took part in the various items milled around Bhagavan when he went up the stage, Parvati, Krishna, Narada, Sur Das and all the rest of them. They recited Jai Jagadisha Hare in such a tumultuous chorus!

Along with the *bhajan* group in the Talkatora pandal sat an old, white bearded Sikh gentleman. He had been wanting to sing, but the *bhajan* leader was doubtful whether the old man would fit into the pattern. Seeing him sitting quietly with the group Bhagavan asked him whether he would like to sing. The old gentleman burst into tears and sang "Vahe guru, Vahe guru."

On 25th morning, Bhagavan inaugurated the kindergarten preschool school named after Bhagavan and run by Shri Ved Prakash Gupta.

Bhagavan's party flew to Jaipur on 26th afternoon but without Bhagavan! He was to have joined the party. But as the plane was indefinitely delayed for technical reasons, he preferred to go by car to Jaipur. The large crowd which had assembled to welcome him at the airport was greatly disappointed. Arrangements had also been made to shower from above a profusion of flower-petals on Bhagavan as soon as he alighted from the plane. The nice display was also not destined to come off. Bhagavan arrived late at night.

The Kamani brothers were hosts at Jaipur. At the spacious pandal put up by them, nearly fifty thousand people had assembled. Bhagavan went into their midst, blessed them and materialised *vibhuti* for some of them. It was announced that he would speak to them and sing some *bhajans* in the evening. The evening crowd was so large that it had to stand around the pandal. The loudspeakers also failed a section of the crowd. It was when Bhagavan went round and moved in their midst that the crowd settled down to his *bhajans* and his discourse.

The Kamanis had established another factory in Jaipur and this was also inaugurated on 27th morning near the factory premises where the workers, officials and their families had gathered together to receive Bhagavan. He spoke here of the need for mutual love and co-operation, fear of sin and the love of God and the three W's: work, worship and wisdom. Just as *swas* or breath is necessary for the body, *viswas* or faith is necessary for the mind.

The same day in the afternoon, Bhagavan laid the foundation stone of the Sri Satya Sai College in Jaipur. The late Shri Punamchand Kamani had planned it. But he did not live to see it through. The brothers had now carried it out as a token of love and respect for him. Shri Rasik Kamani almost broke down with deep emotion when he referred to this fact in his introductory speech. The cream of Jaipur society was present at this meeting. Bhagavan spoke on the deficiencies of modern education and the reorientation that the system needed today. Every one was full of admiration for the discourse. The foundation stone of a Sri Satya Sai Prarthana Mandir was also laid by Bhagavan after this function was over.

Late at night on the 27th came the Bal Vikas programme. The novel techniques used at the performance gave an added colour to it. As usual, Baba went up the stage in the midst of the children. Some members of the party were hurrying away, obscuring the vision of some of the onlookers. Politely but firmly the ladies said: "Please listen. We won't allow you to pass through so long as Baba is on the stage with the children."

Bhagavan paid a visit to the Maharani Gayatri Devi School the next morning. Thousands of school-going boys and girls assembled there along with hundreds of elders standing around. The Principal of the School and the

Vice-Chancellor of Jaipur University extended a respectful welcome to Bhagavan. They said that people had come from hundreds of miles away for Bhagavan's *darshan*. Bhagavan materialised some *vibhuti* for one or two among the audience and spoke to the children about the *panchakshari mantra*, WATCH, and all that it signifies. It was a great meeting.

III

Bhagavan flew to Bombay on 28th afternoon. The visit to Western India began with this flight. There was the crowd waiting for *darshan* at Dharmakshetra. And the pandal holding thousands of devotees for *bhajans*, both morning and afternoon, was full. The public function at Vallabh Bhai Stadium on 29th evening was a colossal meeting. Nearly two lakhs of people sat in utter peace and listened to Bhagavan's discourse and repeated his *bhajans*. Shri Savant and Shri Page made the preliminary speeches.

In the meanwhile, Bhagavan had flown to Poona on the 28th to speak to a public meeting and distribute food to the poor on behalf of the Sri Satya Sai Samiti which had been an agency authorised by the Government of Maharashtra for the purpose. There were *bhajans* there and interviews, and *prasad* was given to the sick.

On 30th morning Bhagavan addressed the office-bearers of the Sri Satya Sai Organisations in Maharashtra. They had assembled at the Aarey Milk Distribution Centre in Worli, Bombay, from all parts of Maharashtra at short notice. Bhagavan spoke to them about their way of work as *sadhana* and about the *padartha*, the essence of spirit, as their goal. The audience were delighted with repeating Bhagavan's *bhajans* for which they were waiting so long. Prof. V.K. Gokak gave an account of the philosophy behind all the Satya Sai Organisations.

There was the Chembur Bal Vikas programme in the afternoon. The Bal Vikas programme for the rest of the Bombay area had already been over on the 29th afternoon. Children recited some verses from the Gita and *bhajans* and also staged a few scenes and dialogues. Thousands of adults had assembled at both the functions for Bhagavan's *darshan* and his inspiring words and *bhajans*. Bhagavan told the children that they should honour, serve and please their parents. "Be cheerful, friendly with all, radiating happiness all around. Cultivate truthfulness. Falsehood is resorted to only by cowards", he advised. "Through your efforts, the great traditions of the motherland have to flourish again", he said.

There was also a public meeting in the Gandhi maidan in Chembur and some forty thousand people had assembled there to listen to Bhagavan. Even the roads were flanked by thousands of men and women who wished to have a close glimpse of him. Here was a mother adventuring with her little son outside the ranks and pointing to Bhagavan in the car. There was an elderly lady slapping herself on her cheeks in traditional fashion and stretching forth her arms in imploration and prayer. It was a touching sight. 3rd April was the eve of Ugadi, New Year Day. A big crowd assembled in the Dharmakshetra pandal to hear Baba and receive his blessings. Bhagavan spoke of the Bhakta. One who does all work as God's, does it in God's name, is a devotee of God and of no mundane desire. He lives a life that is far above the reach of the senses and is an adweshta—utterly free from hate. Prof. V.K. Gokak gave an account of the significance of Bhagavan's tour in the North and West, to the audience.

IV

Bhagavan left by a chartered plane for Rajkot on the morning of 31st March '73 and returned to Bombay on the afternoon of 2nd April. During these three days, it was a great festival of light for people at Rajkot and Jamnagar. The Rajmata of Navanagar had donated 15 lakhs of rupees for the construction of a Digvijaysinh Wing for the celebrated Rajkumar College in Rajkot on the occasion of its centenary and in memory of her late and revered husband. The Rajmata is one of the great philanthropists in India in the sphere of education and a staunch devotee of Bhagavan. It was in response to her invitation that Bhagavan undertook the journey. Hundreds had assembled to welcome him at the airport even in the burning sun. More than fifty thousand people had assembled for Bhagavan's *bhajans* and discourse at the evening meeting. Baba spotted out the sick for interview and materialised *vibhuti* for some others. This was done every morning during his stay in Rajkot and Jamnagar.

Looking at a peacock perched on one of the turrets of the palace 'guest house' in which he stayed, Bhagavan told jokingly that Ravana asked Iswara one day why all beauty was given to women and men looked like logs of wood. At this Iswara answered that the male had its share of beauty and he referred to the gorgeous plume and tail of the peacock and the fan-like plumage of the male parrot as contrasted with the female which has only two feathers. The listeners were all thrilled because, at that very moment, a male parrot came flying, spreading its fan-like plumage.

Later in the evening on 31st March came the tattoo and other items of entertainment organised by the Rajkumar College. There were colourful items staged against the background of the illuminated college building. This institution has been converted into an autonomous public school with an experienced Englishman as its Principal.

The inauguration of the Digvijaysinh Wing came off the next morning. It was a memorable meet. The princely families and the elite of Saurashtra were all there and students with their Phetas—their turbaned heads—in accordance with the princely traditions of the College. The Principal and the Chairman of the Governing Body paid a handsome tribute to Bhagavan. The Principal's remarks were universally appreciated, particularly because some of them were in Telugu, welcoming Bhagavan. Bhagavan dwelt on certain home-truths regarding present-day education. There was prize distribution in the afternoon and it was a colourful ceremony. Students came in groups of four to receive the prizes from Bhagavan and he showered his affection on them by posing with each of these groups. Professor V.K. Gokak spoke to them, telling them about Bhagavan and his teachings. Srimathi Sumathi Morarji, Chairman, Scindia Steam Navigation Company paid her respects to Bhagavan, at Rajkot and received his blessings.

Bhagavan motored down the same afternoon to Jamnagar. There is a Sainik School on the way and the Principal and staff and students had organised a magnificent reception to Bhagavan there. Students had put up a beautiful exhibition of his photographs, his teachings and his books. They also entertained him at a rally in which they put up several group items. Bhagavan addressed them lovingly for a few minutes and told them that S.S.B. (Sainik School Boy) on their sport pullovers meant 'Satya Sai Baba' and showed that he was seated in their hearts as well as outside. He materialised a locket for the student leader whose eyesight was poor and *vibhuti* which was passed round to the boys in the batch.

On the morning of 2nd April, Bhagavan inaugurated the Shri Bal Vikas building that had been built near her palace at Jamnagar by the Shri Rajmata Public Charitable Trust. The Trust has built up a sizable fund of Rs. 60 lakhs to be spent on an educational complex in Jamnagar. Jamnagar came in its thousands to attend the meeting. Bhagavan paid a handsome tribute to the philanthropic and self-sacrificing nature of Rajmata. He told the people: "We come into the world, crying Koham? Koham (who am I)? We should leave the world saying: Soham, Soham (I am He)."

After a reception by the Home Guards, headed by Dr. Chudasama who is the State President of Gujarath Sathya Sai Seva Samithi Organisations, Bhagavan flew to Bombay from the Jamnagar Military Air port. He spent a few minutes there chatting to the airport staff. As Bhagavan said, this was the first time that he ever went inside an airport. Arrangements were usually made to take him straight to the aeroplane in order to avoid crowds at airports.

Bhagavan flew from Bombay to Hyderabad in a chartered plane on the morning of 4th April, Telugu New Year Day. Shri Prasada Rao, the chief architect and engineer of Sivam, Bhagavan's place of residence in Hyderabad like Sathya Deep in Dharmakshetra, Bombay, and 'Sundaram' in Madras, had come to Bombay. He was delighted, as a keen devotee, that his dream of Sivam had come true. Sivam is a distinctive piece of architecture and its most distinctive feature is the Linga symbol that crowns it and rises into the sky. Bhagavan performed the opening ceremony of the building before a large audience and shifted from Prasada Rao's house to Sivam the same evening. The Siva Puranam Week or Saptah began the next morning and Bhagavan materialised a

Linga for worship on that morning. People had the good fortune to listen to his discourse and *bhajans* in the evening. This was the pattern to be followed on succeeding days, culminating in the celebration of Ram Navami.

Certain students from the Sri Sathya Sai College in Whitefield, Bangalore spoke—two on each day—on some days during the Saptah. They gave an account of their hostel life from day to day under the all-seeing eye of Bhagavan, Bhagavan's teachings and of the divine love that was showered on them and the sternness which dealt with their transgressions. They showed how student agitation proceeded from a lack of proper guidance on the part of teachers and elders.

Gorgeous arrangements were made to give a send-off to Bhagavan when he left for Bangalore. There was a police escort, back and forth, for the car and horsemen rode gracefully on either side of it. The procession drew large crowds and thousands gathered together to feast their eyes on it.

V

Now that the narration is over, one might inquire into the significance of these happenings. How to account for these fabulous crowds that came on the scene wherever Bhagavan went and gave him rapturous welcome? The crowds were stationary as well as mobile. Whether in Simla, Delhi, Jaipur, Bombay, Rajkot or Jamnagar, eager faces popped out of car windows to do him *namaskar*. Hundreds collected around Bhagavan's car even if it stopped for a minute. Lakhs of people sat down for hours, wherever he went, to listen to him in reverent silence. One can hardly think of another person in this country who draws such crowds, the common man and the elite alike. Bhagavan's presence answers a long-felt need. He is a cool spring of water for people in a desert.

His appeal is to all age-levels and strata of society. It transcends all considerations of caste, community and language in a country of which they are the warp and woof. Apart from mass-meetings, the elite listen to him and are thrilled. The coming generation—preschool and school children—get together in their thousands and sing his praise. There were *nagar sankirtans* every morning, wherever Baba was. It is a veritable cultural and spiritual revolution that comes in the wake of Bhagavan.

There is an appeal of love and assurance that stirs each one that comes into contact with Bhagavan. The pilot and all on the planes deem it a privilege to fly him and there is a competition among pilots, who should man that particular flight. The police have a hard time of it wherever Bhagavan goes, in spite of the fact that the crowds are spontaneously disciplined. Their rapture sometimes exceeds their restraint. Bhagavan is kind to the police. He materialises rings for their officials and *vibhuti* for them. He invited a group of policemen on the snowy heights of Kufri near Simla to get photographed with him. The District Superintendent of Police at one place was so impressed by Bhagavan that he and his wife followed him wherever he went for nearly a week, taking whatever kind of leave was available.

The sick and disease-stricken people have great hope in their eyes whenever Bhagavan visits their region. They all flock to him for his blessings and *prasad*. The homes of many devotees are rendered sacred by his visit and profound psychological changes are brought about in the interviews. The newspapers, in the region which

Bhagavan visits, bring out special issues, like Shri R. Dhiman's News Chronicle of Ludhiana or publish a number of special articles like Dr. Bhargava's Hind Samachar of Jullundur. This is also true of the papers in Rajasthan and Saurashtra.

The casual conversations that take place when Bhagavan is relaxed, before the day begins or after the day's labours are over, are themselves matchless for their appeal. The parables regarding Hanuman, the monkeygod, when the president of the Jaipur samiti said that he observed fasting on Tuesday because it was a Maruti day; the talk about tube wells, deprecating the exploitation of surface water without providing for pumping an equal quantity into the earth beneath the surface, leading to water-famine eventually; the reference to chemical manures which produce big tomatoes but with very little 'tomatoness' in them; Syam and Laxmi Bai, devoted cooks at the time of the Shirdi manifestation, serving two big bhakris of jowar and brinjal vegetable; the sacrificial priest wanting the performer to repeat "Papoham papasambhavaha" and Bhagavan asking the priest to change it to *punyoham*, etc.; the well-wall distinction, comparing the digging in, to reaching the people and behaving with them and building the wall to raising the spiritual structure; comparing a public lecture to treatment in a general hospital and personal conversation to a treatment precisely directed towards the individual by the *bhavaroga vaidya*; time melting away swiftly and imperceptibly like a block of ice; and the fact that the secret of happiness consists, not in doing what we like, but in liking what one has to do: all this and more was spiritual wealth scattered prodigally, day after day, in casual conversation.

Finally, one remembers what Bhagavan said last year

in a speech at Delhi, that the nations of the world were a railway train, India the engine that drew it on the spiritual path and Bhagavan himself the engine-driver.

A friend said in Saurashtra that Saurashtra was fast becoming Sairashtra. In fact, the whole of India seems to be on its way towards becoming a Sairashtra, judging by the response to Bhagavan and his message in all parts of the country. The late Mr. Winston Churchill called Gandhiji, the father of Indian independence, a half-naked fakir. If a half-naked fakir brought independence to India, a fully clad fakir is sure to bring cultural, moral and spiritual regeneration to India.

IV. Sayings and Writings

26. BHAGAVAN AS PLAYWRIGHT, POET AND PHILOSOPHER

THE table-talk of Dr. Samuel Johnson and S.T. Coleridge has been justly famous. The casual talk by Sri Ramakrishna to groups of listeners that came to him has been collected together as *Vachana Veda*,—Spoken Veda. Baba's talk deserves to be recorded in a similar way. It will be a priceless possession for posterity.

But Baba is not just a conversationalist of genius. He is a brilliant writer as well. Even as a school-going child, he wrote a play which was staged by his school-mates at school: *Do They Practise What They Preach?* This was written in Telugu, the language of his mother and region. There are several other play-lets based on themes drawn from the Indian epics and from legendary lore. A play is no play unless it is staged. Baba is playwright as well as producer. He gets together groups of youngsters, assigns the parts and becomes their instructor as well. He even attends to the make-up of the parts. These plays are staged at the Navaratra festival in Prashanti Nilayam and at the annual socials in Sathya Sai Colleges. •

Each discourse by Baba is prefaced by a verse or stanza composed extempore, on the spot. These stanzas frequently express the core of the discourse that is to follow. Many of them are deeply moving. An anthology of these extempore verses has yet to be published.

Baba has also composed hundreds of *vachanas* or

prose-poems. He uses them occasionally in his discourses with remarkable effect. These are brief and epigrammatic utterances, dazzling the listener or reader by their metaphysical and imaginative brilliance. There are numerous songs that he sings and these have to be identified and published. His *bhajans* are miniature lyrics in themselves. The first of them—*Manasa bhajare*—has been commented on elsewhere in this book.

The Telugu prose-writings by Baba have been more sustained than his poetry. Spearheading, as they do, a consistent exposition of his message and philosophy, they have been translated into many Indian and European languages. He has recently started writing his 'messages' for functions and ceremonies in India and in different parts of the world himself. One or two messages, written by him in English, have been reproduced in this section. Another charming fact about Baba is that he is a prolific and marvellous letter-writer. His colourful personality,—its playfulness, humour, practical and spiritual wisdom, lyricism, banter, sublimity—are all scattered in profusion over his letters. Translations of one or two letters have been included in this section.

Bhagavan's discourses, delivered on various occasions, have been collected so far into seven volumes, englished by Shri N. Kasturi. More are yet to follow. The discourses delivered at the summer courses in Indian culture and spirituality since 1972 have been published in two volumes of *Summer Showers*, translated by Dr. S. Bhagavantham and others will be forthcoming. A talk or a discourse is a congenial mode of expression for Bhagavan and many facets of his personality find expression in these discourses. There are his scintillating parables and anecdotes in the manner of the Buddha, the Christ and Sri Ramakrishna. Almost every discourse sparkles with his puns,—Sivam (the Divine) and *Savam* (the Corpse); *manava* (man) and *Madhava* (God) and so on. The antitheses and parallelisms in his discourses are also noteworthy.

Baba's version of the *Ramayana* is still being published serially in the pages of the *Sanatana Sarathi*. But the *Bhagavata Vahini* has been published as a book and it can be read as a whole. Some of the passages in it have been written with great lyrical intensity and this comes out even in the translation. What Baba has omitted from the original is as revealing as the portions that he has picked out for narration. He has made it mainly the story of Sri Krishna and his comments illumine the contours of Sri Krishna's Avataric personality.

The *Vahinis* like *Prema Vahini* and *Dhyana Vahini* are little gems, classics of the spiritual life from the moment that Baba wrote them. Their simplicity which, at the same time, contains such a depth of meaning, is unique. They speak of Peace, Meditation, Love and Wisdom. They seek to acquaint the reader with the Upanishads and the Gita.

In a class by itself stands *Sandeha Nivarini*, the *Doubt-Dispeller*. It raises various metaphysical problems and answers them. If the reader wishes to experience the toughness of Baba's thinking, he will find it here in abundance.

After reading his writings, especially the plays, one finds that Baba is conservative, a real traditionalist, in an age in which experiments are going on with Expressionism, Symbolism and the Absurd. There are two reasons for this. One is that Baba does not wish to be theatrical, though he has a very fine sense of the theatre. He would rather allow the grandeur of his theme to speak for itself. Each play becomes a morality.

He prefers it that way rather than make it pass through contortions of various kinds. Another reason is the very mission for which he has come,—the spiritual regeneration of the common man. His main stance is not that of a dramatist or poet but teacher. For him, aesthetics is only the most effective way of presenting ethics.

27. BABA'S SAYINGS

(BABA'S talk is oceanic in its sweep of wisdom. It flows like the Ganges ceaselessly. You have to be the river itself if you wish to be in tune with it all the time.

Here are a few pearls gathered from this ocean. They came out in such conversations as I listened to. I happened to note them down. Bhagavan sometimes speaks in Kannada. These have been translated from Kannada into English.)

(1)

A stick floats on the waves of the sea.
So does a swimmer.
It is the swimmer that the sea loves to bear
For he has sensed its depths.

(2)

The current is one
But applied in many ways.
The printing press does not cook food
Nor the stove print a book.
But the current is the same.

(3)

Man is a torch.
His body is the tube
Its switch his will,
His reason the bulb

And his mind the cell
That is charged with the infinite consciousness.

(4)

Rebuked by his wife
For not shedding even a tear
Over the death of their only child,
The Man explained
"I dreamed last night
That I was blessed with seven sons.
They all vanished when I woke up.
Who shall I weep for?
The seven that are vapour
Or the one that is dust?
The seven are a dream
And the one a day-dream."
Though the soul may be born and die
As son or father,
It is immortal in itself.

(5)

Who am I?
The identity that persists
In dream and waking.

(6)

As you say,
The head begins to swim
When you think of the beginning and end
Of the universe.
The only beginning you know
Is when you begin counting the sea-waves.
The only end you know

216

Is when you get bored with counting
And give up counting.

(7)

The sun is gardener.
He draws water from the sea
And distributes it
To all the four corners of the earth.

(8)

When the Battle of the Vegetables was on,
They were all fighting in the Kitchen.
The onion was defending itself in a corner
With its back to the wall.
Brahma, Vishnu and Maheshwara
Judged the contest.
They gave the prize to the Onion
As the longest lasting of them all.
Brahma made its roots look like his beard.
Vishnu imprinted the disc and conch on its core.
Siva gave it the boon of tears:
May he, who cuts you, weep!

(9)

Miracles flow from *sankalpa* Will.
They come from the head to the hand.
A miracle is born
When the moment is ripe for it
And the deserving person has arrived.
What is given must be the right thing
At the right time, to the right person,
For it's a token to my love.

217

(10)

Do I have to do any *sadhana*?
No, I've no need.
I live in the God-Consciousness
And there're no further heights to reach.
I am there in all hearts and one with them.
I am the One in every one and in every thing.

(11)

The snowy expanse of Mount Kailas
Is but the cooling of the restless mind.
Peace is Kailas itself,
Madhurya, the surpassing sweetness,
Intoxicated with which
The drunken bee falls near the lotus-petals.
In the heart of Kailas—
That surpassing sweetness—
Are Siva and Parvati,
Beauty and Friendship.

(12)

Seeing the rose,
Separating it from the thorn and the shrub,
Is Concentration.
Plucking the rose,
Separating the heart from the mind and all,
Is Contemplation.
Offering the rose at the Lord's feet
Is Meditation.

(13)

My friend sat in the second row
For *bhajan* at Nilayam.

218

Bhagavan looked at him,
Tore six petals from a rose
And dropped them on the floor,
Looking at my friend
And saying: "It is empty".
His friends told him
That Bhagavan advised him
To avoid the six deadly enemies.
In his morning worship on the seventh day,
My friend prostrated himself in adoration
And never rose again.

(14)

The Kaurava-Pandava war
Was divine surgery
In the operation theatre of Kurukshetra
With Sri Krishna as surgeon
And Arjun as compounder.

(15)

We should reject the Ego,
Understand the World
And merge in Brahman.
Then is our Ananda complete.

(16)

A man can't run faster than his shoes.
Shoes symbolise *maya*, Illusion.
Illusion must be our footwear.

(17)

Krishna was busy with love or war,
The *gopis* or the *kshatriyas*.
Rama's time was taken up

With family affairs.
Sathya Sai has come for all humanity.

(18)

There are four mothers.
The mother of the body,
The mother country,
Mother Earth,
And the Mother of the Universe.

(19)

The three iron frames
Of *gopuras* or cupolas of the Mandir
Were concrete in 1968.
They were concretised later.

(20)

I am the Dance Master,
Nata Raja, Prince of dancers,
King of cosmic-dance.
You are all my pupils.
I alone know the agony
Of teaching you each step in the Dance.

(21)

There are only two ways to progress
On the path of self-surrender.
One is to know what the Master wants you to do
And do it unquestioningly.
The other one is to get your doubts cleared by him.
And act with full awareness.

(22)

The universe is a university,
The world a school.
Education is the bridge
Between earthhood and heavenhood.

(23)

I am the pharmaceutist chemist manufacturing new
drugs
For this disease called worldly life.
You still cling
To medicines I produced long ago.
Come nearer!
Let each one do his work
With greater dedication.

(24)

When the seer's vision is full of wisdom
The seen universe is full of God.

(25)

One should wake up to Truth
As a man returns with a shock
From a nightmare to the waking state.

(26)

What the thunder said
Gives us the three ancient D's
The Modern D's are:
Duty, Discipline and Devotion.

The prophet is the moon's image in troubled water.
He has yet to grow.
The moon's image in calm water
Is the Son of God, the Individual Divine.
The identity of Son and God
Is the full moon in the sky.

The path of works is like a passenger train.
It stops at every station
And you change at every junction.
The path of devotion is like a through carriage.
It's only the engine that changes.
The path of wisdom's an express train
That takes you straight to your destination.

When one hears the Sound
And wishes to listen to it more intently.
It disappears.
What's the remedy?
Imagine that you're listening to the same sound.
This imitation
Will draw it from its depths.

Today let's worship
The crystal *lingam* of Sivaratri.
Here in a casket of chalcedony
Is water from Gangotri,
Lake Manas:
Here's nectar!

(31)

Concentration is single-pointed vision
As when you stare at a star.
Meditation is single-minded awareness.

(32)

Eleven seconds of attention
Make one concentration.
Eleven concentrations
Make one meditation.
Eleven meditations
Make one *samadhi* or trance.
Eleven *samadhis*
Add up to the transcendental state.

(33)

Meditate both on the Name and the Form.
Conjectured Form
Should be imprinted on the heart,
Turn there into a living image.

28. BABA'S DISCOURSES

(SHRI N. Kasturi has translated many of Baba's discourses and these have been published in the seven volumes of *Sathya Sai Speaks*. More volumes are yet to follow.

I happened to translate Bhagavan's speech on Ugadi Day, 24-3-1974. The speech and translation were taped by Shri R.R. Kamani. I have reproduced the translation here as a specimen of such discourses. It will, of course, be included in the appropriate volume of speeches.)

Speaking on Ugadi or Telugu New Year Day on 24-3-1974, Bhagavan said that modern Indian society is led by self-praise, scandal and ignoble ease. Ancient Indian society cherished great ideals and these were absorbed into the life of society. Today we are rocked by strikes and all kinds of agitations. What is the reason for this fall?

Man has to attain self-satisfaction and peace through service to others. He has failed to live up to this ideal.

New Year comes and goes. It is as old as the hills. The only new thing about a New Year happens if we turn a new leaf in our life that day.

The names of the years of the Calendar are deceptive. This *samvatsara* or year is named *Ananda* or Delight. But this year will be full of monstrosities. Delight springs within ourselves. It does not come from the names of calendar years. A wicked person may have been named Rama. An irreligious person may have been named Dharma. Names are deceptive.

When will man have Peace and Delight as his permanent possessions? Only when his own *dharma* or righteous action supports him and the Grace of God leans towards him. He will never be happy unless these two are his. Happiness does not come from Money. If it did, Dhrutarashtra would have been the happiest of persons, for he was a very wealthy prince. But actually he was one of the unhappiest of men.

Nor are Power, Fame or the Intellect sources of human happiness.

Time slips fast between our fingers. Every moment melts like an icicle. Human life is transient. We must therefore find out our own duty in life and achieve righteousness. It is only then that man can live with the true dignity of a human being. Man must enthrone humanity within himself through self-effort. He must understand the secret of his own personality. This secret consists in the divine principle hidden within man himself and in all the creatures living around him in the universe. He will have delight if he knows himself and knows this Self which resides in the hearts of all creatures.

Man is the target of all misfortunes and sorrows today for he is spending his time in meaningless talk and malicious criticism. That is why he is unable to know himself. Self-praise waters the roots of his vanity and inflates his ego. Speaking ill of others is a great sin because each individual has the divine spark lodged within his breast and to speak ill of him is to speak ill of the Divine. It is the man who is the victim of sins himself that speaks ill of others. He overlooks his own major faults, instead of detecting them and eliminating them, and makes fun of the minor errors of others. The malicious man is ridiculed even in his own family circles. No one speaks well of him. He will be laughed at wherever he goes. If we do not like a particular individual, let us leave him to himself, be indifferent to him. Why single him out for censure and speak ill of him? I do not know myself. How can I know what others are like? It is only irresponsible persons, who do not know either themselves or others and blame others. They behave like mongrel curs, running about aimlessly in the streets. Such persons have no happiness in their own lives. They make themselves more and more unhappy by indulging in malicious criticism.

Then there are the others who indulge in fruitless talk. Such talk leads nowhere. If I believe in any single principle, the best that I can do is to try and realise that principle in my own life,—to achieve something, to measure up to the ideal I have in view, instead of indulging in irresponsible talk and forgetting it all the next minute.

We say that one 'should' do this and one 'should' do that. But have we applied this 'should' to our own lives? Have we realised in our own life what we expect others to do? It is much better to pick up any one maxim and practise it ourselves than utter a million maxims for the benefit of others. We will have fulfilled ourselves if we can introduce this kind of self-consistency in our own lives. Life can even be turned into something divine in this way.

God is everywhere. We do not have to go to far off lands to see and realize God. He is there in the heart of each one of us. We can feel His presence within us if we open our own hearts. Lying concealed there, in a golden casket as it were, is the Supreme Lord. We should experience him there instead of searching for him in all the wide world. We should fashion our daily life in the light of this divine presence within us.

We may know what Love is, and Compassion. But we must know how to express them in our own daily life.

Otherwise we will be utter strangers to them.

Here is a story. A person walking by the riverside saw a fish leaping up and falling on the sand. It was struggling for life and he was full of pity for the fish. He took it home wrapped in a handkerchief and put it on a soft bed. He thought that it would be good for the fish if some coffee were to be given to it. The gentleman meant well. But the few drops of coffee that he pushed into the mouth of the fish were enough to kill it.

Here was a person full of genuine love and pity. But what good was it? He did not know how to make love active in life. He killed the fish with his kindness.

Similarly, the love and pity of a good number of men who mean well but do not know how to translate them into actual life, leads to disaster.

Life is full of paradoxes. Youth contains within itself the seeds of old age and life the seeds of death. They form a continuous chain.

Individuals are going wrong today, because of the impact of the Spirit of the Age and the environment. A good deed done in a particular environment may itself turn out to be a bad one if the setting is changed. The goodness or badness of a particular deed depends, to some extent, on its contextual reference. An article which is good in one place may be dirt in another. Iron which is solid, hard and black becomes liquid, soft and radiantly bright if it is put into a fire, i.e., if its environment is changed. Even a good man who keeps bad company may develop a number of wrong habits and attitudes. On the other hand a bad man in good company may develop several good qualities and eventually become virtuous. Good company is essential for the man who wants to grow.

Good company promotes in us good thoughts and desires, the right inclinations. It removes all wicked

thoughts and holds in check base instincts. Hatred can
lead to nothing worthwhile. But love leads us to the
good foundations of a good life and society.

Man should neither be afraid nor make others fear.
He who makes others fear is an animal. He who is afraid
himself is no less an animal. Neither of them is a cultured human being.

Why should we fear any one on the face of this earth
when the cause we serve is the cause of truth and our
way of life is the way of Dharma? Truth will not bend
before any power on earth. On the other hand, every
one has to bow down before Truth. Like Truth itself,
Sathya Sai also will not bend before any one on the face
of this earth. Others might try to put fear into him. But
he is the most fearless of beings. All that is good, by
virtue of its goodness, draws to itself all attacks from Evil.
Evil just feels like attacking good and does so. This is the
position that Good itself has to understand and recognise
when it wishes to live in human society.

There are many 'insects' of fame in this world who
wish to acquire a reputation. When they see that the name,
Sathya Sai, has caught up in all the four corners of the
world, they wish to affix this name to their own, in the
hope that they may be famous. It is my name, after all,
that they affix to theirs and they feel happy. Their happiness makes me happy.

It is my mission on earth to make every one happy.
If a person finds happiness in blaming me, let him be
happy that way.

There are some who say 'yes' to Sai and others who
say 'no'. Some may describe Sai as good; others as bad.
This has no reference to me whatsoever. The good or the
filth of it proceeds from their mouth, not me. I am a
witness both to the praise and the blame. In all these

matters I am like a fan at work in summer. It gives comfort if it is switched on. It makes one uncomfortable in the heat, if switched off. But heat and coolness are relative terms. They have little to do with the fan itself. But in the way of this world, good and evil are a tangled yarn. Clear as well as muddy water flow together in the running stream.

Always it is the fruit-tree in the orchard that attracts stones thrown by little children. The fruit-bearing trees have to remember this fact. To be subjected to a stone-throw is evidence of fruitfulness, of goodness. Pursuing the path of Love, let us act fearlessly, regardless of any consequence because, ultimately, the Truth will prevail. In fact, Truth will not be Truth and Love Love, unless there are some obstacles in their path.

There are three maxims which you should take to heart on this day, the first day of the New Year. The world is an illusion; do not put your trust in it. Do not be afraid of Death. Do not forget to remember the Divine all the time.

Death is inevitable. If not today, tomorrow or a hundred years later, it is impossible to escape death. Therefore, one should never be afraid of death.

Again, we must always remember God because he is there,—enthroned in the lotus of our own hearts. If only we have a glimpse of Him, it would be impossible to take our eyes away from Him. To be rooted in Him is to be rooted in reality.

Thirdly, do not trust this world because it is changing every moment. It is not stable even for a single second. Every moment the world is changing and we are also changing with it, except the unchanging part in us.

Man will realise his soul if only he remembers vividly all that he has passed through. It was only the other day that he was a child. It was only yesterday that he was young, sowing his wild oats. It was just yesterday that he grew up into manhood. It is only today that he is old and that as an old man, he has begun to repent his misdeeds in youth. What persists through all these stages of growth and decay, when everything is changing, is his own soul.

Sage Purandara Dasa sang of God on these lines. What happiness, after all, does this body offer? It leads us from disease to disease, to more serious diseases; from sorrow to sorrow, to ever-increasing sorrow. Therefore, in the midst of all this destruction and disease, the one thing to do is to remember the Divine, remember Sathya Sayeesha and be true to our own *dharma*. Life can be turned into something sacred that way.

Who is Sathya Sai? This name is not the name of a body. It is the name of the divine consciousness which is enthroned in the heart, *hrudaya sthayi*. This consciousness is universal: it is there for all human beings, not merely the devotees of Bhagavan. Take the phrase, *Sheshashayi*, referring to Maha Vishnu who is asleep on Shesha, the python, in the ocean. Similarly, Sathya Sai sleeps on Sathya or Truth. Truth, which is something universal, is the substance of his bed. It is this truth, this principle of life that animates this body. And this is how you must recognize the inner significance of all persons and personalities.

This is the first day of the New Calendar Year, Ugadi. Ugadi means the beginning of a new epoch. This is how you should understand it,—not as the first day of the New Year but as the beginning of a new epoch in our lives. This is what will make it memorable, not the sweets that we eat on that day. On this day, we should try and understand the roots of our own hearts, the springs from which our sensibility flows, the Spirit within ourselves. Let us at least make a New Year resolution to this effect. Then will the day be significant and mark a new stage in our lives.

Two great forces reside in the body of every human being. One is Matter which is inert. The other is Consciousness which is dynamic. The body is the field and the consciousness is its cultivator. But we have to realise that there is as much force of existence in matter as in consciousness. There is the force of the Divine in both of them. Man fulfils himself only when he realises the divinity of both these principles.

That which is matter consists of bones, muscles, flesh, blood,—the entire physical system. That which is called 'consciousness' consists of the mind and the intellect. There are five *koshas* or sheaths. Of these five, the first is the sheath that envelops the physical system,— *Annamaya*. The second envelops our subtle vital breaths, —the *Pranamaya*. The third envelops our mental aspect,— the *Manomaya*. The fourth covers the archetypal awareness in us, the *Vignanamaya*. The fifth is the Spirit itself which is full of delight,—*Anandamaya*.

Without this aspect of consciousness, the mere assemblage of flesh, blood and bone can lead us nowhere. If we were to choose between the two, it is better to have consciousness without the body than have mere flesh, blood and bone without consciousness. Quite a few great sages sit in constant meditation and forget all about the body. They live in a constant state of bliss. Life is worthless if we cannot experience this bliss, Ananda.

If we wish to experience this Ananda, we must have faith in God and faith in ourselves. We must practise non-violence towards all creatures on earth. We must never hurt the sensibility of any one through word or

231

deed or thought or feeling. *Violence* will make beasts of us rather than men.

Violence of this kind has become a common feature of our lives today through some national misfortune. For every good thing done, there is a bad one that confronts it. We shall all lose human dignity and turn into snakes if we behave in this fashion.

Imagine some one protesting if a hotel charges a few paise more for *idli* or for a cup of coffee or if the Transport Company raises the bus fare by a few paise. Imagine further that this protest takes an ugly form. You eat and drink and don't pay or pay a few paise less. You ride the bus and don't pay. This is different from organised strikes. This kind of irresponsibility will lead society nowhere. Persons who behave in this way are mean and weak. They do not know how to live.

If a man cannot control his impulses or inclinations and restrain himself in the hour of sorrow, how can he ever live a good life? It is this kind of irresponsibility that is weakening humanity in India.

If a mosquito comes and sits on your nose, you wave it off by your hand. Mosquitoes have, however, the nasty habit of settling down on the same point from which they have been chased away. So you wave it off a second time if it sits again on the tip of your nose. The third time you clap your hands loudly so that it moves away. It is only if the mosquito thinks of tipping your nose again that you come to grips with it and finish it if necessary. Self-control is necessary at all times.

If we can keep our mind under proper control, we can discharge any duties efficiently in the interest of society. But man is unable to cope with his problems. To lose one's temper is to lose one's soul. One fit of anger nullifies all the health that a person has gained through proper dieting for three months. In fact, the food that we get today is itself far from nourishing. When in addition, anger consumes our health, loss of life can be the only result.

Man is the child of Rasa or Brahman,—the Divine. He must therefore be healthy and strong, not live the life of a weakling. We should set a noble example to society and not imitate blindly some ignoble action. If a man does not have proper strength of body and mind, how can society, which consists but of a number of such men, have it? If society itself is weak, what else can we expect the nation to be? Therefore, an individual has to safeguard his own health and strength at least in the interest of a stable society and a strong mother-country.

Unfortunately, there are very few individuals today who have the interests of society at heart. They are all self-centred. Office-bearers, leaders and chairmen of societies always think of buttering their own bread and feathering their own nests. None of them have the good of society at heart. How, then, can society come to any good? The members of such societies hang upon the words of their chairmen and behave in a servile fashion because they wish to keep their seats. This kind of selfishness can lead us nowhere.

Bright souls! It is my fervent desire that, today, you should take this oath in all sincerity. Say to yourselves firmly and finally that you will live your lives in the service of Truth and devote every moment of your life to the betterment and regeneration of Indian society and culture. You will experience a supreme sense of fulfilment in an undertaking of this kind. Extend your service and consecration to the welfare of the world itself. Be full-time, and not just part-time, devotees. Whenever we find that Bhagavan's popu-

233

larity has gone down a little because he has espoused truth and not a popular cause, we pack up all the photographs. We put Swami in an envelope and seal him up. This is not what we should do. On the other hand, like the Pandavas, we should be true to our devotion through thick and thin, through happiness and sorrow, through good and bad and cling to God and the Truth. Though their life was full of sorrow, the Pandavas lived their life of exile in the faith that Sri Krishna would, some day, lift them out of trouble. Even if this did not happen, the Pandavas were happy that Sri Krishna was in their midst, for his divine presence itself was a delight. We should live as the five Pandavas lived with Sri Krishna, their Divine Lord and Master.

29. BABA'S ENGLISH UTTERANCES AND MESSAGES

(NOW and then, Baba comes out with memorable utterances in perfect English. Three of them are reproduced here. During the last few years, he has also been issuing messages in English. The fourth and fifth items are messages of this kind.

The sixth item, which is a paragraph on Beauty, has a history of its own. I have weekly tutorials with the hostel students of Sathya Sai College, Whitefield. At one tutorial, I explained to them what beauty is and discussed the four types of Beauty—sensuous, imaginative, archetypal and spiritual. The students went to Baba after the tutorial and he asked them what they were doing so long. On being told about the tutorial on Beauty, he himself came out with a paragraph on Beauty and gave it to the students.)

(1)

Nature is a preacher.
Life is a teacher.

(2)

He who loses his temper at all times is disliked.
He who loses his temper at the wrong time is
ignored.
He who loses his temper at the right moment is
respected.

(3)

Life is a challenge: meet it.
Life is love: enjoy it.
Life is a dream: realise it.
Life is a game: play it.

(4)

Whatever we do reacts upon us. If we do good, we shall have happiness and if evil, unhappiness.

Within you is the real happiness, within you is the mighty ocean of nectar divine. Seek it within you, feel it, feel it. It is here, the self: it is not the body, the mind, the intellect, the brain, it is not the desire or the desiring. It is not the object of desire. Above all these, you are. All these are simply manifestations. You appear as the smiling flower, as the twinkling stars. What is there in the world which can make you desire anything?

It is the heart that reaches the goal. Follow the heart. A pure heart seeks beyond the intellect. It gets inspired.

With blessings and Love
Sri Sathya Sai Baba

(5)

My dears! Accept my Blessings and Love. The fruit is sweet but the rind can afford to be bitter. For, after all, it is the juice of the orange and the sugar content of the sugarcane that counts. Put off the rind of anger, malice, envy and greed and assimilate the sweetness of the fruit so that the sweetness can develop within you.

Be a lotus. The lotus born in slime and mud rises up

through the water and lifts its head above it. It refuses to get wet although it springs up from water. Be like the lotus or the lily of the water, unattached.

Life itself is a market. Giving and taking, bargaining and speculating is part of the game. Life has its ups and downs, its profits and losses, its joys and sorrows, depreciations and appreciations and balance sheets. But the giving of Bhakti in exchange for Mukti is the most powerful business of all.

There are three types of men: those who seek pleasure for themselves only, with no attention paid to the pleasures of others, those who consider the pleasure of others first and derive thereby the pleasure of their own and those who try to prevent others from getting pleasures or benefits even at the cost of their own.

With blessings
Baba (Sathya Sai)

(6)

Beauty is not an independent value but is the manner in which the mind of a subject is affected by an external form which acts as a counterpart of the taste present in the subject.

Objects appear beautiful as long as there is a demand for them from within. When there is no desire, there is no special beauty in anything. It is *maya* that objectifies beauty.

Beauty is not skin deep. Beauty lies in the virtuous deep.

Baba

30. BHAGAVAN'S PROSE-LYRICS

(BHAGAVAN has composed numerous *vachanas* or philosophic prose-lyrics in his incomparably beautiful and expressive Telugu. The philosophic exposition in the *vachanas* is instinct with lovely lyric imagery. His philosophy itself may sound traditional at the first hearing. But it is full of the undertones and overtones of the New Age and the philosophy of Tomorrow. The full originality and brilliance of his philosophy are perceptible in the *vachanas*. A few are given here in translation.)

(1)

The world is not imperfect. There is no remote perfection towards which it will evolve in the millennia to come. We see that it brims with perfection every moment.

Each child is an old man in embryo and each infant carries the seed of death within itself. Immortality lives hidden in the heart of each mortal and divine Grace inheres in each appointed task.

(2)

Ignorance, Sin and Death are, in essence, their own opposites: Knowledge, Virtue and Immortality. All dualities are essential to our growth and structured for our good. To experience antinomies through love is to realise the core of goodness in them. Experienced in this way, even darker antinomies than Sin and Death will bring us a new dawn of Truth.

(3)

There is the keen impulsion of Desire behind Love. And in the heart of Love is the deep power of Life. Do not take Love lightly. Our Life itself is consecrated to Love.

Love is the mainspring of all human activity, be it the highest or the lowest. To know this is the supreme wisdom.

Concentrated pursuit turns the impulsion of Desire into Love, Love into Illumination and Illumination into Delight.

(4)

The dialecticians ridicule the world and call it an illusion. But they will cease to live the very moment that they cease to love it. None can ignore love.

The world strikes us as an illusion when we think of the perishability of the things in this world. But the man of God sees the world as a manifestation of the Real Eternal.

(5)

A granite will turn into dust some day. A sapling may spring from that earth and grow into a tree. Eating the fruit of that tree, a man and wife may bring a child into this world. If a granite can evolve into the warm heart of a human child, why cannot man, endowed with a rare tenderness, become the God-man?

6

Each part has its counterpart and each poise its counterpoise. And the opposite is as true as the thing to which it is opposed.

No man, nothing, is completely pure or impure. Each object is a strange amalgam. The notion of 'pure' and 'impure' arises from lack of a total perception. We should view an object from all sides. Truth is grasped through an integral, not a partial, vision.

Deceptions arise when we fancy that Time is an imperishable reality. Time changes; the Absolute does not.

31. BABA'S LETTERS

(ONE wonders how Baba finds the time to write letters in the midst of his multifarious activities. But he does find the time. Moreover, his letters are not just hastily scribbled. Many of them are real gems of literature and philosophy.

Two of them are given here in translation from the Telugu. One is a letter addressed to the present writer from East Africa. The other one is a letter addressed to the teachers in Sathya Sai College, Whitefield. The personality of the world teacher shines forth in both these letters. The second one has been translated by Professor H. Sunder Rao. I cannot, at the moment, recall who translated the first letter.)

(1)

Sri Sathya Sai Baba

Camp: KAMPALA
East Africa
7-7-68

Gokak! Blessings to you. While thousands and thousands of bhaktas were raising cries of 'Jai Jai', we left Bombay on the 30th by 'Garudavahana' and reached Nairobi at 12 noon. As the plane was landing, cries of "Jai Jai to Bhagavan", "Jai Jai to Sathya Sai Baba", etc., rent the skies. In the meantime a beautiful car decorated with flowers as a palanquin came very near the plane

241

and I got into it. From there the vehicle moved in a big
procession with bugles, music bands and dances, with
thousands and thousands of people on either side of the
road presenting *arathis* and showering flowers. Such
scenes offered a feast to the eye and pleasure to the
mind. While officials were dancing in front of the moving car, it appeared as though Jayadeva and Gouranga
were before us. When the highly inspired officers were
dancing with joy, it appeared as though even the by-
standers were flying above the ground. In this way we
reached an extensive open space where the bhaktas
assembled in such a number that it was an ocean of
humanity, with only their heads rising above   water.
As our vehicle approached the specially erected platform,
the Commander-in-Chief garlanded me. Afterwards, the
High Commissioner, the Ministers, the Inspector General of Police and other high officials followed the Commander-in-Chief in offering the garlands; subsequently
the ministers began to talk to me. When I started to
address the audience, Kasturi was missing. He had to
translate my speech into English. He could not be located in the huge ocean of humanity; he was called for on
the mike and the police also started the search. Even
after an hour's search nobody that had followed me
from India could be traced. Finally it was found that
there was an Air Force Officer there, who knew Tamil
and so I started lecturing in Tamil and the Air Force
Officer began to translate it into English. After a search
for two hours by the police, Kasturi and company were
located. Being unable to pass through the crowd and
being stunned by the devotion and the love of lakhs
and lakhs of people that had assembled there, Kasturi
and company, it appears, were standing at some corner
shedding tears of joy. Such crowds they had not seen

before; no wonder! Even in India such joy and grandeur had not been seen anywhere.

After taking food we reached Kampala in a
special plane. There the 'Jai Jai' welcome was
far more intense than even at Nairobi. Wherever
we saw, there were welcome arches. It was a sight
to see the police *bandobust*, with police cars both behind and in front of our car, and the Inspector General
of Police's escort-car sounding the siren in front.
That grandeur is not of importance to me, but the joy
and happiness of the people moved me considerably. For
the next three days consecutively, meetings were held.
Again yesterday a visit was arranged in a special heli-
copter to the game park at a distance of 600 miles,
where wild life abounds.

There we spent the night in the wooden houses
over the trees. In that area very big lions, tigers,
cheetahs, zebras, bisons, giraffes—why this one or
that one—many other kinds of wild animals, were
freely moving in thousands. The way in which these
various animals were moving about with mutual co-
operation and adjustability appears to suggest that
they are better than the human beings in the present-
day world, where humanism and humanness are altogether dying out. The scenes where these wild animals
were mixing together, eating together, drinking together
and licking each other with friendly feelings, appeared
to me to teach a lesson even to human beings. In all
of them godliness was clearly visible. Thinking about
this strange but holy and wonderful friendship and
adjustability, we reached back Kampala. Today the
Lion's Club, the Doctors' Association, the Lawyers'
Association, the Headmasters' Association, all met together and I presided over the function. It went off

very joyfully. After learning the new way of life and the principles of service, they decided to open a Sathya Sai Association (Sat Sangh), which will be a central association for the whole of Africa. They also decided that Swami should inaugurate the Association on the Guru Pournima day and made elaborate arrangements for the whole function to be broadcast through television throughout Africa. Therefore, I have to remain here on the 10th also. There are several other invitations, but for want of time I cannot oblige them all and consequently they are feeling dispirited. "Bangaru", no one ever imagined that the spread of Dharma will be done in this way in foreign lands. Even Kasturi, Indulal Shah, etc., are getting stunned at this. They are not getting an opportunity even to see me. Only at the time of dinner am I able to see them. Please convey this happy news to all my bhaktas there. I hope to reach India soon. My blessings to your Grihalaxmi.

Baba

(2)

Prasantinilayam
18th Jan. 1974

Dear Devotees of Dharma,

Receive my blessings. Ever since I arrived at Prasanti Nilayam, I have been thinking of writing you a nice letter. But a large number of devotees have come here from distant parts of the country. They have been waiting for a long time. I have had to send them after offering spiritual solace. Hence, the delay in sending this message.

Embodiments of the Divine Spirit,

Open your eyes once and look with circumspection. Contrast our present pitiable predicament with the glory of our ancient heritage. What an abysmal descent! Isn't our situation like that of a man who has tumbled down from the peak of a mountain into a deep valley below? We had, by upholding dharma, attained a pinnacle of perfection in every sphere,—spiritually, materially, scientifically and economically. Our Srutis and Smritis contain the commandments of God. We used to follow with great love and veneration the principles of Dharma laid down in our sacred scriptures. We were bound together by mutual love and affection. Our culture had attained an acme of excellence. But today we are confronted with a terrible situation. Wherever we see, we find men sunk in utter depravity and dissipation. The redemption of mankind by Bhagavan is the greatest need of the day. We have totally discarded the *dharmic* duties prescribed by our ancient Srutis and Smritis. People are jeopardising world peace by spreading mutual animosity and distrust. Violation of the laws ordained by God is the chief factor responsible for the absence of abiding peace in the world.

Isn't the transgression of God-ordained *dharma* the sole cause for present-day poverty, despondency, helplessness and lack of spiritual knowledge? Nevertheless, it is heartening to note that at least a microscopic minority of people in the modern world are, in the logical spirit of "anvayavyatireka", striving for the resurrection of *dharma*, which alone can bring about the welfare of humanity. If the destruction of one particular thing causes the annihilation of something else, then the only method for the regeneration of the latter is the regeneration of the former. Isn't this principle universally valid and applicable? Today it is evident that the decline of *dharma* is endangering world peace. If the welfare of the world is our main concern, then isn't the revival of *dharma* our paramount duty?

Teachers,

Now at least you must wake up. It is your imperative duty to strive for the preservation of *dharma*. Today some people are trying to uproot Bharatiya Dharma. We must resist all such attempts. If we fail to do so, *dharma* may be rooted out.

There are some people who are blindly enamoured of modern western civilization. They pretend to be real social reformers. These so-called, spurious and self-styled social reformers are trying in innumerable ways to pollute society by depriving it of *dharma*.

Champions of Dharma,

That Dharma, for upholding which we have been willing to fight without caring for our wealth, honour and lives, is called *Sanatana Dharma*. "*Sanatana*" means "*Nitya or eternal*". Awake, arise and get ready. The time for demonstrating your indomitable valour and indestructible spirit has come now.

You are born in the ever-effulgent land of Bharat, the abode of dharma and valour. You are the valiant and invincible descendants of great warriors. You are the proud inheritors of the traditions established by Rishis like Bhargava, Kausika, Vashista, Bharadwaja and Kashyapa, who extended their sway over the three lokas and made them tremble by using the spiritual strength of penance. You will be unworthy of such great traditions if you remain indifferent, slothful and apathetic when *dharma* is imperilled. You must become the harbingers of the Great Renaissance of Dharma. You must aim at the welfare of all humanity. Bhagavan will surely help you in your crusade against the evil forces threatening and undermining Dharma.

There have been rapid changes and reforms in all human institutions. This spirit of radicalism is rampant everywhere. Change for the sake of change is the order of the day. There have been several innovations in the educational system also. Sanatana Dharma was an integral part of education in ancient times. Students used to be sent to their gurus for regular instruction, as ordained by the injunctions of the Shastras, after undergoing "Upanayana" or spiritual initiation at the proper age. During the British regime the pattern of education changed completely. The pursuit of the second "Purushartha", viz., "Artha" or wealth assumed great importance. People were lured to the study of English and the pursuit of the western type of education because of the monetary benefits offered by the British regime.

In ancient times devotion to God was a part and parcel of education. Teachers laid emphasis on devotion: That is why students were well-versed in spiritual discipline. All their actions were motivated by spirituality.

Boys and girls used to be instructed by gurus who had a profound knowledge of religion, culture and civilisation. Today the intellectual climate has changed. Preceptors themselves are woefully ignorant of the meaning of culture and the significance of spirituality and religion. Such preceptors cannot transmit sublime thoughts to children. In such circumstances the hearts of little children do not respond to the nobler and higher values of religion and spirituality.

Modern teachers are suffering from a mania for western culture and civilisation. They have become apostles of atheism and agnosticism. They question the validity and authority of the Vedas. Pseudo-historians have distorted historical facts. Can we call such a system of instruction education in the real sense? Can we call those who

247

propagate such falsehoods real gurus? Vidya (education) is God's divine power. Knowledge of the innerself (*Atmatatwa*) alone deserves to be called true education (*vidya*). Modern education is a misnomer.

Neglect of spiritual education is responsible for unrest among students. They are worse than the blind. They are becoming targets of ridicule. They indulge in anti-social activities and bring disgrace to educational institutions.

Dear teachers,

We have to inculcate lofty ideals in our college students. We are embarking upon a noble project. You are all enthusiastic, spiritually-inclined and worthy of Sai's love and affection. I wish to share my thoughts with you.

1. It is not enough to impart bookish knowledge or information to our students. Mere formal teaching will not raise their stature. We should not only inform but also inspire. It is not enough if you plant a sapling in the earth. It will not grow into a tree unless you water it regularly and remove all harmful weeds.

2. It is dangerous to transform our meek rural students into anglophiles or anglomaniacs and make them unlearn the virtues of obedience, humbleness, politeness and fidelity, which alone are essential in life. The acquisition of an academic qualification may be a passport to government service. A degree, however, does not guarantee the acquisition of the noble values of life. Our students should be trained to respect their parents, co-operate with them and earn their blessings.

3. There are about 200 rural students in our college. We should divide them into small groups. Each group may consist of 20 to 30 boys. Each teacher in the college should be in charge of a group. The concerned teacher must pay individual attention to his wards. Special

coaching will have to be provided for substandard students. We must maintain personal contacts with the parents of our students. Personal relations between the teacher and the taught will promote the harmonious and all-round development of a student's personality. We have to humanise and spiritualise the present-day pattern of education.

4. Villages should be purged of evil habits, evil thoughts and evil talk. Our village boys will be useful in this process of purification. This will be possible if they acquire good habits in our college. We should also see that they do not relapse into their evil ways after going back to their villages. We must assist our village boys in establishing spiritual centres in their own villages. Such follow-up work will not only benefit the villagers but also prevent the village boys from relapsing into their former ways.

5. It is desirable for teachers to visit nearby villages once a week or once a fortnight and organise meetings for propagating the teachings of religion and spirituality. Social work and other developmental activities should also form a part of the programme. You may do the necessary spade work and make all preliminary arrangements. I shall return to Brindavan in February. We shall then visit some of the villages and establish spiritual centres there. It shall be our endeavour to transform them into ideal villages. It is only then that education will have fulfilled all its sacred aims and objectives.

6. Teachers will have to develop an exemplary character. They should set a good example to students. Practice should precede precept. It is only then that students will follow the example of their teachers. Our college must become a pioneer in upholding the noblest ideals. It is

not a matter for individual effort. We must work together as a team.

7. Those students who desire to have spiritual centres established in their villages may make the necessary preliminary arrangements. I will pay a personal visit to such villages and inaugurate those centres. I will be extremely happy to provide the necessary facilities for all such centres. These spiritual centres will divert the attention of villagers from petty political bickerings and social squabbles. They will be able to sublimate their pugnacity and develop "Sathvic" qualities.

8. These spiritual centres will provide a reorientation to our education. In course of time many more centres will be founded. Village boys will acquire "Vinaya" (humility) along with "Vidya" (education). This will be followed up by spiritual knowledge. Lack of spiritual knowledge is the basic cause of all our evils. We are producing educated fools. They are blinded by party feuds. It is enough if men can live like men. Let them not become devils. Man's inhumanity to man expresses itself in the form of natural catastrophes like earthquakes. If something is not done to reverse these diabolical trends in modern society, the future of our children may be fraught with grave and disastrous consequences.

9. All of you should meet together and formulate a programme of action which should be implemented in good faith. It is not necessary to compel those who are not earnest. It is enough if we can find a loyal band of 5 or 6 workers who are prepared to devote themselves wholeheartedly to this stupendous task. I will be immensely happy if all those who have a real *penchant* for disinterested service work together with *esprit de corps*. Compulsion has no place in our institutions. I am willing to place a car at your disposal for visiting villages. I have,

during this holy Sankranti, given expression to all those thoughts which I have been turning over in my mind for a long time. I hope you will take necessary steps to implement this great programme.

Your loving Sai

V. Impact

32. BABA'S DEVOTEES IN U.S.A.

(I HAVE compiled this account of my visit to the Sathya
Sai Centres in America partly from the letters that I
wrote to the members of my family. I have reproduced
it here to illustrate the impact of Bhagavan's personality
in parts of the world which he has not even visited as
yet.)

(1)

Early in August 1974, Bhagavan wrote to me: "Mrs.
Cowan wants to welcome you to America. She says: 'If
Swami's coming is delayed for some reasons, kindly send
Gokak; I shall bear all the expenses.' She is praying
intensely for it. You may agree to go. She says that it
would be useful if the topics concerning Swami, our
Samiti organisations and the aims and objectives of
Swami are interpreted properly in that country. She says
that she herself will organise meetings from place to
place. Mrs. Cowan is coming to Brindavan and you may
discuss details with her there. Dussera is ahead of us by
two months from now and it would be good if you will
complete your tour by Dussera."

Naturally, I was excited by this mandate. I had just
pleaded my inability to go as one of the representatives
of India to attend a Conference of World Religions in
Belgium. I received Bhagavan's letter within an hour of
this rejection. And on my birthday!

Mrs. Cowan, Mr. Robert Silver and others came and

I was told that plans would be made accordingly. I was to arrive in New York by 12th September 1974. I was busy arranging for my passport and visa.

I meet the hostel students of Sri Sathya Sai College twice a week in the evenings and talk to them about the spiritual life. I told them briefly about this contemplated visit and I asked them what I should do during the month. I was surprised at the maturity shown in their replies. They anticipated practically all that I said or did for a month in America.

Towards the end of the month, I went to Puttaparthi to take Bhagavan's blessings since I was not sure that he would come to Brindavan before I left for U.S.A. He blessed me and asked me to dig and make an outline of the roads. He would go and tar them at a later date. He said he would be in Brindavan before my departure. He was far too busy in Prashanthi Nilayam and so he wrote to me on 4th September 1974: "I can't come over there. Go with joy. It is my desire that you should return laden with joy and victory and in good health. Swami is with you and in you. I will be in all that you do from moment to moment and be helping you. Do not have any anxiety." Armed with these blessings, which were as life-giving as a diamond-hard armour given by Sri Krishna to Arjun, I proceeded to Delhi and then to New York. I had prayed to Swami, while taking leave of him, that, during the month that I went as his delegate to the States, I should do nothing that was unworthy of a devotee of his. He granted my prayer.

After my 'altercation' at Palam airport with the Exchange people who, I thought, were deliberately withholding American dollars from all passengers and giving them German coins in exchange for Indian money, I waited in the immigration lounge and boarded the PAN

AM plane at about 4 A.M. My seat was one in a row of
four and I was alone in that row. When the plane was
about to start, there came an American girl in a *saree* and
occupied the seat at the other end of the row. She recognised me as soon as she saw me and namaskared to me.
I also recognised her. She was Leila Fazio whom we had
admitted to the Sri Sathya Sai Summer Course in Indian
Culture and Spirituality! She had been to Rishikesh after
the Course was over and studied the *Chamakam* and some
other Vedic recitals there. She was the second American,
along with Smt. Kanta Devi, to join the group that
gathered to study the recitation of *Purusha Sookta* under
Shri Kamavadhani Shastri.

My presence there acted as a tonic on Leila. She had
just been discharged from hospital after treatment for a
stone in the kidney bladder. But she had not been
operated on and there was still some pain in the system.
She felt that I was a Bhagavan-send, a God-send to her.
My presence made her cheerful throughout the journey.

On my part, I had an open ticket from New York
onwards. I did not know whether I was to stop over for
the night at New York or proceed straight to Los Angeles.
The journey was also trying. After having spent a sleepless night from R.K. Puram in New Delhi to New York,
another sleepless night would floor me. Miss Fazio invited me of her own accord to stay overnight in her father's
house. I felt that Bhagavan had sent her expressly to a
seat near me (she said that she even quarrelled with the
plane staff to give her a window seat and not the one in
my row) in order to take care of me. Between us were
two vacant seats that were unoccupied till London. It was
my feeling that Bhagavan was sitting on these two seats
as *ayi* and Baba and helping us from moment to moment.
He said in his letter to me on the eve of my departure,

257

dated 4-9-74: "Gokak! I waited upto now to see whether my work would be finished, so that I could go to Brindavan. The construction work is going on. It won't now be possible for me to go over there. It is my desire that you should go full of joy and return laden with victory, health and delight. Swami is going with you, he is in you. I shall enter, from moment to moment, into your duties and activities and I will be there helping you all the time. Do not doubt this for a moment... I wish I had more time to write to you which I haven't.

                                    With blessings and love,
                                    Baba."

With this divine assurance coming from Bhagavan, how can we say that this meeting with Miss Fazio was a mere coincidence? I was of some help to her in clearing her luggage through the Customs. She was of some help to me by way of an assurance that I would not be stranded in New York if Hilda and her group had not been informed about my arrival.

There was another link in this chain which was equally full of Providence. Shri S. Sitaram, of the Sathya Sai Samiti in London had expressed a desire to see me at the London airport on my way to New York. I had cabled to him from Bangalore about my plane and date and time of arrival. As we were alighting from the plane at the London airport, there was the usual announcement about transit time, etc. and I also understood the announcer to say: "Dr. Gokak should wait at the Grand Stand." Leila Fazio heard this and said: "Ah, your friend has come to see you!" And so we went hopefully to the Immigration Lounge to see Shri S. Sitaram. But he was not there. I was not aware of the fact that he might be waiting outside. There was a chubby-faced

258

British officer going there and I wished to accost him and request his help. He tried to avoid me, divining my intention. But I left him no room for escape. When I told him my difficulty, he very willingly agreed to announce my name, calling my friend to meet me. There was an announcement. But it brought no response. I explained this to the officer when he came to see me. "I'll ask them to announce again. How do you pronounce your name?", he asked. I told him that the typical English mispronunciation 'Gokyak' would do! The second announcement also was still-born. I was disappointed and Miss Fazio and myself were thinking of moving on to the canteen for a cup of tea when—hurrah! the British officer appeared on the scene with a beaming face, leading Shri S. Sitaram and Shri Shah, who had worked as a Yoga teacher on our Summer Course, towards us! We were all overjoyed. The British officer then explained to the Customs official there that he had allowed the two visitors inside on his own responsibility and that we might be permitted to speak to each other, sitting there, till the transit time was over.

I discussed with Shri S. Sitaram his plans for a conference of all the devotees in England on 9th October in London. I would attend the Conference. It was clear, in the course of our discussion, that Shri Shah had mentioned to the girl at the PAN AM counter that he wanted to see a friend who was on the 001 PAN AM flight. But he had not given my name to her. How, then, was my name announced on the plane? Nobody can say! Was it an illusion of the ear? If so, this illusion had been shared at least by two persons,—Miss Fazio and myself!

Equally revealing was the more than genuine solicitude revealed in the matter by the British official. He somehow took it into his head to be personally involved in

259

the whole affair. He placed himself as hostage before the Customs official in order to enable my friends to sit with me in the immigration lounge. Because my friends called me Dr. Gokak, he asked them whether we were all medical men. He was pleased when he was told that we were followers of the same Master and when Shri Sitaram showed him a tiny photograph of Bhagavan. When the transit passengers were called back to the plane, the officer appeared punctually before us and led our friends away. I was deeply touched. I said to him: "I do not know how to thank you. I am deeply grateful to you." I wanted to add: "It is such acts of kindness coming from Britishers like you that make me love your country so deeply." But I felt a little shy. And I shook hands with him with great warmth. He too was visibly moved.

This is how Bhagavan was helping me from moment to moment.

After catching some glimpses of a magnificent aerial sunset, we arrived at New York at about 9 P.M. There was the usual trouble about 'printing' my name, etc. on the Customs papers. But the Customs inspectors themselves felt sure of our honesty and never checked our luggage. As we crossed the Customs barrier, there was Hilda, with a group of ten or twelve friends, waiting to receive me. Mishal was there. And I knew I was in the midst of friends and that there was nothing to be worried about.

After resting on 10th night as the guest of Mr. Joseph King, an eminent citizen of New York, I went with Hilda Charlton to see Sita. I had two memorable days with the Kings. They are a most cultured and charming family. And the entire family is devoted to Bhagavan. When the Kings had come to Bhagavan in India, the doctors had told Mrs. King that an operation on her eyes was imminent for cataract. But Baba had told her that no operation was necessary. He produced fortyfive pills for her and some *vibhuti* in Madras in the presence of all the conference delegates. The doctors examined Mrs. King after she returned to New York. They were surprised to find that the cataract had stabilised and that no operation was necessary.

Heidie King, the daughter, is a crusader in Baba's cause. She has surrendered herself totally to it. She is a gifted artist and it was a pleasure to see her paintings of the Buddha and of Siva. It was a real privilege to spend two days with these chosen spirits and to be driven about the crowded streets of New York and Brooklyn in Leila Rubenstein's car. She is a radiant storm trooper of the Divine and once you have known her, you cannot miss her. She was in India in 1969 and she was very keen on being admitted to the Whitefield College.

Who is it that has shaped such youngsters and been an inspiration to them? It is Hilda Charlton, the dedicated and missioned spirit that is the soul of the Sai Baba Centre in New York. She came for Baba's Darshan as far back as 1965 or even earlier. She was a gifted dancer and, in her early years, she organised a Greek pageantry in Los Angeles for some fifty thousand spectators. But she gradually became aware of her mission in life and the free spiritual centre which she runs in New York, with its weekly meetings now in the basement of a West Village Church, is drawing four hundred youngsters as well as grown-ups. She conducts meditation classes with great earnestness and dignity and several participants have experienced a real inner-opening. The illnesses of the dear ones of the participants are put to the general 'Aum' at every meeting and it is quite an experience to hear this thrilling chorus of

'Aum' echoing and re-echoing in the hall. Many cases of healing are reported by participants each week.

Her comrade in spirit, though much younger in years, is Sita.

Sita's inner and higher consciousness have opened up and she is constantly in *samadhi*. Her daughter was telling us that Sita was seen eating out of a plate which contained nothing. She is almost every day a denizen, more of the supra-terrestrial world than of the terrestrial.

It has happened that some priests came to know this lady and they have been initiated into a state of illumination by her. They, it seems, took her to their bishop and the bishop said that Sita was in a state of grace. One of the priests wrote to Sita a letter at the time of his death, acknowledging her to be his spiritual master. She has seen the gods of the Hindu pantheon. Garuda has appeared to her in vision and she has seen Brahma, the four-faced God, with his 'girl-friend' who sits holding a banjo in her hand. Going deep into ecstasy once, as we were sitting talking to each other, I heard her repeating "Kalyanam, Kalyanam, Kalyanam!" as we do: "Shantih, Shantih, Shantih!" It was not she who uttered the word. It was some great one who visited her in her consciousness that must have said it.

She teaches *tantra* and the pupils in her class are well advanced spiritually. Several of them have experienced *samadhi*. Hilda is a chosen spirit come to earth for certain missioned work. So is Sita. They have now realised that, when they came to earth, they had agreed in heaven that they should work together on earth. Sita's problem is how to stay on earth, for heaven is so much more real to her than this world.

I addressed two meetings in New York. One was

262

held at the house of the Flags, a family of devotees. *Vibhuti* had appeared there in Baba's photographs and on the heads of devotees in meditation. We had exquisite *bhajans* sung by Mishal and other American singers, producing the right atmosphere. There were many familiar faces there and one could see the genesis of 'Baba' devotion in a meeting of this kind. A confirmed devotee holds *bhajan* sessions in his house and he informs his friends about it. They join in and freshers also put in their appearance. Those who are regular in their attendance at *bhajan* sessions gradually feel like going to India for Baba's darshan. This is how the movement has grown. A few devoted Indians are also found in these centres. I had lunch with the Ganeshans. Shri Rajah is busy planning a world society for orphans and for giving them Sai education at various national centres.

Heidie King, my host's daughter, has been painting and wood-cutting. She has pictures of the Buddha, Siva, Baba and others. She lives like a celibate and as for the world, a home and family, she just says: "Forget about it." It is a pleasure to see such a self-effacing worker.

The Sathya Sai Baba Centre working under Hilda meets every Thursday evening in the basement hall of a church in one of the suburbs of New York. The church authorities have allowed the centre to function there on Thursday evenings and one may occasionally listen to Hilda's announcements that members of the Centre should not stray into other parts of the church building. Any disturbance caused by members may make the church authorities think of cancelling the concession altogether.

A wonderful group gathers there every evening. Some three hundred were there as we entered the hall.

Americans young and old, a real 'melting pot'; some Indians and possibly some persons of other nationalities too; but mostly vibrant American youngsters—boys and girls—long-haired, earnest, enthusiastic, free—who had heard the call of spirit and responded to it with their whole soul. It was a fascinating group.

The meeting began with the singing of a few songs by young songsters with a guitar in their hands. One of them was Mira. There were other names and they all gave us soul-stirring songs. A few *bhajans* were sung and repeated enthusiastically by the audience. Hilda asked for narration of any self-discovery that might have taken place during the week. A young man narrated how 'high' he had gone in his meditation. A girl narrated how, in hospital, she saw an aura of light around a patient's head. Another lady narrated how there had been a bitter quarrel between herself and her husband. The apple sauce now tasted all the sweeter for that interlude.

Cases of illness concerning the intimate relatives or friends of those present were then put to the general AUM. Names were mentioned and followed by an overwhelming and prolonged chorus of AUM,—an impressive tumult of the soul from its very depth. The healings which followed as a result of this AUM would be reported on the succeeding Thursday.

Hilda introduced me and I spoke for about an hour. I spoke about the Avatar and the path that took me to Baba. This talk was greatly appreciated. As Mr. Joseph King told me later: "It was a masterly speech. You bellowed and continued to do so and there were tears in everybody's eyes."

It was with a heavy heart that I took leave of Hilda and the Kings. I left for Washington D.C. the next morning and I was received at the airport by Shri Radhakrishnan, a friend of Dr. Pani, Convener of the Sathya Sai Centre there. Both these gentlemen are from Mysore, the one an engineer and the other an important official of the federal government in U.S.A. I found a lovable host and hostess in Dr. and Mrs. Pani and they made me very happy in their home.

Mrs. Pani, a medical graduate and medical practitioner, has had a mild paralytical stroke and she has been confined to bed for some weeks. But her cheerfulness even in this predicament is something to be admired. Dr. Pani and Mrs. Pani are full of intense devotion for Baba. They are the moving spirits of the Sathya Sai Centre in Washington.

There was a meeting of the Centre at Dr. Pani's home in the evening followed by dinner. The four or five American youngsters that came for the meeting were full of an intense love of the spiritual life and they were eager to know all about Baba. I had a sitting with them for half an hour. The Indians were a mixed group. Some of them had probably no more than a conventional interest in spirituality, let alone Bhagavan Baba. A few were genuinely interested. One or two even seemed to think that spirituality should be concerned only with the salvation of the individual and that it should have nothing to do with the re-ordering of society. Any way, we had a hearty talk and meal. Dr. Pani's unobtrusive way of offering *arati* and *prasad* to all had a soothing effect on everybody and we dispersed after a friendly chat. I left for the airport to fly to Los Angeles after a fine *idli* breakfast with the Srinivasans. I reached Los Angeles after five hours of non-stop flight. Mrs. Cowan, Mr. and Mrs. Robert Silver, Mr. and Mrs. Crystal, Mr. and Mrs. Frizzell, Mr. and Mrs. Reeves and other friends from the Sai Centre were there to welcome the representative that it had pleased Bhagavan Baba to send to the U.S.A. They were all delighted that it had pleased Baba to send some one here to represent him in the States. This was an indication that he might himself visit the States in the near future.

As we drove along, recalling old happy memories, we reached Tustin and had tea with Mrs. Cowan, head of the Sathya Sai Book and Publication Centre in U.S.A. She is the wife of the late Mr. Walter Cowan, who died in Madras in hospital when he had gone there from the States to see Baba. Baba resurrected him and sent him back to the States to do his work. This figures prominently in a television film prepared in Los Angeles on Baba. The film is going to be released shortly for the public. Mrs. Cowan is the head of the Sathya Sai Book Centre which publishes and distributes Sai books all over America. She has invested a good part of her fortune into this service and turned her spacious house into a temple, with fine photographs of Baba placed prominently in each room. It was, in fact, Mrs. Cowan who organised my visit to the States, with Bhagavan's sanction. At the age of eighty, she has energy, vivacity and zest for work which can put young men to shame.

(2)

I had to leave for Hawaii the next day. It is a five-hour non-stop flight from Los Angeles to Hawaii. There is nothing to see on the way except the 'watery waste' of the Pacific and passengers are given 'old movie' entertainment with earphones for a fee, if one is inclined to have them. Mr. Terry Payne, Mrs. Burroughs and several others came to receive me. I was garlanded in Hawaii fashion and taken to the residence of Mr. Terry

Payne. It is perhaps worth noting here that the original inhabitants of the Hawaii islands are said to have come originally from Kerala in India.

The plane had been five hours late in Los Angeles and I had to wait at the airport. My task was made much lighter by friends who came to see me off and spent those five hours with me,—Mr. Frizzell, Mr. Miles, Mrs. Reeves and of course, Mrs. Cowan who had adopted me as her own baby and looked after me with motherly care and tenderness. We spent five hours talking about the Vedic view of the origin of the universe and Baba's philosophy.

The devotees at the Sai Centre in Mr. Terry Payne's home had waited for me for more than three hours and then proceeded to eat their food, which they do here in silence after *bhajan* and meditation are over. We joined the group and they were delighted to have me with them. Rama, Terry's son, was such a delightful child. I exchanged greetings with the members, recited the Sai Prayer, had a pleasant time with Mr. Stanley A. Burroughs, a well-known naturopath, author of *Living Creatively* and retired for the night.

Terry does contract work for Government in roofing. He carries his Sai sincerity and honesty into his work too. He is so devoted to Lord Sathya Sai that his entire house takes on the look of a Sai temple, with photographs of Baba in every room and at every angle. Through an American disciple of Baba in New York (Kriyananda) who observes silence and lives away from people on an island, he received divine grace at a critical moment in his life and all his life now is a gratitude for that blessing. Mrs. Payne is full of the same Sai devotion. She was eager to know what other Sathya Sai activities could be pursued besides the *bhajan* centre. I spoke to her of Bal

267

Vikas, a Sai Centre for children, which could grow naturally in their home around little Rama.

Terry's house is right on the sea-shore, hardly thirty or forty feet above the sea-water level. He has built a small wooden cabin for meditation and this is the Baba room in their home. My bed had been made here and I could go to sleep being lulled by the low and soft and gentle sound that the waters made a few feet below. I could wake up as the soft colours of sunrise suffused my room and revealed the bay which had lulled me to sleep.

Mr. Steve Au and Irene, his charming wife, had also been present at the meeting held at Terry's on the previous night. I was to stay with Steve for the next two days. He is a well-known architect in Hawaii and he and Irene had spent quite a few months in Brindavan in our vicinity in the presence of Baba. Srinath, my son-in-law, also knew him when he and Sarala were there in Hawaii for Srinath's postgraduate degree in engineering and his employment later. Steve was such an unobtrusive and obliging host. We called on two of the eminent professors of the East-West International Centre at Hawaii. Irene then took me to Steve's office where Timmy, an apprentice cook of the Sheraton group and a very sincere Sai devotee, joined us. We all had lunch in a near-by restaurant and proceeded then to Steve's home. Situated on the shady summit of a hill, with a banian tree in the compound, it is built out of wood in a new and convenient style.

The Aus spoke with great enthusiasm of their days in India and of the well-timed manner in which Baba had sent Steve back to his profession in Hawaii in spite of his protests. Irene said how, a week before she knew of my schedule in the States as a representative deputed by

Baba, she saw Baba alighting from a plane at the Hawaii airport. This was thrilling. Timmy would come out now and then with his dreams about Baba,—revealing his childlike innocence. We spent an enjoyable afternoon.

In the evening, we moved on to another Sathya Sai Centre in Honolulu. Some fifty or sixty persons were there, eager for *bhajan* and for listening to my talk. We had a wonderful time together and there was something truly lifting and moving in the atmosphere.

The next morning we called on Dr. Mrs. Diegel in her Central Bookstore and Centre, Honolulu at 1418, Kapiolani Building.

In addition to running a bookstall and reading room, mostly concentrating on oriental wisdom, spiritual life and allied subjects, Dr. Mrs. Patricia Diegel and her husband John Diegel also organise classes in astrology, yoga and other similar subjects. She showed us round the place. Some classes were in progress then. The reading room bids fair to develop into a yogic institution,—the University of Metaphysical Arts and Sciences.

It was Steve's bright idea to see whether a public talk by me could be arranged. Hawaii had a very, very late intimation of my arrival and there was not much time. Steve told me that, when he approached Mrs. Diegel about it, she seemed to feel me physically for a moment and asked a few questions about me:

"Is he tall?"
"Yes."
"Does he carry a walking stick when he goes out for a walk?"
Steve had seen me carrying one in India.
"Does he wear a cap and scarf?"
"Yes, o Yes."

Though this was not the basis on which Mrs. Diegel decided to arrange for my talk in her pretty hall, she did agree to arrange for it. She telephoned a number of people for two days and secured for me a wonderful audience,—office-bearers of the many spiritual organisations functioning in Hawaii. This was a real opportunity.

On the second day in Hawaii, I had lunch with the Aus and with Mr. Landon Carter, a young American friend of mine when I was in India, the Paynes and a few others. Landon is working now with Werner Erhard in a movement which aims at bringing about a spiritual awakening in individuals. He wrote to me in a note later: "I really experienced Baba through you in our brief meeting... I love you."

In the afternoon we drove round one of the other islands where the vegetation and landscape are quite different. We had an early dinner with Mr. and Mrs. Robert Burroughs. It was a unique dinner, for milk and milk products even are banished from the table of this eminent naturopath and I felt honoured, as a vegetarian to have been invited to dinner by a super-vegetarian. It is interesting to see how, in spite of this rigorous self-denial, there is such a great variety in the menu. Mr. and Mrs. Burroughs are ardent Sai devotees.

We then left for Mrs. Diegel's hall for the talk. There was a good gathering and I also felt like speaking to them. I spoke to them on my discovery of the identity of Sri Aurobindo, the Mother and Baba and of the opening of my heart to Love. The listeners were fascinated. There were a few questions at the end of the talk. The whole atmosphere was elevating and ennobling. Several members of the audience were introduced to me by Mrs. Diegel after the talk was over. One of them, still visibly under

270

the spell of the experience, took out a ring that she wore on her finger and wanted to hand it over to me, saying in words full of emotion: "Give it to him!"

I hesitated, saying that I did not know what Baba would think of me if I accepted it for him.

She just said in a tone full of intensity and possibly very slight impatience: "Give it to him! He will understand!" I was simply overawed into accepting it, listening to her.

Before I left Hawaii, Timothy Wilson handed over to me a poem by a member of the Sai group in one of the other islands. These groups attended the meetings held in Honolulu as I could not go to some of the other islands. The person who wrote it was Faina Tackaberry. I reproduce it here because of the poignancy of the writing:

"The world is a hall of radiant mirrors reflecting
Thought and action. We are aware of processes
Of consciousness flowering all around us."

"Teachers appear as sudden jewels shooting
Through our dark night. In their presence
We come to know the true meaning of
Divine Love. Here and here alone is diamond-clear
perfection...and we experience that there never
was a speck to mar the purity."

"And the shining stranger
You've been tracking
Turns his face and it's you."

I sat chatting with the Aus and Timmy late in the night, for I was to leave for Los Angeles the next morning.

I had given a talk in the Philosophy Department of the University in the afternoon. There were about a hundred students there. One of the professors of Philosophy, a man of Indian origin, had handed over his students to me for that period. It was nice of him. But the students seemed to have had a heavy lunch and my talk possibly weighed heavier with them. I could catch some of them napping. I had to cut a few jokes to wake them up, and when they were wide awake, lay it on more thickly than ever in a loud voice.

My daughter was in Hawaii with her husband, a structural engineer, for about four years. I very much wanted to call on her landlady. But I had left my address-book and reading glasses at the house of the Kings in New York and I had yet to receive them back. I was so sorry I could not call on that family. My visit to Hawaii was a last minute fixture and my daughter also did not know that I would go there.

The Aus narrated to me another incident that was highly revealing. They have constructed a nice new house for themselves. The roof-laying was being looked after by Mr. Payne's men. They are Samoans and they had to pass, from one on to another, hot tar for being poured on the roof. They were doing this work, repeating, all the time to themselves: "Sai Baba! Help! Sai Baba! Help!" This was how the common man in Hawaii had taken to Sai Baba.

Mrs. Irene Au could recite *bhajans* beautifully, with Timmy and myself joining in. This was what we did when we were driving up and down the island during those two days.

I had such a delightful time at Hawaii and I did not feel like tearing myself away from friends there. Kanta Devi, such an ardent devotee of Baba now, had joined the Summer Course in May 1974 as an observer. It was a real pleasure to see her and her mother (who, alas, is no more) in their own charming home in Hawaii and have tea with them. Kanta Devi is so sincere and so full of the genuine Hawaii mysticism. She seems to have inherited the tradition and it should be possible to know more about it from her.

The next morning I took leave of my friends and I was driven back to the airport by the Aus and Timmy. I was received at Los Angeles airport by the Silvers. Mr. Robert Silver is a prosperous lawyer and Mrs. Jerry Silver a teacher. Both are wonderful Sai devotees. The Silvers have their home in Ojai, a pretty little town which has been a centre of many spiritual activities,—Amerindian mysticism, theosophy, J. Krishnamurti and now Baba. The highest mountain-peak in Ojai, Topa Topa, was a sacred spot for Amerindians. Shri Rajagopal, one time Secretary to the J. Krishnamurti Foundation, has still his home here.

We stopped, on our way to Ojai, at the home of Dr. John Roger Hinkins, leader of the M.S.I.A., a popular spiritual movement in America. Many spiritual movements are on in the States now. There are liberal Christian movements like those represented by the Church of Religious Science, the Unity Church and the Eucumenical Centres. Then there are the organizations which present spirituality in near humanistic terms or branch off into the provinces of the Psychic and the Occult. The M.S.I.A. movement of Dr. John Roger Hinkins and the yogic approach advocated by Eugene Roy Davies are also there. Sikhism, Sufism, Vedanta established all over U.S.A. in the form given to it by the Sri Ramakrishna Mission, the Ashram of Paramahamsa Yogananda and his disciples, Maharishi's International University and its science of creative intelligence,—all these have a strong foothold in the States. There is the

273

World Institute of Avasthology recently started by Dr. B. Reyes and his associates in Ojai. Visits by Swami Muktananda and others, yoga centres started by persons like Yogi Amrit Desai (Shaktipat Kundalini Yoga) also attract people. California is full of such attractions and each one of them has persons that respond to it.

Dr. John Roger Hinkins came out to receive us and he showed us round the house. Mrs. Jerry Silver attended a seminar in the M.S.I.A. Asram and she was very appreciative of the M.S.I.A. movement. Dr. John Roger was enthusiastic about Baba and he offered to keep his 'caravan' at the disposal of Baba for tours when Baba visited America.

The M.S.I.A. (Movement of Spiritual Inner Awareness) Prana Asram is run on a voluntary basis. The people living there provide almost all of the services required to run it. The asram has group chants in the mornings and evenings and there are classes in Creative Dance, Hatha Yoga, taped seminars and so on.

Dr. Roger Hinkins has a spacious home and it is also the headquarters of the movement. All the gadgetry required for tapes is here. The house is situated at the foot of a picturesque hill, with a large compound and swimming pool. He has a 'caravan', complete with radio, television and all. We listened to some fine hymns and devotional songs after dinner at Dr. Roger Hinkins' and moved on to Ojai. Roger had been to Puttaparthi to see Baba. Baba materialised a ring for him.

It was late in the evening when we reached Ojai. The Ojai *bhajan* group, some fifty or sixty people, were waiting there patiently for our arrival. *Bhajan* began after we had rested a little, followed by my talk. Lawyer Silver has an old mother who is also full of devotion for Baba. She suffers from rheumatic pain. Most of the

274

bhajan groups squatted on the floor-carpet wherever I went. They did so here too. But the old lady sat in a chair because she could not bend her knees. It happened that, in the course of my talk, I narrated what happened in March 1974. Baba had taken on himself the desperation of a devotee and both his legs were paralysed. He had to crawl to the bathroom with a pair of wooden legs, as it were. On the third day of the attack, he said he was fed up with lying down in bed. He asked for a glass of water, sprinkled a little water on each one of the legs, got out of bed and walked freely about the room. He did not do this earlier because he should suffer like his own devotees.

Something strange happened as I narrated this incident. The old Mrs. Silver had, without her own knowledge, slid down from her chair and she was sitting on the carpet, folding her legs like the others! After the meeting was over, she was profuse in her expression of gratitude to Baba for this miracle, for this was nothing short of a miracle. In fact, Robert Silver said that she had not been able to bend her knees till now, for the last fifteen years!

The next morning, we moved on to the World Institute of Avasthology, of which Dr. Benito Reyes, a native of the Philippines and sometime President of the University of Manila, is President. He was guided by the voice of his Masters to come to Ojai and start this Institute. It has been planned to develop the Institute into a World College in 1975 and into a World University in 1976. *Avastha* is a Sanskrit word meaning a stage in spiritual awareness. Dr. Reyes has coined the word *Avasthology* to mean the science of consciousness. Dr. Reyes has written some interesting books in English on the spiritual life and he is also a poet. Mrs. Reyes shares all his interests and she is his spiritual comrade.

Lawyer Silver, who is one of the members of the organizing committee of this Institute, had taken the Reyeses to Indra Devi's Asram in Tecatee, Mexico. A Baba film was being shown there. At one point, Dr. Reyes saw in the picture, not Baba, but Christ. Mrs. Reyes also did so independently but at the same moment. And a voice said to Dr. Reyes that he should be able to see the Divine in another form too.

The Reyeses then came over to India and had Baba's *darshan* and interview along with Dr. John Roger Hinkins and Mr. Silver. It happened that Baba was going to Anantapur and the party was asked to follow him in another car. On the way, Dr. Reyes desired that he should have a ring from Baba. At that moment, Baba's car stopped and he sent for Dr. Reyes and materialised a Krishna ring for him. When Dr. Reyes said that he would have preferred to have the Baba image on the ring, Baba quipped: "What's the difference?" Baba further told him that, if he wanted anything, he did not have to express it orally or in writing. All that he had to do was to think about it. The thing would then be immediately given.

A few days before I went to the Institute, on a Sunday, Dr. Reyes had the thought: Why should not *vibhuti* appear in our residence as it has done in so many other places? How nice would it be if it did! The Reyeses then went out for a morning walk. By the time they returned, the fire-place, the floor of the sitting room, were all full of *vibhuti*. Persons from far and near came to see this phenomenon which was unprecedented in Ojai. The owner of the house was greatly concerned and sent for fire-experts to see whether the house had caught fire at any point. We had a lovely lunch in this house, prepared by Mrs. Reyes with the help of one or two students.

At the Institute, the morning was well spent. There were some fifty teacher-trainees anxious to learn all about the art and science of spiritual education and quite a few other 'auditors' had also dropped in. Dr. Reyes had just entered the class and I also sat in there for a while. I then spoke of the gradations of the human personality and Baba,—the psychicised man, the spiritual man and the God-man. I thought the talk was very well received. It was a pleasure to meet the Babbs and other selfless workers at the Institute. Mr. Babb told me that it was a joy to breathe the clear air of Ojai and bask in its bright sunshine. Nothing would take him and Mrs. Babb back to the smog of Los Angeles.

We had another *bhajan* meeting at lawyer Silver's house in the afternoon. I took leave of the four pretty little Silvers, the old mother and the Silvers after dinner. Mr. Eric Petersen, a government official and a Sai devotee from Santa Barbara, some forty miles away, drove me to that city. As the car moved up a hilly track, Santa Barbara was spread out like a carpet before us,—a real festival of lights. Mr. Petersen's family was there in the car along with Miss Chandler, the daughter's friend. Miss Chandler had an inquiring mind and she was asking me interesting questions on Time, Space and such other entities. This was the curious thing I noticed in the States at various meetings which I addressed: the alertness of youngsters and their desire to know. This is a hopeful sign of the times.

Mrs. Helen Vreeland, with her team of devoted youngsters, was there to receive me. The Santa Barbara

Sathya Sai Centre is housed in her residence. She is such an ardent Sai devotee.

Next morning, after breakfast, John, Susan and Mrs. Vreeland took me round to see three halls one of which could be tentatively regarded as the venue for a grand Sai meeting at the time of Bhagavan's visit to the States and to Santa Barbara. Mrs. Vreeland had spotted out possible venues of various dimensions and it was a pleasure to feel her earnestness in the matter and to listen to her comments. The matter could, of course, be clinched only when Baba's visit to the States was fixed. We also visited the Museum and some interesting buildings in the city.

The *bhajan* group met in the afternoon. Some sixty people were there, including Sai devotees well known to many, like Miss Muriel Engel, University of Santa Barbara and others.

A remarkable feature of this group meeting was that Sai *bhajans* were sung so beautifully. Mrs. Denise Riversole sang them with great feeling and made me feel that I was really back in India, listening to *bhajans* in Prashanti Nilayam. She also recited a *bhajan* composed by her in English:

I love Thee, Sathya Sai,
I love Thy blessed face.
I love Thee, Sathya Sai,
I live upon Thy grace.
I love Thee, Sathya Sai, in flaming bliss, I sigh;
My heart in longing cries, I love Thee, Sathya Sai.
I love Thee, Sathya Sai,
Thy truth I live to know.
I love Thee, Sathya Sai,
I need Thy light to grow.

In cycles calm or stern, I know just where to turn;
Thy home is in my heart, I love Thee, Sathya Sai.
This world is just a stage,
A play within Thy mind.
I but an actor am,
Within Thy play divine.
I act my part in Grace, my gaze upon Thy face;
To Thy feet, let me race, I love Thee, Sathya Sai.
I love Thee, Sathya Sai.
I love Thee, Holy Lord!

'Petrouchka' sang the following hymn so feelingly and
beautifully that I was moved to request her to write it
down for me:

We are one in the Spirit.
We are one in the Lord.
We are one in the Spirit.
We are one in the Lord.
And we pray that our unity
Will one day be restored
and we'll know we are brothers
By our love—by our love
Yes, we'll know that we are brothers
By our love.
We shall walk with each other
We shall walk hand in hand
We shall walk with each other
We shall walk hand in hand
and together we'll spread the word
that God is in our land
and we'll know we're His children by our love
By our love
Yes, we'll know that we're His children by our love.

Kent, one of the youngsters in Mrs. Vreeland's team of volunteers, had collected a few children for a Bal Vikas class. This was the only Bal Vikas class that I saw in the States. I wished him every fulfilment in his endeavour and I had a lively chat with him. I appreciated deeply the earnestness and enthusiasm of these young people gathered around Mrs. Vreeland.

The next morning we were off among the mountains. This was a gorgeous experience, for, near Santa Barbara, men meet the mountains as well as the sea.

I addressed a second meeting of the group in the afternoon. Many more persons had come. The hall was full and the audience overflowed into the other rooms. I loved to speak to that group.

(3)

It was with a heavy heart that I took leave of Mrs. Vreeland and her group the next morning. They were such dedicated workers and so full of devotion. Mr. Eric Petersen drove me to Los Angeles, to the hotel where Mr. Eugene Roy Davies, editor of *Truth* and a famous American teacher of yoga, was staying in the course of his lecture-tour. Mrs. Elsie Cowan, Mr. Crystal, a distinguished lawyer in Los Angeles, the Alexanders and a few other friends were also there. Eugene Roy Davies had been to India to see Baba. He has published a slim volume of selections from Baba's speeches and writings. He had some useful suggestions to make regarding the proposed visit of Baba to the States.

We all went together after lunch to see a film on Baba to be shown in one of the studios in Hollywood. It was a kind of selection and amalgamation made out of the many shots taken by Richard Bock while in India. There was a select audience invited to see the film and Mr.

Bock's friend, who had planned the picture, was happy to have me there. The telescoping of the various shots was good. But the preface, tagged on to the film, consisting of tourist attractions like beautiful buildings and jugglers, struck one as irrelevant and likely to be mis-understood.

We moved on to Tustin after the picture and here I was, in the care of Mrs. Elsie Cowan, treated to genuinely considerate and generous hospitality, breathing an atmosphere of great kindness and love. The few days that I passed here flitted by like minutes. There were friends all around me, Mrs. Cowan herself who, unobtrusively, took every care of me, including the dietetic chocolates that I should eat, members of her family, the Frizzells, the Reeveses, the Mileses, Dr. and Mrs. Hislop (the former with his warm and spiritual companionship and the latter giving me a foretaste of the curries which she was going to cook for Baba when he would visit America), Mr. Skibbler with his forthright and transparent affection and several others whose contact I deeply cherish. We sat around after breakfast and talked about Baba. In the evenings particularly, we all had dinner together and sat talking. Some one, diplomatically, raised one point or the other about Baba and the spiritual life and this was enough to get me going, for an hour or two, into a spontaneous flight of philosophy, poetry and mysticism. All that I had read and brooded over for years and tested in my own crucible of experience, found expression in those glowing and expanding moments. My experiences with Baba flavoured the entire exposition. I forgot myself in my happiness and I believe I carried all these friends with me too. The month I spent in America this time I regard as a memorable one in my life, for I was dipped in one surging river of love after another, every two or three days. Mrs. Elsie Cowan has said that, if ever there was heaven on earth at any time, it was there during that month. During the other days of the month, though not exactly in heaven, I was hovering somewhere near heavenly regions. But the days I spent in Tustin, first immediately after my arrival, second, arriving after the visit to Santa Barbara and then during the days of the conference, were nothing short of heaven itself.

Mrs. Frances Reeves, holding the balance even between reason and emotion and finding at last, an intuitive opening to the Divine; Rita Reeves, her daughter, wanting to dedicate her life to the service of Baba and realising that research on "New Pathways in Indian and American Education" could be the first step in that direction; Joe Frizzell, moved to tears of gratitude by the sacred, ruby-studded image of Krishna that \he received from a holy man in Los Angeles from Calcutta; the Alexanders (Vince and Marge) from Florida, who attended all the meetings I addressed from New York to Los Angeles, except Hawaii, and who have sold away all their property and given up their jobs in order to replan their lives and dedicate them to Bhagavan and to doing his work; and Mr. Skibbler whose transparent sincerity and affection were deeply moving: all these and other friends were there in these after-dinner gatherings. The mansion of Mrs. Cowan turned out to be the Peacockian Abbey, where all could assemble care-free and speak heart-to-heart, but without the string or malice or anti-romanticism of T.L. Peacock. No words are adequate to convey what we all felt about it.

Mr. Robert Dane of the East-West Cultural Centre and Mr. Mario Valez came to Tustin to take me to Dr. Judith Tyburg's great institution. I spoke there in 1958.

Intelligence men and clergymen harassed her then. But this was her life's mission and the institution grew. Today, Universities in U.S.A. vie with each other in inviting her to lecture under their auspices. The Centre has developed into a prosperous institution. Dr. Tyburg had come to India in 1967 and I had taken her to Prashanti Nilayam for Baba's *darshan* at her request.

This is a strong Sri Aurobindo Centre and I spoke here on Sri Aurobindo and Baba and explained how I myself had been moved to equate the two in my life. Dr. Tyburg was lying in bed with a fractured leg. The wound had healed, but she was advised to rest. Nevertheless, she could not resist the temptation to pull herself to the height of the window near her as we drove in, to have a look at me.

Dr. Tyburg has compiled a very fine glossary of metaphysical Sanskrit terms. I have written a foreword to this volume. It is useful, not only to American readers but to many Indians as well.

Dick and Janet Bock picked me up from the Centre and I was taken to the Crystals to be their guest for the next two days. Mr. Crystal, as has been said before, is a distinguished lawyer and Mrs. Crystal, English by origin, is a charming lady. The English I speak has, naturally, its roots in British English and this was a matter of joy to her because it reminded her of her early years in the United Kingdom. They lived on the twelfth floor of a magnificent mansion in Los Angeles and one could have a lovely view of the city from that height. I was moved to write the following lines:

When the city, smeared with smog,
Is clear and sun-smitten at noon,

283

Clumps of white-roofed red-tiled houses
Peep amid clustering trees.
Down-town Century city skyscrapers
Scratch their signatures in the sky.
Cars in ferment on the Free Way
Ape galectic speed
As Beverley and Hollywood hills
Look on amusedly.
And the sea conspires with the horizon
And, sphinx-like, keeps her secret.

We had a fine dinner party here, at which we met quite a few Sai devotees.

Dick and Janet Bock are missioned spirits. They have organised a pretty Sai Baba Centre in rented premises. A number of Sai devotees meet here every week for *bhajans* and Mrs. Janet Bock herself leads them with the greatest earnestness and devotion. They prepare tapes of Baba's discourses and *bhajans* and of talks on Baba. What is more, Mr. Richard Bock has prepared a few films on Baba,—*The Advent of the Avatar, My Life Is My Message* and so on, which capture effectively the spiritual atmosphere which Baba radiates around him wherever he goes. It is difficult to film a spiritual leader and much more difficult to film his spirituality. But these films do it.

The Bocks took me to the Penns in Santa Monica the next day for lunch and *bhajans* in the afternoon. On the way, we stopped at the Self-Realization Fellowship Lake Shrine where the mortal remains of Paramahamsa Yogananda have been laid to rest. It is a beautiful spot.

Mr. Charles Penn, Mrs. Faith Penn and her mother, Mrs. Taylor, are devotees of long standing and it was a pleasure to have lunch with them and to meet their meditation group in the afternoon. Bob Reimer, an old friend, was also here. Mr. Penn is an air pilot like Mr. Reimer. Readers of Sai literature know Mr. Penn as a frequent contributor to *Sanatana Sarathi.*

There were a number of lively questions asked by the members of this group and I was sorry to be hurrying away. But we had to be in time for my speech and film-show at the Religious Centre of the University of California, Los Angeles. There were some four hundred people assembled in this hall, eager to see the Sai film and listen to me. There were a number of youngsters willing to learn and anxious to know about Baba. To talk to them was a rewarding experience.

Professor Samuel Sandweiss took me to San Diego in his car after I spent two more days in Tustin. Professor Sandweiss is a practising psychiatrist and he teaches psychiatry to students in San Diego University. He came to see Baba with Indra Devi to find out whether all that was spoken about Baba was true. He and Mrs. Charon Sandweiss have grown into ardent Sai devotees and their four pretty daughters, little girls, are also in tune with Baba. Professor Sandweiss is now busy with a book on Baba, spelling out the challenge that Baba is to psychiatry and to our notions about life generally. The Sandweisses lavished their generous hospitality on me and it was a real joy to stay with them.

I stopped for some hours on the way at Santa Bernardo, a small village for retired people, to see Dr. and Mrs. Wesley La Violette. He was president of a college of music and author of *The Crown of Wisdom* and other books. He had also been to India. But he has not seen Baba. Dr. Sandweiss took me home in the evening and we had a hearty meal together.

Mr. Popoff drove me the next morning to Dr. Jack

Hislop's in Mexico. Mr. Popoff is an American gentleman of Russian origin and an ardent devotee of Baba.
He has his business in San Diego. We crossed the
border and then drove amid picturesque Mexican
scenery. Mountains towered on one side and grew larger
and larger and on the other side was the sea. The road
picks up in between and it was a lovely drive.

No one is more delighted than Mr. Popoff when he
hears a good speech about Baba. This I noticed at
several meetings. As Indra Devi says, he is an uncut
diamond and he has a heart of gold. But his English is
not quite what it should be. His Mexican is equally
uncertain. As we drove down the Mexican road after
crossing the border, there were a number of toll-stations
that we had to pass. Mr. Popoff had paid toll at the
first station and all that he had to do thereafter was to
show the receipt at the others. But he either forgot to
take the receipt or wanted to be kind to the toll-
officers. We used to see little cottages around us, a
poverty-stricken scene like in India. Mr. Popoff told me
that the Mexicans were a starving people. If they got
some money, they drank it all and danced and then
starved again. The Mexican officers, he said, had large
families and their salaries were not adequate to meet
their expenditure. Mr. Popoff said that it was generally
recognised that some money should be paid to the
officers. As he paid a dollar to each of the officers at the
toll-stations, Mr. Popoff said: "Gratis, gratis" and the officer smiled back courteously at him. I was wondering. On
my return journey to San Diego, I travelled with Indra
Devi and I heard her saying to the Mexican officer who
let us cross the border: "Gracias, gracias." It meant:
"Thank you." I now understood what Mr. Popoff had
been wanting to say. Instead, he was saying "Gratis,

gratis." and paying a dollar every time.

It was noon by the time Mr. Popoff dropped me at Dr. Hislop's house and took leave of us. Dr. Hislop is close to Baba and the notes he has maintained of his talks with Baba get published in *Sanatana Sarathi*. A widely travelled man, he practised meditation under a Buddhist monk in Ceylon and came to Baba when he was ripe for the contact. He was a commerce teacher and now he is in business. The house he has built on top of a mountain peak overlooking the sea is a marvel to behold. Mrs. Hislop planned it all and it has been dedicated to Baba and a deed passed in his name. The house cost them something less than a lakh of rupees. But the marble flooring inside the house and the combination of Hindu and Muslim styles· of architecture introduced to emphasize the unity of religions for which Baba stands, is truly impressive. At the foot of the mountain, on which this house stands, is the sea. A poet has said that great things happen when men and mountains meet. Greater things can be expected to happen when the sea also is present at such meetings.

I had a perfect time in this house of the Faithful. Mrs. Hislop gave me exquisite Indian food and I had the urbane and friendly company of Dr. Hislop throughout the day. To walk around the house was to feel the breath of the mountain air and the sea and at night, when the stars came out, a golden mystery joined the dark mysteries that surrounded us. I was the first guest to spend a night in that lovely house in which a suite of the most excellent rooms with gorgeous furniture has been reserved for Baba's stay when he comes to bless that house.

The Hislops took me the next morning after breakfast to Indra Devi's *asram* at Tecatee, some forty miles away. Indra Devi, popularly known among Americans as Mataji, has been a famous teacher of yoga, in Europe and America, for many years. She is in her seventies now, but young rather than old. She is a lady of Russian origin, domiciled in America. But she loves India as her own homeland. She fled from the Russian Revolution along with her parents as a girl. She studied yoga in India under capable masters. In 1966 she came to Baba and she has been an ardent devotee ever since. She organizes seminars on yoga in the U.S.A., Canada and other countries and she holds them every three months in her own *asram*.

Her *asram* was a spacious ranch before it changed hands. It is situated at the foot of a rocky mountain slope and a beautiful vineyard grows on one of its sides. There are lovely pomegranate trees, with their fruit breaking into shining cracks of red. The grapes are protected from bees by being covered with old socks. There is a hostel for about thirty seminarians on the premises and the basement of the asram is reserved for seminars, with a hall and a worship room in which Baba's photograph is kept, with incense-sticks, *arati* and all. Exactly on the other side of this Mexican *asram* is the fence that divides the U.S.A. from Mexico. Even a baby can leap over this fence. The upper slope of the mountain is American. The base is Mexican.

Dr. Knauer, Indra Devi's husband, is a famous consulting physician. By the time we reached the Asram, quite a few persons had assembled there. The Sandweisses, the Bocks who brought with them from Los Angeles Mira Bharani, the talented daughter of Shri C.L. Bharani of New Delhi, Mrs. Babb, wife of the seminarian who happened to walk alone into the basement worship room where he saw an Indian in a long robe and with a shock of hair, sitting along with him and who realised later that there was no Indian on the seminar and that the person he saw sitting was the same as Baba seen in the photograph; and some others. It was a fine group,—neither the self-impeaching group that assembled in Peacockian Abbey nor the self-effacingly devotional group that met in Mrs. Cowan's Tustin mansion but a lively, self-conscious group that had its convictions as well as questions, devotion as well as intellectual curiosity. In any case, the more vocal members of the group answered this description. Dr. Knauer was himself the foremost among these, ready to give a knock-out blow and to take one if it could be given.

We had a stroll through the vineyard along the border-line in the afternoon, when Indra Devi took me right on to the fence, leaping over rocks with the agility of a girl. Her yogic discipline has helped her to maintain good health and vigour. In the evening, Mr. Bock showed us a Baba film and I gave a talk. This was in the seminar hall. Some local dignitaries from Tecatee were also present at the function. One of them spoke in Spanish at the end, thanked me for telling them about Baba and wanted me to convey an invitation from the Mexican people to Baba to visit Mexico. I replied suitably. The next day, after lunch, I left with Indra Devi and her adopted daughter for San Diego. I have had very pleasant memories of this visit. I could see the setting in which Indra Devi works and realise how, through her seminars, she has trained a number of men and women in different parts of the country in yoga and inspired them with her love of Baba. I was now back in San Diego.

It was about 12.45 A.M. on the morning of 2nd October that I dreamed a dream. A few acquaintances, possibly admirers, had gathered together to listen to my poems. I had agreed to recite them. But, somehow, it took me an unconscionably long time to find them. When I did find them, my eye-balls seemed to lose their sight so that I could not read them. Then I thought of reciting poems that I knew by heart but could not at all remember even a single line or half-line. When this failed, I desired to compose poems extempore and recite them, as I had done so often among friends. But I realised that this too was impossible.

Bitterly disappointed, I did not know what to do. Then I learnt to my horror that, all the time, Baba had been waiting patiently to recite some songs after I had finished doing so. Actually, I was told that he was to have begun the recitation. But when he learnt that I had volunteered to recite, he did not desire to come in my way. He was quietly sitting there unobserved in a corner, waiting for me to finish.

I had been unable to 'deliver the goods'. What was more, I had made him wait endlessly and fruitlessly for me to finish, when I had not even begun. I felt guilty and I was deeply ashamed. I fell at his feet, praying to him to forgive me. He smiled gently towards me, lifted me and embraced me and led me towards the holy of holies. The message of all this during the first hour of 2nd October, '74 was that I should realise my identity with him if I wished to succeed supremely in my task. To stand on my own was to court disaster.

Sitting there on that chair, Baba was himself. But he had the features of Bendre, the seer-poet of Karnataka and of Datto Pant Balekundri, my father's preceptor and a gifted *bhajan* composer and singer.

I was, throughout the visit, a transmitter, a news-bringer, a mouth-piece of Baba, but not a merely mechanical contrivance. Baba's message had sunk into my soul.

It was in my own soul's light that I transmitted the message.

San Diego is a beautiful city. Professor Sandweiss's house is right on the sea-shore and at the foot of a hillock. It was fun climbing that hill with him.

A public meeting had been organized that evening and there were some five hundred people present to see the film and to listen to me on Baba. It was a very successful meeting and there were many wanting to know how to go to Prashanti Nilayam, attend the summer course and so on. The effort of selfless workers like Sandweiss, Popoff and others had been well rewarded.

The local newspaper sent a representative to interview me the next morning. This was a Philippine gentleman and we had an interesting discussion. He made the point that Love is the common gospel of so many schools. How is there anything distinctive about this Sai philosophy? Surely, the one distinctive feature is that Baba teaches us how to love selflessly. It is not a philosophy of information but transformation.

In the evening was the Sandweiss *bhajan* meeting. A number of people turned up. The *bhajans* were wonderful. I still remember the peace and serenity that soaked me that night as I spoke. The atmosphere had been charged with Baba's presence.

Dr. Sandweiss took me the next morning to Tustin and I started the day there with an interview by *The Movement*. The leaders of all the American *bhajan* groups had arrived here by that time and a business meeting began with Mr. Alexander in the chair. Mr. Terry Payne had come from Hawaii. Mrs. Cowan and Indra Devi, Mr. Robert Silver and Mr. Popoff, Mrs. Helen Vreeland and Professor Robinson,—all were there discussing, participating. I spoke at the beginning, conveying my impressions and appraisal of possibilities. It was agreed that the Sai Baba Book Centre, of which Mrs. Cowan is the chief and the SAI Foundation, of which Indra Devi is president, should continue to function in their own way. In addition, there should be formed the Sathya Sai Society of the Americas and Canada, with representatives from all the *bhajan* groups. There should also be a Sathya Sai Committee managing such property as may be donated to the cause all over the States. Panels were proposed for both these bodies.

The final meeting came off in the Church of Religious Science, Laguna Beach, California. Devotees from all the bhajan groups in America had assembled here on 6th October 1974. The Rev. Henry Gerard, who was clergyman, was also present here with Mrs. Gerard and about four hundred people attended. Dr. Hislop introduced me to the audience after Mrs. Gerard had sung a beautiful hymn. The Rev. Henry Gerard then spoke eloquently. He referred to the visions he had seen and the voices he had heard and then said that in the coming of Baba we had the second advent of the Christ. He referred to my role as that of the forerunner, John the Baptist.

I explained, when I spoke, that I was a runner carrying Baba's message rather than a forerunner announcing his coming. I said that I had brought for them the love and blessings of Baba, like the Holy Grail that Sir Galahad saw, the Grail that contains the blood of Christ. It is his own life-blood that Baba offers to us as love. I spoke for more than an hour. There were several questions at the end and I had a lively time answering them. There was a big ovation as I sat down. Leave-taking was a touching and enormous task. Nothing could be more genuine than the love that glistened in the eyes of these fellow-devotees and lived in the words that they uttered with such feeling.

As we went home to Tustin, Mrs. Cowan had ordered to be prepared for us a regular banquet by way of farewell. Most of the delegates were there. At an informal gathering after dinner, I was presented with a poem composed by Mrs. Karen Shultz:

Envoy of the Lord
October 1974

How would Sai fare on American land?
Were westerners ready to work in God's plan?
Replies to such queries Sai sent one to find—
A dear, trusted servant left India behind.
The Messenger journeyed and found many jewels—
Satsangs of bhaktas: Sai culture schools!
Then gently, he strung them, gem upon gem,
Into one splendid gift to lay at the Lord's Hem.
Thank you, Dr. Gokak, for bringing us Sai,
And the wisdom of your own soul...

(4)

I left for Chicago the next morning. Dr. Hislop, Mrs. Hislop and Mrs. Cowan were in the car with me. Dr. Hislop drove the car. Though we left early, there was such a traffic-jam on the way that, in spite of all that Dr. Hislop could do to reach early, I missed the plane by three minutes! It was as well that I missed it, for Mr. Don Marginson rushed up to the airport to give me a letter to Baba and he would have missed me had I not missed the plane. He arrived hardly within a minute or two of my missing the plane. We all had breakfast together and I went by the next plane which left half an hour later.

I was received at Chicago airport by Mrs. Robinson. Professor Robinson arrived soon after we reached home. Devotees from Illinois and other places also came. We all had dinner together and then proceeded to Yoga Retreat Hall at 57E Walton Place. A good number of devotees had assembled there. There were also present some friends from India and it was a fine group to talk to. There were interesting questions asked at the end. Chicago was cold, for winter was making itself felt, with a nip in the air and the turning of the leaves. But nothing could be warmer and more full of affection than the farewell that the Robinsons gave me at the airport. Even the lady officer, who stood at the entrance to the plane and who knew nothing of the bond that held us together, smiled warmly in approval of this international gesture of goodwill. I was received at Washington airport by Dr. Pani. I spent a few hours with the Panis, discussing their plans of going to India to see Baba and I was put back at the airport on a BOAC plane bound for London in the evening by Dr. Pani. I reached London the next morning.

A strange incident relating to my bunch of keys, I shall narrate here and leave it to the reader to account for it as he likes. As we reached London, I took out my coat which I had folded and kept in the space above the seat. I felt for the key-bunch in my coat pocket and found that it was missing. I searched for it in the locker, the toilette room, the space beneath my seat and between the seats. I found it nowhere. I was desperate and I reported the matter to the officer on the plane. He also searched for it, but in vain. I thought that the bunch might have dropped down on my seat in Dr. Pani's car when I got out of it. In the meanwhile, as everybody had

294

to get off the plane, I was advised to contact the BOAC counter at the airport. I had to push the small handcart on which I had dumped my luggage, to which I had no key. How was I going to pass through the Customs? I explained to the Customs officer that I had lost the keys. He said something in a high tone which I could not understand. So I went ahead and the officer seemed to have been glad to get rid of me. I went to the BOAC counter and I was none the wiser for it. As I had no change, I bought a few chocolates and I wanted to telephone to Shri S. Sitaram, President of the Sathya Sai Organization, who was to receive me. I had lost an hour in all these movements and he might have returned home, thinking that I hadn't come. I did not have his telephone number. So I rang up Shri Lakshmipathi instead. He received the message and promised to inform Shri Sitaram. I then turned to the Information Counter. I wanted to request them to announce that I was there, waiting for Shri Sitaram. I was visibly shaken and I wondered how Baba, who had assured me that he would be with me from moment to moment, had deserted me so cruelly.

It seemed as though Baba was playing a prank with me. For, the very moment I walked up to the Information Counter, Shri Sitaram also came there and we met each other. He was frantically searching for me all the time and he had come over for a similar announcement. As we proceeded towards his home in Pinner, Middlesex in his car, I spoke to him about my misadventure with the key-bunch. He took out his own bunch of keys after going home and we could open one of the two bags I carried. The big one had been opened and I took it upstairs in order to change my clothes. Shri Sitaram brought the smaller one, which had still remained locked and oh, wonder of wonders, he held forth his hand to give me my bunch of keys! I was stunned. I asked him where he had found it. He said that it was lying on the floor on the spot on which my big bag had stood.

There is only one possible explanation to this. This bag, made of some plastic material, has its two zip ends which can be locked together. The lock can then be covered by a big flap of the same material which can be fastened on the top side by a brass hook. Did it happen that, as I locked the bag, the bunch fell inside the flap unnoticed and remained there as I fastened the flap to the topside hook, coming down on Mr. Sitaram's floor as I loosened the flap? This seems unlikely. I carried the bag to the ticket counter at Washington airport. It was obviously dumped along with other luggage in the luggage room on the BOAC plane. Luggage may not have been handled roughly to the extent to which it is on Indian planes. Nevertheless, there must have been some moving about which might have resulted in the bunch sliding down the flap. If so, the bunch would be lost to me, for it would lie on the floor of the luggage room in the plane, recoverable later if the matter was pursued and if the Inspectors on the plane found the bunch. It would be a miracle even if the key-bunch were to be held in its place by the flap, coming down on the floor in Shri Sitaram's house after the flap had been loosened. This *might* have happened. If this is regarded as outside the sphere of practical realities there is no other explanation possible. I don't think I forgot to put the bunch into my pocket after locking the bag. I must also confess that I saw nothing sliding down as I opened the flap of the bag in order to try the keys from Shri Sitaram's bunch on the lock.

I have narrated this trifling incident in all its detail in order to invite the reader to solve it as he would a puzzle. My bunch consists of two small keys in a ring, with a little crystal-like bar containing four little steel pieces for boring holes, cutting and such other mini jobs.

The Sitarams were in Burma for a number of years. After leaving Burma, they bought a house in Pinner and settled down in England. Shri Sitaram is an auditor. He and his associates have done significant work by way of spreading the Sai movement in England.

Arrangements had been made for my talk in a hall near-by, which could hold some three hundred people. But we found in the evening that some four hundred people were jam-packed in that hall. Devotees from other centres, like those in Bradford and Birmingham, had come in special buses to attend the meeting. *Bhajans* were sung by Shri Sitaram and others and also by some youngsters who had come from the other centres. I spoke on Baba and on the organization of Sathya Sai centres. There was a great deal of enthusiasm. A snack was served.

The idea was mooted that there should be a Sathya Sai Samiti for all U.K. like the one proposed to be organized for all U.S.A.

Vibhuti came out from a Gujarathi lady's palm at this meeting. I had heard about this before. It is, no doubt, a remarkable happening. But people go into hysteria over such things. It is better to leave the persons chosen for such happenings alone, for, otherwise, their vanity may be aroused.

Indians who live abroad suffer naturally from nostalgia, particularly when their sense of security is not satisfied. Baba's grace becomes all the more precious in their eyes for this reason.

There were genuine overtures from fellow-devotees. A lady walked up to me and said: "You said your daughter's name is Sarala. My name is also Sarala. Please consider me as your daughter and convey my *pranams* to Baba!" I was deeply moved and I assured the lady that this would be done.

Unlike as in the States, there are very few native devotees in the U.K. Most of them are Indians. But a few Britishers were present in the hall and I telephoned Mr. Grossman who, Mr. Sitaram told me, was writing a book on Baba and spoke to him the next morning. Shri Mukund has been giving musical concerts in Great Britain and Europe and organizing Sai centres. He and Mr. Grossman may succeed in spreading Baba's message in the U.K.

There were quite a few visitors the next morning. Shri C.L. Bharani and his brother took me out for a little 'wool-gathering',—buying in London shops woollen sweaters, cardigans and pullovers for which Great Britain is so famous. In the evening, we proceeded to Bharatiya Vidya Bhavan where I had to give a talk.

Shri M. Krishna Murty, who is the first registrar of this London branch of the Bhavan family, is an ardent Sathya Sai devotee. I have also known him as a Kannada litterateur. The Murtys were very happy that I was able to go there. A good audience had gathered, including some old friends. There were some Britishers too. Mr. King was there, the moving spirit behind the New and Free Country Project. There was an Australian gentleman who had a few minutes with me, discussing a miniature photograph of Baba on which white rays had started darting from Baba's head. He had a desire to come to Prashanti Nilayam and see Baba.

We had the usual session of a talk and some interesting questions and answers. *Arati* was performed at the end.

Shri M. Krishna Murty told us the next morning how, when he prayed on the morning of his birthday anniversary, *vibhuti* had materialised on his diary page. We had

298

a long chat and a nice Indian lunch which Mrs. Sitaram had taken great care to prepare. Since the Sitarams were also leaving for India the same day by the same plane, we left for the airport together. The BOAC engineers announced a lightning strike even as we stepped into the airport. Negotiations were afoot for seven hours and we did not know what was going to happen. The crowd of passengers gave a joyous shout when it was finally announced that our plane would take off. We were soon up in the air, on the airway to India.

This travelogue with a purpose has now come to an end. Looking back on the month that is over, I cannot help feeling that it was a month which brought me great experiences. Baba's impact had been felt so widely in spite of the fact that he has not stepped as yet on British or American soil. Change itself is an illusion and Time is the magic prince of illusions. We are, for ever, what we are in the pristine depths of our being. No change can ever enter there, for eternity is law. Nevertheless, it happens once in a while that the moon, who waxes and wanes, is lit up with the full splendour of the sun of eternity. Consequently a *moon-th* or *month* can enable us to hold eternity in an hour. This was what happened to me in September-October 1974.

I am happy that I was enabled to lay at the lotus feet of Bhagavan—*patram*, a leaf, the personal warmth and love which I conveyed to his devotees in the New World; *pushpam*, the flower of the exposition of his philosophy of love; *phalam*,—the fruit, the National Society and Committee which, it was agreed, should be established; and *toyam*, the sprinkling of the holy water of love all over the States. He allotted this work to me and I have offered it at his feet in a spirit of dedication.

299

APPENDIX

LANDMARKS IN THE LIFE OF BHAGAVAN BABA

SATHYANARAYANA, now known as Bhagavan Sri
Sathya Sai Baba, was born in a Raju family on 23rd
November 1926 in a village called Puttaparthi, Andhra
Pradesh, South India. That day was a Monday of the
Holy Month of Karthika. The ascendant star was Ardra
and the year was Akshaya, the "Never-declining, the
Ever-full". Pedda Venkappa Raju was his father and
Eswaramma his mother.

Of the many incidents that took place at the time of
his birth, which proved amply the advent of the Avathar,
two are worth recording.

1. In the house there were two instruments, *thambura*
and *maddala*. The household was awakened at midnight
and sometime early in the morning by the *thambura*
twanging melodiously and rhythmically and the *maddala*
softly beating, as though they were in expert hands.

2. A cobra was found under the bed in the lying-in
room in which the child was placed.

The child started growing and the jasmine bud was
slowly blossoming filling the air with fragrance. Sathya
was full of love towards animals which made his neighbours call him "Brahmajnani", a "Realised Soul". He
was the idol of his family and became the pet of the
entire village of Puttaparthi.

He had his early education at Puttaparthi and Bukkapatnam. He accompanied his brother Seshama Raju, a Telugu teacher, to Kamalapur and Uravakonda to have High School education. But generally he was listless in the class, engaged most of the time in what he later described as composing chants and copying them for distribution among his class-mates, for was he not their Guru? When he was ten years of age he formed in Puttaparthi a Pandhari Bhajan group, for the presentation of songs of love and devotion to God.

On 8th March 1940 at about 7 o'clock in the evening, a "big black scorpion" stung Sathya. He shrieked. Although no scorpion or snake was discovered, he fell as though unconscious and became stiff. Was it the first instance of his leaving the body for the rescue of his devotees?

Sathya revived in a day or two. He then began to behave in an extraordinary manner. This was sometimes explained as "a complete transformation of the personality —the occupation of Sathya's physical form by SAI BABA of Shirdi."

On 23rd May 1940 Sathyanarayana announced: "I AM SAI BABA." "I belong to Apasthamba Sutra, the School of Sage Apasthamba and am of the Spiritual Lineage of Bharadvaja."

It was on 20th October 1940 that he left his brother's house at Uravakonda, announcing "I am no longer your Sathya. I am Sai." "I don't belong to you, my devotees are calling me. I have my work, I cannot stay any longer." He moved out into the garden of Sri Anjaneyulu's bungalow where he sang his immortal song "Manasa Bhajare Gurucharanam..." (Meditate in thy mind on the Feet of the Guru).

He came to Puttaparthi and stayed in the house of Subbamma, the village accountant's wife.

He shifted to Old Mandir (Old Temple) built in 1944.

Prasanthi Nilayam—"Abode of Tranquillity"—the present abode of Bhagavan—was inaugurated on 23rd November 1950—on his 25th birthday.

Three festivals are celebrated every year at Puttaparthi since the very beginning of his manifestation.

1. Dasara.
2. Birthday of Bhagavan (23rd November).
3. Mahasivarathri.

Amongst innumerable miracles which have emanated from Bhagavan all these years, the following are worth recording.

During the latter part of the year 1953 Bhagavan brought back to life one V. Radhakrishna, a well-known citizen of Kuppam, whose body had started decomposing at Prasanthi Nilayam. A similar instance took place in the case of Mr. Cowan, an American, in the latter part of 1971 at Madras, who was pronounced dead by the doctors in the hospital there.

In 1957 he presided over the deliberations of the All India Divine Life Convention held at Venkatagiri.

He established a hospital on the hill behind Prasanthi Nilayam in October 1957.

Left on his North Indian tour on 14th July 1957 and visited places like Delhi, Rishikesh, Sivanandanagar, Mathura, Srinagar.

Inaugurated the Sanathana Sarathi, the monthly magazine, devoted to the moral and spiritual uplift of humanity through Sathya, Dharma, Santhi and Prema on 16th February 1958, the auspicious day of Mahasivarathri. It is now published in eleven languages—Telugu, English, Tamil, Malayalam, Kannada, Marathi, Gujarathi, Bengali, Hindi, Assamese and Nepali.

On 29th June 1959 Bhagavan planted the banyan tree

in the grove behind the Nilayam, placing under it a thick copper plate, materialised from the sands of the River Chitravathi, about 15″ x 10″ in size. It contained mystic markings and letters of many known and unknown alphabets.

On the 26th day of February 1961, while installing the marble image of the Previous Sai, the Shirdi Sai Baba, at the famous Nagasai Mandir at Coimbatore, Bhagavan said, "This day deserves to be inscribed in letters of gold, for this function is the beginning of the New Era, the Sathya Sai Era, when Sai will become Hrudaya-Sthayi, the Inner Motive Force of all. The only other instance of a similar kind, of an Avathar installing an idol of the Lord, is that of Rama installing the Linga at Rameswara. That was done as a preliminary to the destruction of the demons. I am doing this now as a preliminary to the other task of all Avathars, the establishment of Dharma in the World." An Epoch-making declaration indeed!

Visited the great Shrine of Visveswara, the Lord of the Universe, at Banaras on 2nd April 1961.

Proceeded to Badrinath on 7th June 1961 with devotees. Consecrated the Nethra Lingam (Eye Linga) which Sankaracharya had brought from Kailasa and installed it inside the Badri Shrine.

On the very first day of the Dasara festival held in 1961 Bhagavan declared: "Rama was the embodiment of Sathya and Dharma; Krishna of Santhi and Prema. Now, when skill is outstripping self-control, when Science laughs at Sadhana, when hate and fear have darkened the heart of man, I have come embodying all the four—Sathya, Dharma, Santhi and Prema."

Released the first volume of Sathyam Sivam Sundaram —the life of Bhagavan Sri Sathya Sai Baba written by N. Kasturi in English—on 23rd November 1961.

While hoisting the Flag of Prasanthi on the Nilayam on 23rd November 1962 Bhagavan referred to the Chinese attack and announced: "My Birthday festival will not be marred by any dispiriting news; you will get positive chearful news. Sanathana Dharma will suffer no harm." And, true to this declaration, the Chinese, who were rushing into this country like locusts, had started withdrawing since the midnight of 22nd-23rd, beyond the mountain ranges.

29th June 1963—Bhagavan took on himself one of the deadliest diseases—Tubercular Meningitis—from a devotee dear to him and suffered from it for eight days.

On Guru Pournima Day—6th July 1963—Bhagavan declared: "I am Siva-Sakthi born in the Gothra of Bharadvaja according to a boon won by that Sage from Siva and Sakthi. Sakthi herself was born in the gothra of that Sage as Sai Baba of Shirdi; Siva and Sakthi have incarnated as myself in his gothra now; Siva alone will incarnate as the third Sai in the same gothra in Mysore State." (Bhagavan has said on many an occasion that he would live in the present body for 96 years and that he would be born again as Prema Sai in Mandya District—Mysore State—the present Karnataka State.)

Bhagavan announced in 1964 the establishment of Prasanthi Vidvanmahasabha, an All India Academy of Vedic Scholars—who will strive to awaken humanity to the need to attain Prasanthi—Inner Harmony and Equipoise—which has its Nilayam—Abode—in the Sanathana Dharma, formulated in the ancient scriptures of India, at Rajahmundry on the sacred day of Ramanavami. (It was formally inaugurated during the Dasara festival in 1965.)

On 23rd November 1964, on his 39th birthday, Bhagavan announced himself as Srinatha and Lokanatha and Anaathanatha, the same who saved Gajendra, the boy Dhruva, the poor Kuchela and helpless Prahlada.

Visited Pandharapur Vittala temple on 13th June 1965; materialised Mangala suthra and placed it round the neck of the Goddess Rukumayi.

During the Dasara Festival in 1965, Veda Purusha Sapthaha Jnana Yajna was performed and it consisted of two sections; the Morning Sessions for seven days of Athi-Rudrahoma with all its complementary rites and the Evening Sessions of Jnana Yajna where distinguished exponents of the Vedas explained to the vast gathering, the meaning and significance of the scriptural rites.

Established Sathya Sai Veda-Sasthra Patasala, the Academy for Vedic and Sanskrit study, at the Nilayam on 23rd November 1965, on his 40th birthday. On that occasion Bhagavan said, he had four missions, 1. Veda-poshana, 2. Vidwatposhana, 3. Bhaktarakshana, 4. Dharmarakshana.

On 4th August 1966 Prasanthi Nilayam was separated from the Puttaparthi village and constituted into an administrative unit, named the Prasanthi Nilayam Township.

The first All India Conference of Bhagavan Sri Sathya Sai Seva Organisations was held in Madras in the divine presence on 20th April 1967.

The second part of Sathyam Sivam Sundaram in English, written by N. Kasturi, was released on 29th March 1968, the New Year Day.

Inaugurated Dharmakshetra, his abode when in Bombay, on 12th May 1968.

Bhagavan inaugurated the first World Conference (and second All India Conference) of Bhagavan Sri Sathya Sai Seva Organisations held in Bombay on 16th May 1968 at Bharatiya Vidya Bhavan Campus. On this occasion he declared: "This is the first time in the history of "this world that a World Conference of the devotees of an Avathar is being held, in the immediate physical presence and under the direct supervision and observation of the Avathar Himself."

Left for the first time the boundaries of India on 30th June 1968 to bless the devotees of the East African territories. Visited places like Nairobi, Kampala, etc.

Established Sri Sathya Sai Arts and Science College for Women at Anantapur on 22nd July 1968. It was at this hour that Bhagavan announced that he was planning a college or two in every State of India, all to be knit together later into a university as an instrument forged for his Task.

Founded the Sri Sathya Sai Arts and Science College at Brindavan, Whitefield on 9th June 1969.

Inaugurated the third All India Conference of Bhagavan Sri Sathya Sai Seva Organisations on 20th November 1969, at Prasanthi Nilayam.

Inaugurated the fourth All India Conference of Bhagavan Sri Sathya Sai Seva Organisations at Prasanthi Nilayam on 20th November 1970.

Inaugurated the fifth All India Conference of Bhagavan Sri Sathya Sai Seva Organisations on 22nd December 1971 at Madras.

Blessed the third part of Sathyam Sivam Sundaram in English written by N. Kasturi which was released on 16th March 1972.

Guided the first Summer Course in Indian Culture and Spirituality—1st May 1972 to 31st May 1972.

The second Summer Course was conducted at Brindavan between 21st May 1973 and 21st June 1973, under the supervision of Bhagavan.

The sixth All India Conference of Bhagavan Sri

Sathya Sai Seva Organisations was held at Rajahmundry on 2nd January 1974.

The third Summer Course was organised at Brindavan from 20th May 1974 to 20th June 1974. Bhagavan was the moving spirit of the Summer Course.

In spite of his stupendous work Bhagavan could still snatch some time to write books for the guidance of the sadhaks. The books he has written—*Prema Vahini, Jnana Vahini, Prasanthi Vahini, Dhyana Vahini, Dharma Vahini, Sandeha Nivarini, the Geetha Vahini,* and *Bhagavatha Vahini* —are treasures that shed light on intricate problems of spiritual discipline. Bhagavan has retold the Bhagavatha and the Ramayana, in a manner which makes them invaluable guides for aspirants to liberation. Seven volumes of his speeches have also been published.

Compiled by
D.S. Habbu